Essentials
of
speech communication

Other books by Raymond S. Ross:

Persuasion: Communication and Interpersonal Relations, 1974
Speech Communication: Fundamentals and Practice, 6th ed., 1983

and with Mark G. Ross
Understanding Persuasion, 1981
Relating and Interacting:
An Introduction to Interpersonal Communication, 1982

2nd edition

Essentials of speech communication

RAYMOND S. ROSS Ph.D.

Professor of Speech Communication, Theatre, and Journalism
Wayne State University

PRENTICE-HALL, INC., ENGLEWOOD CLIFFS, NEW JERSEY 07632

Library of Congress Cataloging in Publication Data

ROSS, RAYMOND SAMUEL
    Essentials of speech communication.

    Includes index.
    1. Oral communication. I. Title.
P95.R67   1984   001.54'2   83-24633
ISBN 0-13-289173-5

Printed in the United States of America

10   9   8   7   6   5   4   3   2   1

Editorial/production supervision: Jeanne Hoeting
Page layout: Gail Cocker
Cover design: Ben Santora
Manufacturing buyer: Ron Chapman
Business agent, Ross Enterprises: Ricky Ross

ISBN 0-13-289173-5

PRENTICE-HALL INTERNATIONAL, INC., *London*
PRENTICE-HALL OF AUSTRALIA PTY. LIMITED, *Sydney*
EDITORA PRENTICE-HALL DO BRASIL, LTDA., *Rio de Janeiro*
PRENTICE-HALL CANADA INC., *Toronto*
PRENTICE-HALL OF INDIA PRIVATE LIMITED, *New Delhi*
PRENTICE-HALL OF JAPAN, INC., *Tokyo*
PRENTICE-HALL OF SOUTHEAST ASIA PTE. LTD., *Singapore*
WHITEHALL BOOKS LIMITED, *Wellington, New Zealand*

Contents

chapter 3
NONVERBAL COMMUNICATION 55

chapter 4
LISTENING BEHAVIOR 85

PART TWO: INTERPERSONAL AND GROUP COMMUNICATION

chapter 8
LEADERSHIP AND INTERPERSONAL INFLUENCE   161

PART THREE: PUBLIC COMMUNICATION

chapter 9
AUDIENCE PSYCHOLOGY   181

**chapter 10
PREPARING AND ORGANIZING**   **206**

**chapter 11
PRESENTING INFORMATION**   **236**

chapter 12
THE PSYCHOLOGY OF PERSUASION

Preface

The major questions guiding the researching and writing of this introductory text have focused on how people are able to responsibly coordinate their language, thought, voice, and actions across a variety of settings—from dyads and small groups to larger audiences. The pedagogical aim is to discuss these *how* questions without being overly prescriptive.

The parts and chapters support one another. That is, the specific encoding, decoding, linguistic, and nonverbal behaviors discussed in Part One, (Chapters 1–4) relate directly and crucially to the interpersonal, group, and public settings that follow in Parts Two (Chapters 5–8) and Three (Chapters 9–12).

This text does not avoid all the complex concepts found in such a broad coverage of the field. It does, however, make a real effort to sort and select them based on many years of teaching and writing experience.

Nor is the text meant to be an encyclopedia of current research. It does include, however, many references to recent work as well as to the classic works. It is meant to be a current statement about a broad, realistic perspective on human communication. It is designed to introduce students to the field of speech communication and to have them better appreciate its concepts, skills, and ethical responsibilities.

A useful *Instructor's Manual* by Mark G. Ross featuring test items and model examinations is available to professors.

R.S.R

1

The process
of human communication

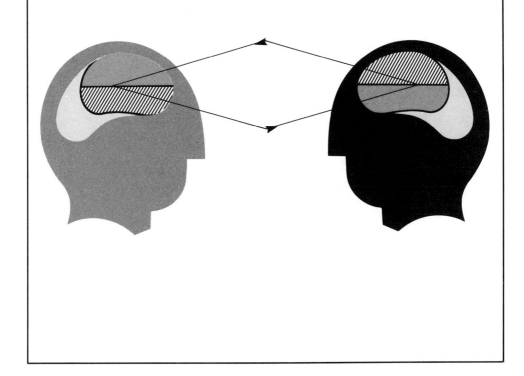

General learning outcomes

- We should learn the influence of context, setting, purpose, and situation on human communication.
- We should learn the process nature of human communication.
- We should learn how our perceptions of people affect our relating and understanding.
- We should learn four characteristics of ethical communication.

Suppose you communicate a rumor to two of your friends; then suppose that they each relay the rumor to two of their friends. Allowing fifteen minutes for each communication and assuming a hypothetical chain of contacts that is neither duplicated nor broken, this rumor would reach every person in the world in only eight hours and thirty minutes. Talk about a grapevine! If you have ever played the game of passing along a message orally to see how much distortion takes place by the time the message reaches the last person at your party, you can guess what would probably happen in our hypothetical, worldwide grapevine. One wonders how we achieve any understanding at all.

If you would like to speed up the rumor mill, consider that newspaper pages and photographs are now transmitted from coast to coast, using regular telephone lines, in about four minutes.

That is slow compared with a new laser-writing method which takes just four seconds. The device also can transmit documents, X-ray photographs, color photographs, and a three-dimensional "stereo" picture.

We first need to know something about the communication process, which more than anything else gives humans their special place among all living things. Our overwhelming need to communicate and express ourselves is as characteristic a part of our nature as is our physiology. We are unique among all other forms of animals because of our rationality and our sophisticated system of communication. These assets have permitted us to record the discoveries of yesteryear so that others yet unborn may profit from the past. This ability, in conjunction with human creativeness, has led to an information explosion.

The amount of material to be stored and communicated in this period of our history is enormous. One scholar has estimated that we have accumulated more knowledge within the last fifty years than during all the centuries before, and that knowledge has more than doubled within the last century! Furthermore, it is estimated that 95 percent of all the world's scientists are alive today! Our libraries at Wayne State University alone house some 1300 technical journals. The costs of American scientific research exceed $25 billion a year. Our present specialization of knowledge adds to our problems. Communication must somehow bridge these isolated islands of specialization.

The sheer amount of communication is fantastic. Surveys indicate that we spend 75 percent of our waking time in some communication activity: in listening, speaking, reading, and writing. When one considers the telephone system and the mass media, the volume of messages becomes astronomical. It is estimated that the American public makes some 288 billion telephone calls a year, or nearly 6000 per second. Washington, D.C. has over 130 phones per 100 persons.[1]

10 LEADING NATIONAL ADVERTISERS[2]
(Ad dollars in millions)

1	Procter & Gamble	$671.8
2	Sears, Roebuck & Co.	544.1
3	General Foods Corp.	456.8
4	Philip Morris Inc.	433.0
5	General Motors Corp.	401.0
6	K mart Corp.	349.6
7	Nabisco Brands	341.0
8	R. J. Reynolds Industries	321.3
9	American Telephone & Telegraph Co.	297.0
10	Mobil Corp.	293.1

Consider the $400,000 cost of a thirty-second spot commercial during the Superbowl. If one assumes that there are 90 million viewers, that is $8.88 per 1000 viewers per minute (CPM). The average viewer is exposed to more than 500 commercials a week; production costs can average $10,000 for a day of shooting; a thirty-second spot often requires a fifteen-member production crew and a ten-hour day.[3] This kind of communication is indeed big business, and somebody thinks it is effective.

One scholar defines speech as "a tool of social adjustment, which reflects the efficient personality." Others suggest that "physical, social, and mental existence depend upon communication. Each affects the other until it would be foolish to try to distinguish where one begins and the other leaves off. Communication shapes personality and personality determines the pattern of communication."[4] Perhaps for our purposes we can say that speech training can have as much impact on personality as personality can have on speech.

[1]*Detroit News,* January 8, 1975, p. 12C.

[2]Reprinted with permission from the September 9, 1982, issue of *Advertising Age.* Copyright 1982 by Crain Communications, Inc.

[3]*Detroit Free Press,* May 18, 1981, p. 2C.

[4]Gordon Wiseman and Larry Barker, *Speech—Interpersonal Communication* (San Francisco: Chandler, 1967, 1974), p. 5; see also Lee Thayer, *Communication and Communication Systems* (Homewood, Ill.: Richard D. Irwin, 1968), p. 17.

COMMUNICATION CONTEXTS

1. "I love you John."
   "I love you Mary."
   Applause, sobs, the movement of many people.
2. "I love you John."
   "I love you Mary."
   "We love you too Father."
3. "I love you John."
   "I love you Mary."
   The birds sing; the air is heavy with jasmine.

What is happening here? It could be a lot of things. It would help if we knew the context, setting, and purpose better.

In 1 we are in a theatre, the curtain is coming down, and the actors are ending a tear-jerker play.

It's a public or media context, at least in one sense. If the actors really experience their roles, it's an intimate, interpersonal context for John and Mary. So you see, nothing is easy about human communication.

Number 2 is easier. We have more information about the context. We have a small group of at least three (it turns out to be four). Father (could it be a priest?) apparently loves John and Mary. How did you attribute "We love you too Father"? Did John say it? Did Mary say it? We look at more of these problems later.

How about number 3? "I love you John." "I love you Mary." "The birds sing; the air is heavy with jasmine." They are alone. (Aren't they?) Lovers? Are we into intimate communication?

All different contexts, yet the words and messages are so very similar.

In the most general sense, all communication must occur somewhere in some context. It takes place in all kinds of organizations, groups, settings, and even in the media. It is dyadic, interpersonal, small group, and also public speaking.

According to Littlejohn these various contexts all overlap and they should be viewed ". . . as a hierarchy of nested contexts in which the higher level includes the lower but adds some additional constraints and qualities."[5] Littlejohn illustrates how interpersonal communication cuts through and is a part of other contexts including group, organizational, and mass communication. Since organizational contexts are thought to be largely involved with small-group communication, let us consolidate Littlejohn's explanation as follows in Figure 1.1:

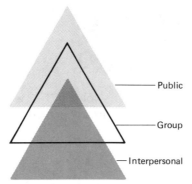

Public

Group

Interpersonal   **Figure 1.1**
The hierarchy of communication contexts.

Interpersonal communication and contexts are clearly a large part of what goes on in small-group interactions. Most small groups depend on face-to-face, interactive, oral exchanges.

The last context shown (there are others) is public communication or "relating to audiences." A public speech to a large audience is obviously quite different than an intimate, dyadic interaction. However, many of the basic speech-communication processes and behaviors are involved. Language is still critical (sometimes more critical). Voice is special; so are all of your nonverbals. Remember that you are also part of the context. Listening (especially if you're in the audience) is involved; so are all the problems of messages, attitudes, perception, attraction, and so on. Audience-participation contexts may call for applications of interpersonal practice as well as integrations of interpersonal theories and processes. Public communication finds dyadic communication models valuable instruction devices for the same kinds of reasons just discussed.

Intrapersonal communication is also vital to all levels and contexts of communication. It is the thinking or "talking to oneself" that goes on internally—that is, within one's self. It is a large consideration in the chapters that follow, which will hopefully help you gain insight into your *intra*personal behavior in such mat-

[5]Stephen W. Littlejohn, *Theories of Human Communication* (Columbus, Ohio: Charles E. Merrill, 1978), p. 204.

ters as ethics, people perception, management of meaning, self-concept, rhetorical sensitivity, internal conflict, problem solving, personal style, audience assessment, organization of ideas, controlling fright, and logical thinking.

The major parts of this book address the largest social contexts: interpersonal, small-group, and public communication. The basic speech behaviors discussed run through all contexts.

SETTING AND PURPOSE

Visualize an impressive church or temple complete with stained-glass windows, exquisite statues, and a high-arched ceiling. In it we feel close to our creator. There is a temptation to whisper—a rock group would surely be out of place here. The speakers seem to alter their voices, their language, and their dress to meet the communication requirements of this powerful setting. The ritual associated with this setting also dictates much of the verbal as well as the nonverbal communication. Even an empty church or temple is a powerful communication setting, and we adjust our signals accordingly.

Ceremonial settings such as weddings, funerals, initiations, and graduations are important influences on human communication wherever they are held. Weddings are held in gardens, living rooms, and woods, as well as in churches and temples. Graduations may take place inside, outside, in a gym, in an auditorium, and so on. Part of the influence of such an occasion comes from its obvious purpose, but much of the influence is also tradition and ritual, which seem to go

Figure 1.2   **Figure 1.3**

beyond the obvious. Human communication in such settings is somehow different.

Think about the last funeral you attended and consider your total verbal exchange. Being present at the ceremony had a strong impact on what you said. The same holds true to a lesser extent at weddings. However, once you are out of the setting, the controlling aspect of place and ritual disappears.

Even the dinner hour is a rather formal setting for some families. It is a time for prayer and thanksgiving and not a time for deep conversation or heated argument. Of course, this setting varies considerably, as we see in Figures 1.2 and 1.3. Test the wind of this setting when you are a dinner guest, or you may very easily break the ritual and therefore much of the communication that otherwise might have been possible. You are also part of the setting.

The purposes of communication in the public-communication setting (discussed in Chapters 9–12) are to inform, persuade, and entertain. In some inter-

personal, group, and ritualistic settings, the purpose agenda is so important that it has a greater impact on communication than the place has. If the purpose is strictly or mostly social, the loud and aggressive advocate who can't adjust may find him- or herself poorly received.

Some interaction purposes seem obvious: social, ventilating, help seeking, bargaining, evaluating, and so on. But are they always obvious?

Rodney is invited to a party and that's strictly social, right? If the guests are a group of friends who have just failed their midterm exams, it might be more of a ventilating and commiserating situation. If the party is with Rodney's new employer, it may involve some subtle evaluation or even bargaining. The setting has a lot to do with how one "reads" the purpose. A social gathering in formal clothes at the college president's campus home may be quite different from a peer-group get-together in jeans and T-shirts. The point is that purposes overlap, change, and are sometimes even disguises for hidden purposes. The new boyfriend or girlfriend may find that the party is really going to be mostly for evaluation.

For all of the changing and overlapping purposes, some parties are sincerely called for fellowship, fun, and a good time. We judge how good a time we had in terms of fun. Of course, what's fun for one person or group may not be fun for another. One side of Rodney's family socializes in a loud and active way—backslapping, arguing, even some mostly good-natured fighting. However, the other side of Rodney's family comes from a more introverted heritage and finds parties frightening and threatening—no fun at all. Understanding these different approaches goes a long way toward improving communication and perhaps even having a good time.

Have you ever been misunderstood by parents or friends when your purpose was really simple ventilation? You're trying to blow off some steam, but your listener misinterprets the situation and proceeds to give you point-by-point arguments on all the gross generalizations you've blurted out. All you really wanted was a quiet, sympathetic listener and now you've committed yourself to an emotional argument you really didn't need or want! Clearly, another reason we interact is to unload gripes and generally express pent-up feelings—to unwind. In such situations we are usually looking for a sympathetic ear. We are not interested in

having our statements and viewpoints challenged, at least critically. Take care with *whom* you ventilate. Some people really don't discount for your blowing off. Some may encourage you to say more than you really intended. "I don't know what I said exactly, but I feel I exposed too much." Sometimes our need to ventilate causes us to misinterpret and overreact to even the simplest questions: "Daddy, where did I come from?" After a long and detailed lecture on the birds and the bees comes the reply: "Golly, I meant was it Chicago or Toledo?"

Responsibilities run both ways in these ventilation situations. Try to determine how much of what you are hearing should be discounted as ventilation and how much is a sincere call for help.

Have you ever asked one of your classmates a simple question, only to receive a lecture on transcendental ontology? Your classmate may honestly have misunderstood the intent and scope of your question, or he or she may have found a victim on whom to try out his or her new learning! That's not all bad either—communication most often *is* a compromise of purposes and intentions. Previously, we discussed seeking a listener who did not interfere continually as we griped, vented our emotions, or otherwise used him or her as a release for accumulated strong feelings. Other types of circumstances may lead to a more specific call for help—a call for a response, information, support, or reinforcement. There are many

such situations, ranging from simply requesting the time, date, or directions to asking a person to assume a more emotionally complex, supportive role. Once again, the *why* is the influencing factor. Some call these types of purposes therapeutic, in that the asker is seeking a cure or answer for a difficulty. It is quite important and sometimes difficult for a receiver to really know whether someone wishes help and support or prefers only a sympathetic ear.

Sometimes the real help we seek is a nonverbal presence, not talk at all. When the play is a bomb, the team has fumbled near the goal line, your speech was a mess, or you've flunked the exam, you may just prefer silent, miserable company, unless you're ventilating. Misery does love company, especially people with the same problem.

Bargaining is working out differences together. This purpose is sometimes evident, as with known, honest differences of opinion. However, it may also operate quite subtly, sometimes by design and sometimes quite by accident. In bargaining, the response to a statement often determines the next response. A statement may contain a specific intent unknown to the receiver. This intent may be concealed in some code or message intended to have persuasive effect on the receiver. Notice the bargaining influence in the communication when you're buying a used motorcycle. The seller may suggest $800 as an asking price. You're interested in determining just how low the seller is really willing to go in price. In this special kind of setting there is often a hidden motive and a payoff (which we expect as part of the game). The setting is sometimes called a game because of this payoff aspect. Unless you recognize this purpose and adjust accordingly, you may come off second best in the negotiation without really having played the game.

Sometimes we bargain without knowing it. Asking to use your big brother's car may really be more bargaining than a simple request for help. If this is so, your initial purpose may be to seek information. You may then shift to an expression of feelings as you attempt to establish common ground. You may then prepare

to move into the bargaining stance. Whatever your line will be, you must be aware that in this type of context the receiver may not always give you the specific answer you want. (That's part of the game, too.) If, after several exchanges, you sense that your goal is not likely to achieved, you may decide to offer more in exchange, modify your time requirement, or do whatever is possible to work out the bargaining together.

Bargaining among unions and employers is a similar communication interchange, except that it is much more formal. Most of these bargaining situations are worked out cooperatively. We usually hear about the few that are deadlocked as if they were typical!

That bargaining is often unsuccessful is another fact of life! Most bargaining would probably be more successful if the participants knew more about the process and recognized a bargaining situation when they were in one. Lucy doesn't bargain well . . .

Figure 1.4 Peanuts © 1962 United Feature Syndicate, Inc.

"John, it's '*doesn't* not *don't* make any difference.' *Don't* is a contraction of *do not*."

"Really? Well, up your nose with a rubber hose!"

Even feedback on something relatively trivial, such as grammar or spelling errors (which would not be trivial in the setting of an English class) or even minor arithmetic mistakes, may be surprisingly threatening to some people. If you are in a position which requires you to give negative feedback—such as an umpire, referee, traffic officer, or teacher—and everyone expects this kind of discipline or feedback from you, it is one thing. When you offer such advice freely, in a different setting, and with a less specific purpose, it is quite another thing! *How* you do it, expected or not, has a lot to do with your success.

The evaluative or negative-feedback setting is never easy, even for professional counselors and skilled teachers. When your purpose is to direct negative feedback at someone else, you must work especially hard at being your best self, your most sensitive self. When you *ask* for evaluation or feedback, prepare yourself for some blunt remarks: Most people will be quite honest, but not always objective, and rarely as kind as you think they should be.

Do not be too eager to evaluate others. The counselor Carl Rogers was known to say, "The older and wiser I get, the less eager I am to rush in to fix things."[6] Objectivity is critical to sensitive feedback situations, but so is tact.

Our communication, whether public speaking, group discussion, or informal interaction, is often limited by where we are. Some settings may restrict communication, whereas others may aid it. We may not always like or approve of certain settings, but sensitive human interaction demands that we take them into account. We should take the setting into special account when we evaluate a person's social adjustment. A "nut" may not be a "nut" when he or she is out of the special setting or context you are observing. The berserk football fan may be Mr. Cool when you find him or her in church or temple.

[6]Carl Rogers, *On Becoming a Person* (Boston: Houghton Mifflin, 1961), p. 21

COMMUNICATION MODELS

The Role of Models

The boat is going in the water . . . "Scott, bring a short line to tie us up." Scott arrives with six feet of 5/8-inch manila rope. No way will it work. The spiling is two feet in diameter; six feet of line won't get him around the post. How do we know that? How can a verbal model or theorem assist?

"There's nothing more practical than a good theory." In geometry we accept the theorem $C = \pi D$ or the circumference of a circle equals its diameter multiplied by the transcendental 3.14159265 . . . (3.1416). Just a rough estimate (2 × 3) is a help, with closer figuring indicating 6.28 feet. With knots, scope, and all, Scott had better figure on at least twenty feet of line.

If Scott were going to sail this boat on a triangular course he could figure the long leg if he knew the lengths of the short ones. Assuming that the course is a right triangle (90°), he could use the Pythagorean theorem, which states that the square of the hypotenuse of a right triangle is equal to the sum of the squares of the legs. The statement is a form of verbal model. If we draw a picture of this theorem as well (Figure 1.5), we have a verbal-pictorial model. Communication experts have used primarily verbal-pictorial models in trying to give us a closer look at the communication process.

We can, then, make models with words, numbers, symbols, and pictures to illustrate things, theories, or processes. We can also learn much about how trains, boats, and airplanes work by building working models of them. The famous America's Cup sailboats are precisely modeled by naval architects and then carefully tested in wind and wave machines. These models offer low-cost predictions of what the big sail machines *might* do. We say *might* do because models are, after all, not the real things and often the predictions are not accurate.

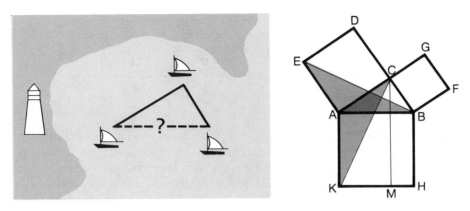

Figure 1.5   The square of the hypotenuse of a right triangle is equal to the sum of the squares of the legs, or *AKHB = ACDE + BFGC*.

When we try to model more abstract things like human communication, we often oversimplify to the point that we develop wrong predictions. We may not even always agree on what it is that we are modeling. Or we may try to fit the physical model notions (boats, trains, planes, etc.) completely into the abstraction models. We can *convey* an automobile from one part of a production line and actually *see* the auto while it is in conveyance, so that its meaning is clear.

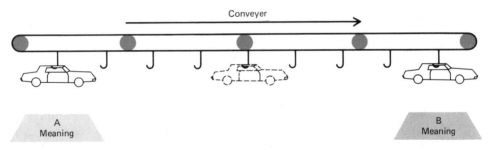

Figure 1.6

But how do we convey an idea, a concept? Where is the meaning? What does an idea look like?

Figure 1.7

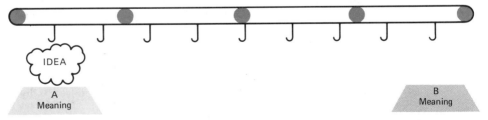

Figure 1.8 Carroll model. From John B. Carroll, *The Study of Language* (Cambridge, Mass.: Harvard University Press, 1955), p. 88.

We cannot actually pick up meaning and move it like we can an automobile. We can *convey* or transfer speech sights and sounds, but not meanings. Somehow the meanings have to be at both ends of the conveyer system. Communication must *elicit* meanings already at the destination which are intended or sought by the source. It is clear that the encoding part of communication is largely *intrapersonal.*

Despite these problems, a model does give one another look—a perspective. A model can provide a frame of reference, show information gaps, and allow us to express a problem in more precise figures or symbols. Communication experts have used mostly verbal-pictorial models in trying to give us a perspective view of the communication process.

Some models are pretty much one way or linear. The Carroll verbal model shown in Figure 1.8 does, however, alert us to the *encode-decode* notion of human communication.

Most engineering or mathematical models are essentially linear—that is, they go from a source to a destination. There is no clear representation of a circular response or feedback, and no clear explanation of the transactional nature or mutual involvement we find in human communication. But then, that was not their major purpose.[7] Engineering models do, however, give us insights into part of the process in which we are interested.

A process notion is what we're following. If we accept the notion of process, David Berlo has told us ". . . we view events and relationships as dynamic, on-going, ever-changing. Continuous . . . it does not have *a* beginning, *an* end, a fixed sequence of events . . . The ingredients within a process interact: each affects all the others."[8]

Wilbur Schramm was one of the early theorists to demonstrate circularity and process in his models (see Figure 1.9).

The decoding of a message by the receiver starts that person's intrapersonal process of encoding. Whether or not this encoding results in an overt communication depends on the barriers to communication. The communication process is continuous. A single communication is merely part of a greater network of communication.

[7]Some writers are interested primarily in mathematical theories and models applied to electrical engineering: See C. E. Shannon and W. Weaver, *The Mathematical Theory of Communication* (Urbana, Ill.: University of Illinois Press, 1949), p. 98. Others are interested in animal communication: See Jon J. Eisenson, J. Jeffrey Auer, and John V. Irwin, *The Psychology of Communication* (New York: Appleton-Century-Crofts, 1963), Chapter 10.

[8]David K. Berlo, *The Process of Communication* (New York: Holt, Rinehart & Winston, 1960), p. 24.

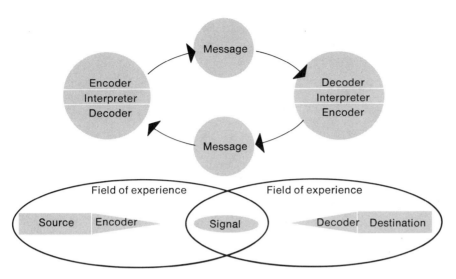

Figure 1.9 From Wilbur Schramm, "How Communication Works," in *The Process and Effects of Mass Communication,* ed. Wilbur Schramm (Urbana, Ill.: University of Illinois Press, 1955), pp. 4–8.

The roles of encoder and decoder are interchangeable. Thus, each person in the communication process is encoder and decoder as well as interpreter. The tripart circle also suggests the interesting notion that these functions can go on simultaneously for the most part. While someone is talking, the listener is not only breaking the speaker's code and trying to make sense of it but is also considering his or her next transmission. Meanwhile, nonverbals may already have been encoded and interpreted before verbal messages.

In the second diagram Schramm suggests that the encoder and decoder can perform their functions only in terms of their own fields of experience. In this sense, then, both the decoder and encoder are limited by their experiences. Nevertheless, there must be some experience common to both in order for the communication to be useful for the intended message to be conveyed.

There is also the lesson here that we may sometimes have to build bridges or overlaps before we can have truly interpersonal communication. Furthermore, for your signals—that is, your message, language, nonverbals, and so forth—to be most effective, they must somehow fall in the area of overlap.

Because no model of anything, much less a complicated process, can ever be completely accurate, you are not expected to agree totally with the previous models or with the one about to be described. However, with the previous material as a frame of reference, perhaps more insights are now available to you as you decode the instructional model in Figure 1.10.

The Ross Communication Model

Let's start with a person, Mark, sending a message to a receiver, Sue. The model suggests what's going on intrapersonally in Mark's brain (top) and what kinds of knowledge and experience he has to work with (bottom). The loop between

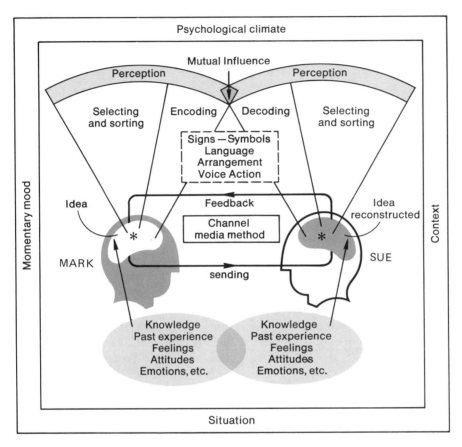

Figure 1.10 Ross communication model.

Mark and Sue suggests that human communication is a *mutual* process, that it works both ways. Mark is both a sender and receiver at the same time.

THE MESSAGE. Let's suppose the idea being sent is an abstract one such as *love*. Mark proceeds to sort through and select from his storehouse those items that help him refine and define what he is trying to say. He really needs something similar to a computer program to help assess, cross reference, and bring together his material. This is essentially an *intra*personal process.

Now let's look at Sue's part. Sue's role in the model is similar to Mark's, but her specific knowledge, experience, attitudes, and such are not identical. Note how the fans overlap. The overlapping area indicates mutual experience. If there were *no* overlap, communication would be difficult indeed—Mark and Sue would have practically nothing in common. Sometimes in human communication we spend most of our time building a core of common understanding before much else can happen.

Mark's computer program must assess what he knows, or thinks he knows, about Sue and about love before he chooses his codes and proceeds to send them. We're assuming a face-to-face communication. Mark could seek a different channel. He could write a letter or hire a plane and write across the sky!

THE FRAME.   The model tries to show everything, including the world in which this communication takes place. The picture frame suggests the importance of situation, mood, context, and climate.

The *situation* could range from being a date to being a simple exchange of homework information. It could then make a real difference. The *mood* of Sue or Mark refers to feelings of the moment. At different times one's mood might be happy, angry, tense, or so on. One's mood can greatly affect what one says or hears and how one says or hears something. *Context* is the framework of other words or ideas into which one's words or ideas fit. If someone is talking about paper, note how the word changes in these contexts: The paper was late today (newspaper). The paper is crooked (wallpaper). It is an A paper (homework). *Psychological climate* is a lot like weather or physical climate. Just as our weather might be bitter cold, so too might the psychological mood (climate) of a classroom, a meeting, or a date be cold. An unhappy, impersonal (cold) psychological climate would hurt rather than help communication. Sometimes climate (psychological) is the most important part of a message.

ENCODING AND TRANSMITTING.   Let's return to Mark and his computer program. We really can think of the brain in some ways as a computer. The forebrain (which is a kind of regulator for received information) can be thought of as an automatic device into which we feed the information (called a program in computer talk). We can now see that Mark's program had better include at least three instructions or he is already in trouble! They are: (1) What information do I, Mark, have stored under love? (2) What do I really know about Sue? (3) What roles do this particular situation and context play? One can picture the program evaluating the storehouse, saying *yes, no, maybe,* cross-checking, organizing—in short, selecting and sorting the best facts, thoughts, past experiences, and so on.

Before Mark gets even the first few words out of his mouth, he should evaluate his *codes*—that is, his language, voice, gestures, and so on—using almost the same program.

DECODING.   At last Mark sends out the codes, which are mostly oral. Finally (and the whole operation takes but a few seconds), the codes strike Sue's senses. This is the first part of human perception: *sensation;* the second part is *interpretation* of what the sensations mean.

The model suggests that Sue now proceeds to decode the signs, symbols, language, and so on. She then draws from her storehouse of knowledge and experiences those meanings that will allow her to create a message concerning love.

If her idea is similar to what Mark intended, we have communication. Sue's understanding of Mark's message, then, depends on what she already knows.

FEEDBACK. Mark also has the advantage of *feedback* if he chooses to use it. In engineering, feedback refers to sent-out energy that is returned to the source. The automatic pilot used in airplanes and the thermostats on furnaces are examples of machinery that use feedback. For human communication purposes Mark should think of feedback as useful in a "Sue-adjusting" sense. As his signals are bounced off Sue, they feed back information that allows him to adjust, refine, and improve further messages. A puzzled look, a frown, a yawn, the sound of Sue's voice (or his own)—any of these may cause Mark to rethink and recode the signals that he sends out.

We should now be able to define what we're talking about.

The model shows, as stated earlier, that communication involves the assigning of meaning, and that it *works well* when the person receiving a message interprets it in the *same* way the sender intends it. It is clear that human communication is not really a transfer of meaning at all. It is *a process involving the sorting, selecting, and sending of symbols in such a way as to help a receiver find in his or her own mind a meaning similar to that intended by the sender.* That we seldom have perfectly clear communication and probably should not expect it now seems obvious.

Definitions of Communication

Definitions of communication range from "speech is the great medium through which human cooperation is brought about"[9] to the more specific definition of the American College Dictionary: "the imparting or interchange of thoughts, opinions, or information by speech, writing, or signs." Let's look at some other useful definitions.

Human communication is a subtle set of processes through which people interact, control one another, and gain understanding.[10]

Communication is social interaction through symbols and message systems.[11]

Communication has as its central interest those behavioral situations in which a source transmits a message to a receiver(s) with conscious intent to affect the latter's behaviors.[12]

---

[9]Grace A. de Laguna, *Speech: Its Function and Development* (New Haven: Yale University Press, 1927), p. 19.

[10]Alfred G. Smith, ed., *Communication and Culture: Readings in the Codes of Human Interaction* (New York: Holt, Rinehart & Winston, 1966), p. v.

[11]George Gerbner, "On Defining Communication: Still Another View," *Journal of Communication*, 16, no. 2 (June 1966), 99.

[12]Gerald R. Miller, "On Defining Communication: Another Stab," *Journal of Communication*, 16, no. 2 (June 1966), 92.

Speech is ongoing multisymbolic behavior in social situations carried on to achieve communication. We define communication as a social achievement in symbolic behavior.[13]

Communication is a social function . . ., a sharing of elements of behavior, or modes of life, by the existence of sets of rules. . . . Communication is not the response itself but is essentially the relationship set up by the transmission of stimuli [signs] and the evocation of responses.[14]

Communication occurs whenever persons attribute significance to message-related behavior.[15]

Over ninety-five serious attempts at defining communication have appeared in print. Although they differ in many respects, all the definitions agree that ideas must in some way be shared before communication can exist. They agree further that communication should be thought of as a process and not simply as a transfer of meaning from one mind to another. Let us explore this idea of process and develop a definition that will help us in this course.

There is something *mutual* about human communication—that is, each party influences the other. Let's assume we have a message (an *idea* or *meaning*) that we wish to get to another person. We must sort through our storehouse of knowledge, experience, feelings, and previous training to select and refine the precise meaning we are seeking. Then we must encode it—that is, put it into verbal and nonverbal signs and symbols. We might transmit our meaning by sign language, a foreign language, or even Morse code. The way in which we code the message, the channel we choose, and the skill with which we send it help determine the meaning our message will have for the receiver. Assuming we are face-to-face with the listener, we now have the encoded message, its transmission, and its reception. The listener then attempts to decode it. The listener sorts out and selects meanings from *his* or *her* storehouse of knowledge, experience, and training until he or she creates in his or her own mind an idea of the ideas contained in the mind of the sender. If the idea we send and the idea the listener receives are similar, we have achieved communication. The idea received, or meaning in the mind of the listener, is therefore dependent upon the knowledge and experience the listener can bring to bear on the code. If we send the signal in an unfamiliar code, such as a foreign language, not much happens. The value of knowing your listener and of analyzing your audience becomes clear.

Thus, our working definition of communication is *a process involving a sorting, selecting, and sending of symbols in such a way as to help a listener find in his or her own mind a meaning or response similar to that intended by the communicator.* We now see why meanings that seem obvious to us are often misun-

[13]A. Craig Baird and Franklin H. Knower, *Essentials of General Speech* (New York: McGraw-Hill, 1968), p. 9.

[14]Colin Cherry, *On Human Communication* (Cambridge, Mass.: M.I.T. Press, 1966), pp. 6–7.

[15]C. David Mortensen, *Communication* (New York: McGraw-Hill, 1972), p. 14.

derstood by others. Perhaps this is what is meant by the saying, "One cannot teach a man what he does not already know," and perhaps this better explains the old teaching rule, "Go from the known to the unknown."

PERCEPTION AND HUMAN UNDERSTANDING

Sensation and Interpretation

You're at a stop sign with cars to the left and cars to the right. You depress your brake pedal with more force because you appear to be creeping forward but nothing happens. You press still harder on the brake. What is going on here? A pedestrian crosses in front of your car and it's clear that you're not moving. The light dawns: The cars on either side of you were slipping backward on the slight incline. You weren't moving; *they* were. You were tricked by your own experience. Perception is like that. First we *sensate* something; then we interpret what it means based on previous experience (or lack of experience). Your language and writing experience should help you interpret the following visual sensation (Figure 1.11). Your *lack* of experience with optical illusions may confuse your interpretation. Block out the bottom half and the interpretation of these markings becomes obvious. Now block out the top half.

Another closely related problem in interpretation arises from our normal tendency to "read in" what is left unsaid: We close the gap. If we cannot achieve a sense of completeness, we often feel upset, ill at ease, confused, and unhappy. This tendency can be a motivator. A teacher can give us just enough knowledge in a stimulating way to motivate us to do further study to complete the picture or close the gap. A problem arises, however, when we close gaps in ways not intended by the speaker or when we become frustrated by a lack of details. It is easy to see Figure 1.12 as a *complete* circle and its companion as six strange marks—or can you fill in the missing information and find the scissors?

With enough key features, we can even recognize faces. (If you still don't recognize the portrait, try looking at it from 15 feet or more, or while it's in motion, or while you're squinting, or with your eyeglasses removed.)

A person's set or mood may cause him or her to select for attention those things that agree with such a set. The three photographs in Figure 1.14 are re-

Figure 1.11

Figure 1.12   Pattern-closing tendencies help us close the gaps between these marks.

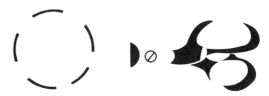

Figure 1.13
Portrait courtesy of Bell Laboratories.

| A young man "on the town" | A person needing to cash a check | Someone who is late for an appointment |

Figure 1.14 Selective perception. Reprinted with permission of Macmillan, Inc. from *Communications: The Transfer of Meaning* by Don Fabun. Copyright © 1968, Kaiser Aluminum & Chemical Corporation.

produced from the same negative; they are shown as they might appear to three different mental sets.

The complexity of human communication is also indicated by the various levels of perception now thought to exist. *Subliminal* or *subthreshold perception*, for example, is the reception of impressions below the level of conscious awareness. This is not to be confused with so-called extrasensory perception. Many experiments have been conducted in this field, most of them with images projected so fast that, although we are subconsciously aware of them, we cannot consciously recognize them. Such experiments are complicated by the fact that people vary in their perceptual abilities, and that a person perceives better at some levels of perception than at others.

The best-known of all subthreshold experiments was the projection of nonsense syllables and the simultaneous application of an electric shock to the subject. When these stimuli were later presented at speeds so rapid that the subjects could not consciously identify them, the subjects' emotional reactions were more intense than their reactions to nonsense syllables not previously associated with a shock. The subjects were thus able to identify the stimuli unconsciously before they could do so consciously.[16] During a six-week experiment in a New Jersey theater in 1957, sales of popcorn and soft drinks were allegedly increased by the use of subthreshold messages superimposed over the regular film. No adequate account of the procedures used is available for us to examine, however.[17] Another study of subthreshold perception that flashed the word *doctor* on one person in a videotape discussion indicated significant influence.[18]

If these problems of perception aren't enough, visual distortion can be caused by simple distance. For an example, bring the circle that follows in Figure 1.15 to about 1½ inches from one eye and watch all of the curved lines "square up."

Figure 1.15

[16]R. S. Lazarus and R. A. McCleary, "Automatic Discrimination without Awareness: A Study in Subception," *Psychological Review*, 58 (1951), 113–22.

[17]H. Brean, "'Hidden Sell' Technique Is Almost Here," *Life*, March 31, 1958, pp. 102–4.

[18]J. Douglas Gibb, "An Experimental Study of the Effects of a Subthreshold Prestige Symbol in Informative and Persuasive Communication" (Unpublished doctoral dissertation, Wayne State University, 1966).

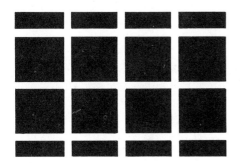

Figure 1.16

Sometimes we really do "see" things that are not there. Do you see the gray dots at the intersections in Figure 1.16? Stare at one of them. Does it disappear?

Perhaps one of the famous Escher prints says it all. (See Figure 1.17.)

A person's mood (or set) along with climate, context, and situation also affect perception. Sometimes we try to defend ourselves by refusing to perceive: "What problem?" "What cheating?" "He didn't look angry to me." Sometimes we want something so strongly that it distorts our perception: "I thought you said it was OK." "You said the assignment was due next week." One of the great barriers to good communication is the tendency to hear what we wish to hear, see what we wish to see, and believe what we wish to believe.

Understanding the way people perceive their worlds is also critical. Just as listening is much more than hearing, so all of our senses may be called upon to help us interpret the sensations we receive. To perceive is to become aware of meanings through our senses. The meaning, as we learned from our communication model, is supplied primarily by learning and past experience.

Figure 1.17 No matter how objective or how impersonal the majority of my subjects appear to me, so far as I have been able to discover, few if any of my fellow-men seem to react in the same way to all that they see around them[19].   M.C. Escher, © BEELDRECHT, Amsterdam/VAGA, New York. Collection Haags Gemeentemuseum, The Hague, 1981.

[19]Maurits C. Escher, *The Graphic Work of M. C. Escher* (New York: Ballantine Books, 1967), p. 8.

People Perception

Much of the meaning we assign to communication comes from the notions or perceptions we have of others. The content of what people say is obviously important, but not always. *How* a person says something may affect your relationship more than the stated or worded message. Perhaps the *how* (inflection, tone, facial expression) is the message. "Do you like large dogs?" said to the owner of a large dog may be an innocent question meant to start a conversation at the barbecue or it might be an expression of an attitude: "I don't like large dogs and people who do must be somewhat unusual." After fifteen minutes of smiling "dogtalk" the dog lover leaves and mutters intrapersonally, "What a bore, why can't she be more tolerant of me and poor old Goliath?" Goliath may not have been an important part of this interaction but don't rule that out. He was the vehicle for a lot of relationship communication and people perception.

Our perceptions of others affect not only our relationships, but often our communications: how much we say, how we say it, or even *if* we speak. Charlie Brown gets caught up in this bind.

Figure 1.18

Peanuts © 1960 United Feature Syndicate, Inc.

Another perspective on people perception can be gleaned from an analysis of the impressions and notions two interacting individuals might have of themselves and of one another.[20]

Suppose Mark and Sue interact again. There are really three Marks: (1) Mark's Mark, who Mark thinks he is (his self-percept); (2) Sue's Mark, who Sue thinks he is; and (3) Mark's Sue's Mark, who Mark thinks Sue *thinks* he is. There are also three Sues, following this same pattern (see Figure 1.19).

Mark's circles could, of course, all overlap if all three notions were the same. If Sue's also overlapped, they would know each other very well indeed. "Sue's

---

[20]Oliver Wendell Holmes, *The Autocrat of the Breakfast Table* (Boston: Phillips, Simpson, 1858); also see Paul Watzlawick and Janet Beavin, "Some Formal Aspects of Communication," in *The Interactional View*, P. Watzlawick and J. H. Weakland, eds. (New York: W. W. Norton, 1977), p. 61.

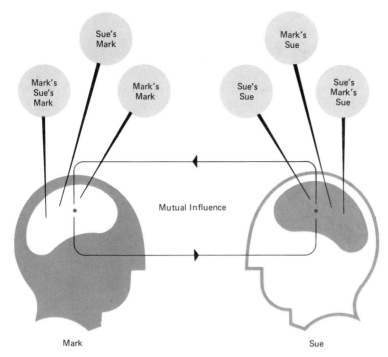

Figure 1.19
People perception.

Mark" may or may not be an accurate picture, depending, as it does, on how well she knows Mark and how objective she is. If Sue didn't know Mark at all, she would normally proceed with a very tentative or general notion. The danger of stereotypes is now obvious! Our notions of each other certainly affect our interaction with each other.

Now let's consider what Mark and Sue *think* the other person thinks of them. From Mark's point of view, it is what Mark *thinks* Sue thinks of him (Mark's Sue's Mark). If either's notion is badly in error, Mark and Sue may have some very unusual, confusing, perhaps even unfortunate interaction ahead of them. Little wonder we have misunderstandings with one another.

Feedback, both verbal and nonverbal, also shapes Mark's and Sue's attempts to communicate in an objective and nonthreatening way. It is important that we present our best *selves*—yet these must be honest best selves or we may quickly turn people off. Even if phony selves are initially successful, they will almost always catch up with us.

These evaluations of ourselves and others, along with all the "other selves" we like to play on the stage of life, complicate human interaction. If a third or fourth person is added to the interaction, the complications really increase!

And there's still another aspect. Perhaps Mark just doesn't like Sue; on the other hand, he may be infatuated.

How good we are at *people* perception clearly has a lot to do with our communication with others.

ETHICS AND RESPONSIBLE COMMUNICATION

Distorting or Falsifying Evidence

LIES AND FALSE FACTS.   "He tells a lie who has one thing in his mind and says something else by words or by any signs whatsoever" (St. Augustine). To some moral philosophers the natural end of speech is to communicate our thoughts, and a lie is evil because it frustrates the very end and purpose of speech. A communicator is morally responsible for telling the truth and for the social consequences that result if the truth is not told. This critical statement is meant to include not only our words but all the nonverbals as well.

Being honest and fair to the facts are obvious moral obligations. We must play by the game rules and obey the law. Using outright lies, manufactured facts, and "dirty tricks" is clearly unethical. Even here we encounter some problems. Prudence is a virtue. Can the ethical person be honest without being unkind? Can he or she be both tactful and forthright? When does strategy become unfair distortion? We address these questions, and more, shortly.[21]

Figure 1.20   Wright Angles © 1982 United Feature Syndicate, Inc.

USE OF EMOTIONAL APPEALS.   This is not a new ethical question. Plato and Aristotle argued it long ago. Plato counseled that emotional appeals should be avoided because they detract from the truth. Aristotle felt that it was a persuader's moral purpose, not his or her art that made such appeals unethical. If you use emotional arguments when there is *no* evidence to support your point, it is, for Aristotle (and most modern rhetoricians), unethical. It is also unethical if the emotional argument clearly flies in the face of what the receivers, given time, would find in their own investigations.

In a heated interaction one is not always searching for truth. One may not intend to distort unfairly, but it happens. As receivers we should be reminded that humans are emotional as well as rational, that free citizens have a right to sound off, and frequently do. Our ethical tolerance should include a healthy discounting of legitimate emotional appeals. As receivers[22] we also have moral obli-

---

[21] For a detailed discussion of lying, see Sissela Bok, *Lying: Moral Choice in Public and Private Life* (New York: Pantheon Books, 1978).

[22] See Franklyn Haiman, "Democratic Ethics and the Hidden Persuaders," *Quarterly Journal of Speech*, XLIV, no. 4 (December 1958), 385–92. See also Richard L. Johannesan, *Ethics in Human Communication*, 2nd ed. (Prospect Heights, Ill.: Waveland Press, 1983), pp. 124–26.

gations to give fair hearing once we have committed ourselves to some legitimate interest in the issues. We must make efforts to understand the senders' biases and intents. We should show tolerance and work at understanding intents. Fair hearing replaces force in a free society. Ewbank and Auer reminded us years ago that "no code can be legislated or imposed to relieve the listener of the duty of analyzing the speech and deciding for himself what constitutes valid proof and a legitimate appeal to the emotions."[23]

To give fair hearing we must also analyze our own range of acceptance. Are we really stuck with "hard" attitudes? Is there some latitude in our positions? To give a fair hearing also means allowing the other person some chance to talk. Ethical interpersonal communication doesn't outlaw aggressive arguing, but it does outlaw excessive monologuing; it does necessitate giving the sender some chance to make and explain his or her point. Fair hearing also calls for fair fighting. Sandbagging or setting people up for obvious embarrassment borders on unethical entrapment. Dragging in every superfluous issue to deliberately confuse is another question of ethics. These unfair interpersonal conflict techniques are discussed in Chapter 6.

CONCEALMENT OF TRUE PURPOSE.   "It is unethical for a speaker to conceal his or her real purpose, or the organization represented, pretending to speak objectively when really an advocate of one point of view."[24]

This guideline is obvious in some contexts but not as clear in others: a man posing as a minister to bilk a senior citizen of her money; a Marxist pretending to be a capitalist—these are unethical if the concealment is *total*, whether it be purpose, organization, or point of view. But what of strategy? Perhaps rhetorically one should not be too quick to shout out one's point of view or purpose. To do so might prohibit any kind of a hearing. You are rhetorically ethical as long as your concealment is not total or delayed to a point or time when it has no chance of being heard.

As receivers we should be on guard and perhaps expect some overstatement when listening to a person with an obvious ax to grind—a politician, salesperson, or promoter. If that person is within the law (false claims, slander, etc.) and does not falsely or totally conceal his or her purpose or the organization represented, he or she is probably on ethical grounds.

Mental Reservations, Strategy, and Secrets

SPECIAL SITUATIONS.   Are some broad mental reservations allowed? Yes, say the ethiticians, in the same way that a defendant pleads not guilty, or a doctor, questioned about professional secrets, replies I don't know. Yes, they say, because there were fair and sufficient *clues* within the special contexts and situations. A courtroom would not allow for any kind of mental reservation (a very special con-

---

[23]Henry Lee Ewbank and J. Jeffery Auer, *Discussion and Debate: Tools of a Democracy* (New York: Appleton-Century-Crofts, 1951), p. 258 (slightly edited for clarity).
[24]Ibid.

text). According to moralists, the common good is at stake here and it supersedes the private good of the individual.

A strict mental reservation without any clue is a lie in any context. So too are all communications that are grossly unfair to the facts, or so subtle that they give the receiver no clue about possible alternatives.[25] The clue is important, as is the context. Notice in Figure 1.21 how the message is changed when the clue and the context are manipulated. The last picture of the series, Figure 1.22, shows the true context; the other three pictures, using restricted clues, are unethical because they suggest different contexts.

Honest clues protect the receiver's fundamental right of choice. Even in social compliance situations there is usually some choice. When choice is minimal, at least there are some alternatives (the courts when necessary). The ultimate decision of how to behave, act, interpret, or believe must in some way, however small, be left to the receiver. That choice must be a viable one. "Your money or your life" is no real choice.

If moral law permits some concealing of the truth, to what situations does this pertain? What are some guidelines? First, some generalizations with wide ethical acceptance in a democracy are the following:

> We have a right to do what is necessary or helpful to preserve our own personal dignities and independence.
> We have a right to keep our private affairs secret.
> We should do that which promotes mutual trust among people. (Doctors, lawyers, and others should not reveal secrets except in extraordinary circumstances in which the common good demands it.)

All of these generalizations deal with situations in which trust and some kind of *secret* puts us in a double bind.[26]

SECRETS (DEFINITIONS).   Joseph Sullivan, S. J. deals forthrightly with the ethical principles that should govern the keeping or revealing of secrets. We offer them for your consideration:

> *Secret*—is a truth which the possessor may (right) or ought (duty) to conceal.
> *Natural Secret*—is a truth, which *from its own nature* gives the possessor said right or duty.
> *For example*: One's own or one's neighbor's private affairs, the revelations of which, at least in ordinary circumstances, would cause reasonable offense or injury.
> *Secret of Promise*—is a truth, which *because of a promise made*, possessor has a duty and therefore a right to conceal.

[25] See James Jaksa and Steven Rhodes, "A 'Content-Ethic' for Interpersonal Communication," *Michigan Speech Association Journal*, 14, 1979, 80–88.

[26] For an excellent discussion of situational perspectives, see Johannesen, *Ethics in Human Communication*, Chapter 5.

| Candidate | On the town | Solid citizen |

Figure 1.21

Figure 1.22 Photojournalism at the edge of the 1980s.   *Popular Photography*, December, 1979, pp. 79–80. Photography by Walter Oates, *Washington Star*.

Secret of Trust—is a truth, which, because of the fact that it was confided to one by another on the express or tacit agreement that having been communicated for a serious purpose it be held in trust, possessor has a duty and right to conceal.

For example: Knowledge communicated to a lawyer or doctor, or even in some circumstances to a mere friend.

At *times permits*—i.e., man sometimes has the *right* to keep a secret.

At *times commands*—i.e., man sometimes has *more than a right,* he has a *duty.*

Question: When are these times?

Answer: a) *Man has a duty* to keep:

1) *a natural* secret—as long as
   a) the truth is not made common property by some one else;
   b) he cannot reasonably presume the leave of those concerned, to reveal it;
   c) concealing the truth works no serious harm to a community;
   d) he is not questioned about the matter by legitimate authority;
   e) it can be kept without serious inconvenience to himself or another.
2) A secret of *promise* as long as
   a,b,c,d, as above.
   e) it can be kept without serious inconvenience to himself or another; and even at the cost of such inconvenience, if he has—*expressly promised* to do so.
3) A secret of *trust*—as long as
   a) *revelation is not necessary* to avert serious and impending harm from
      1) the community,
      2) the holder of the secret,
      3) a third and innocent party who is endangered by the person who has confided the secret in another,
4) the one who confided the secret.

The reason why the obligation of keeping a secret, even of promise, ceases in the circumstances mentioned above, is because, even when assuming obligations of a strict contract, no man can reasonably be thought to intend to bind himself in such circumstances. Cf. approved authors in Moral Theology.

   b) *Man has a right* to keep all secrets
      1) in all the above-named cases where he has a duty;
      2) in some of the cases mentioned where he has no duty.[27]

False Pretense and Ad Hominem

POSING AS AN AUTHORITY. A person posing as a doctor of medicine may do considerable harm through such a charade. Speaking as a qualified economist or engineer when one is not so qualified is also dangerous and unethical. This is not to say (when one is not posing) that we must remain silent on taxes, wage concessions, automotive engineering, and the like. The point is that we should not

[27]Joseph F. Sullivan, S. J., *Special Ethics* (Worcester, Mass.: Holy Cross College Press, 1948), pp. 26–27.

mislead others about our *qualifications* to expound. A concert pianist may be a brilliant piano player, but not an expert on foreign policy. He has a right to speak his mind but not if he's posing as an authority and probably not if we've paid $30 to hear him play the piano! There are, however, many considerations here: He may be guilty of poor judgment but not unethical communication (unless he was grossly in breach of his contract). We'll have more to say about these matters under credibility in Chapter 12.

UNSUPPORTED PERSONAL ATTACKS. An unsupported attack on personality is also known as *ad hominem*. When a communicator attacks the personal character of an opponent rather than the issue at hand, that person is guilty of *ad hominem* argument. If the character of the person *is* the issue, that is another matter. When, however, *ad hominem* is used solely to change the issue from an argument on the proposition to one of personalities, it is unethical. Our legal system calls such an attack slander if the personal charges are unsupported. Public figures have less protection from *ad hominem* than other citizens, as we learn in the next section. To argue the stage-and-screen abilities of Burt Reynolds by referring to him as "that self-centered woman-chasing traitor" is a good example of *ad hominem* because such a description is irrelevant if not unfair and unethical. Mr. Reynolds' stage-and-screen abilities have no direct, logical connection to his alleged off-stage pursuits. That is not to say that every personal attack is illogical or unfair. If Mr. Reynolds were being evaluated on off-stage matters it might be a different situation. Although Mr. Reynolds might have problems getting even with you if you made these remarks, the same kind of unsupported personal attack on a neighbor will probably earn you a legal suit for slander or libel if you put it in writing—clearly serious matters of ethics for responsible communicators.

Restating Ewbank and Auer: "It is unethical for a speaker to divert attention from weaknesses in his or her argument by unsupported attacks on an opponent or by appeals to hatred, intolerance, bigotry and fear."[28]

Culpable Ignorance

The intent of the sender is, of course, critical to an evaluation of the morality of his or her message. Equally important is the *role*, or *status*, of the sender. A person qualified to serve and serving in a leadership role has special ethical obligations. We expect our political and religious leaders and our professional people to be responsible, regardless of intent. A doctor convicted of malpractice rarely *intended* to do harm. An incompetent teacher may have *good intentions*. We judge such people harshly and hold them ethically responsible, even though their intent may have been good. Our laws accommodate this notion, not just for professionals, but for political leaders as well. Senators, congresspeople, and other public figures have less protection from libel and slander than does the average citizen. (They do, of course, have their protective immunities, however.)

All of us have some ethical obligations beyond intent. Many people have been hurt by those who "meant well." All of us have some obligation to get our

[28]Ewbank and Auer, *Discussion and Debate*, p. 258.

Figure 1.23 Peanuts © 1964 United Feature Syndicate Inc.

facts straight before sending messages that might capriciously misinform or injure the receiver. Moralists call this *culpable ignorance*—that is, ignorance usually from carelessness deserving blame.[29]

Most often we have an ethical responsibility to rhetorically analyze our receivers. For one not to care how people are apt to decode a message borders on immorality. A child may decode a message quite differently from a mature adult. How a particular person will interpret a particular message is an ethical consideration. Responsibility is often a frustrating question, as Lucy illustrates in Figure 1.23.

SUMMARY

Human communication is capable of fantastic speeds. The amount of communication we use is tremendous. Practices in government, industry, and colleges and universities reflect the growing importance of speech and communication training. The literature cited in this chapter underlines the growing systemization and the interdisciplinary character of the study of communication.

Communication occurs in context. Some important contexts are: interpersonal, small group, and public speaking. There are also intrapersonal dimensions to context and communication.

[29]Lawrence J. Flynn, S. J., "The Aristotelian Basis for the Ethics of Speaking," *The Speech Teacher*, VI, no. 3 (September 1957), 179–87. See also Johannesen, *Ethics in Human Communication*, p. 30.

In some settings, the purpose of communication is so important that it outweighs the impact of place. Some purposes are: ventilating, seeking help and information, bargaining, and evaluating.

The point of view of this book is that communication is not simply a transfer or transmission of meaning from one mind to another. It is a process intimately related to human perception, and it involves the sorting, selecting, and sending of symbols in such a way as to help a listener elicit from his or her own mind a meaning similar to that contained in the mind of the communicator.

A knowledge of the processes of communication and perception is essential to those who want to learn communication skills. The model we have used to analyze the communication process (Figure 1.10) includes: (1) an idea or concept; (2) selecting and sorting; (3) encoding; (4) transmitting; (5) receiving and decoding; (6) selecting and sorting; and (7) a reconstructed idea or concept. Feedback is information being returned from our receivers that is vital to the correction and refining of the signals we send.

Perception may be divided into (1) sensation and (2) interpretation. Past experience, knowledge, set, all have a great impact upon perception. Wishful thinking is the cause of much distortion in perception and therefore interferes with communication. Perception is a result of internal as well as external signals or forces. Much of the meaning we assign to communication comes from the notions or perceptions we have of others.

A communicator is morally responsible for telling the truth and for the social consequences that result if the truth is not told. Using outright lies, manufactured facts, and dirty tricks is clearly unethical. Some mental reservations are allowed as long as there are fair and sufficient clues within the special contexts and situations. A strict mental reservation without any clue is a lie in any context. The ultimate decision on how to behave, act, interpret, or believe must in some way, however small, be left to the receiver.

Responsible speakers have ethical obligations to try to match their messages to the specific audience, context, and situation. A given message does not mean the same thing to all people, and perceptions and understandings vary with contexts and situations. We have the ethical responsibility to analyze our audiences and their circumstances. A qualified person serving in a leadership role has special ethical obligations. All of us have some obligation to get our facts straight before sending messages that might capriciously misinform or injure the receiver. Moralists call this culpable ignorance—that is, ignorance usually from carelessness deserving the blame.

To be truthful we should consider such factors as: the difference between facts, inferences, opinions, and generalizations; moral principles; and the immediate and long-range effects of what is said and what is not said.

As receivers we have the moral obligation to give fair hearing once we have committed ourselves to some legitimate interest in an issue. Morally good communications preserve the integrity of the ego, provide the information needed, permit and encourage the expression of thought and feeling, and reveal respect for the person as a person.

STUDY PROJECTS

1. With a classmate, prepare an eight- to ten-minute dialogue in the form of an interview or role play (for instance, a job interview, a dialogue with an arresting officer, a doctor's appointment, a conversation with a friendly bartender), so as to introduce yourself to the rest of the class.
2. Attend a meeting of a relatively ritualized group setting (for instance, a church or temple service, award ceremony, graduation, or funeral service) and write a short report on its influence on human interaction.
3. In a small group, develop a communication model capable of discriminating interpersonal from noninterpersonal forms of communication. Be sure to address the process notion of communication, circularity, mutual involvement, and so on.
4. Reread the various definitions of communication offered in Chapter 1 and be prepared for a classroom discussion of the drawbacks and merits of each.
5. Using the illusions in Chapter 1 or other perceptual abnormalities you may find, test a few people outside class and record what they see. Assess the reasons for any differences and be prepared to share your experiences in class.
6. Discuss a real or hypothetical, "allowable" mental reservation. Explain when it becomes a lie.
7. Prepare to discuss the ethical principles that should govern the keeping or revealing of secrets. (See pp. 30–32.)
8. Locate a case of culpable ignorance; describe it and explain how it might have been avoided.
9. Keep a communication log. The communication log is a record and analysis of your personal communication experiences. Minimum standards (for a grade of B on the log) are as follows:

1. *Number of entries:* Entries should be made on *at least* four days of each week. Date your entries.
2. *Nature of entries:* Each week, at least one entry should describe something that occurred in class, and at least one entry should describe something that occurred outside class. Some of the entries may be brief (for example, one sentence). Other entries should be much longer in order to demonstrate that you are growing in the ability to understand and analyze the communication problems of both yourself and others. In either case, try to explain why a speech or discussion went well or poorly. Your efforts to explain what occurred are the principal criteria for distinguishing between A and B logs.

    In the first two weeks of the course, you *must* make one entry that describes your strengths and weaknesses in communicating with others and that states what you expect to accomplish in this course. Be specific.

    During the last week, one entry *must* describe again what you think your strengths and weaknesses are and what you think you have accomplished during the term.
3. *References to the textbook:* The log must show that you have read this text. This requirement can be met by making a *minimum* of ten references to the text in your log entries.

2

Language habits
and meaning

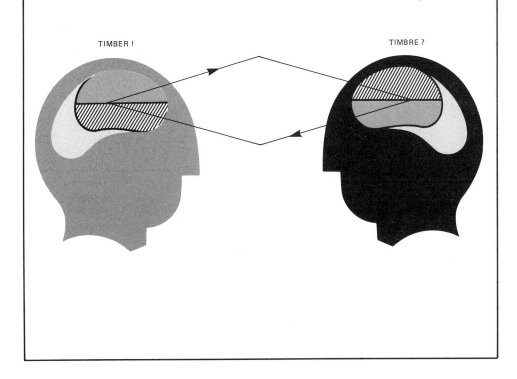

General learning outcomes

- We should learn the importance of language habits as they relate to communication.

- We should learn about the sensitive nature of words and language segments.

- We should learn the basic premises of general semantics.

- We should learn that meaning has basic dimensions: content and relational; digital and analogic; and behavioral.

- We should learn to use syntactical, semantic, and relationship rules to coordinate meanings.

- We should learn that language habits affect and reflect our personalities.

CODES AND SYMBOLS

Before we can have oral language, we must be able to recognize speech sounds (*phonology*), and eventually we must be able to combine these sounds to form words (*morphology*). Meaning can be attached to these different codes and symbols. The meaning attached to words is called *semantics*; the ordering or grouping of these words is called *syntax*. These four—phonology, morphology, semantics, and syntax—are the heart of language. An unspoken language does not have the phonetic component, but it is otherwise similar (for example, Morse code, sign language for the deaf).

Words

Words are central to spoken languages. They are symbols commonly agreed upon to represent certain things. They are the labels that help us classify. The heart of the difficulty with language is the confusion (and sometimes the emotion) of the word with the thing for which it stands. We have more to say about these semantic matters shortly.

"Elmo" or "Mo" makes clear that words are arbitrary symbols. Dictionaries try to regularize the assigned meanings of these symbols. With all of our interest in context and attributed meanings of the moment we sometimes become careless in our choice of words. The term *disinterested* counselor may be decoded by some as meaning an "indifferent" counselor, when, in fact, it means that the counselor is interested in an impartial and objective way. *Infer* and *imply* are frequently misused. To *imply* is to state indirectly, hint, or intimate: "Tom's voice implies distrust." To *infer* is to draw a conclusion or make a deduction based on facts or indications: "I infer distrust from Tom's voice."

Figure 2.1

An outdated dictionary can also cause you trouble in interpreting words' meanings; some words take on different meanings over time. For example, *fabulous* once meant false and fictional; *silly* once meant blessed; *portly*, dignified, and so on.

Problems in understanding meaning can also result because there are obviously more things and concepts in the world than there are words. If you think a cat is a cat, consider all the definitions listed in Figure 2.2.

In short, if we didn't use our limited number of words to represent an unlimited number of things, we could hardly communicate at all. Despite our useful and necessary dictionaries, no word has real meaning except in the particular context in which it is used. The meaning of a word is never quite the same from one situation to another. A good communicator must always ask, "What does *this* word mean to *this* audience in *this* situation, in *this* context, as used by *this* speaker at *this* time?"

Figure 2.2   What is a cat?

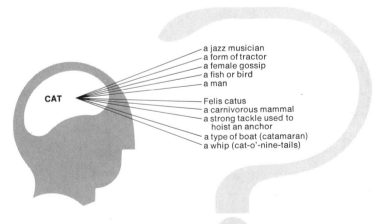

Figure 2.3   Wizard of Id.   By permission of Johnny Hart and Field Enterprises, Inc.

Oral language provides a larger number of signals than written language, simply because nonverbal signals can accompany your words. Your voice has a powerful influence upon the meaning the listener attaches both to your words and to you. So does your appearance—dress, movements, facial expressions, and gestures. However, when words of different meanings happen to sound the same, the written form may be superior. Try these:

FROM TIMBER TO TIMBRE

Figure 2.4   By permission of Steinway and Sons.

Sometimes verbal and nonverbal codes work together and strengthen meaning. At other times they conflict to the point at which they confuse the listener: the sloppy student presenting a speech on the value of personal neatness or the professor with a frozen grin discussing the possibility of a student's failing a course. How we act often contradicts what we intend to say. The cause for such inconsistency may be tension, emotional involvement, or simply poor speech training. Nonverbal codes are discussed in more detail in Chapter 3, *Nonverbal Communication*.

Elaborated and Restricted Codes[1]

Person A:	Aye, roger-dee, good buddy. How we hittin?
Person B:	A full ten-pounder, don't you know, come on.
Person A:	Aye, we thank yee.

"Mellowspeak, surf talk, talking iron, red neck chic," and so on, are all examples of language codes.[2] Different types of social systems or social structures tend to generate different speech systems, ways of talking, or language codes. Our particular language habits sometimes function to label us as members of certain speech communities. People often make initial attributions about us based on our particular language habits.

In restricted linguistic codes, experience is not verbally elaborated. The "CB'ers" had already shared this special linguistic experience—they had common meanings. Their words functioned indexically. That is, a small number of words (or numbers) functioned to index a realm of common experience (hittin, ten-pounder, your twenty?, ten-four).

Figure 2.5   B.C.   By permission of Johnny Hart and Field Enterprises, Inc.

[1]Basil Bernstein, "Elaborated and Restricted Codes: Their Social Origins and Some Consequences," in *Communication and Culture, Readings in the Codes of Human Interaction*, ed. Alfred G. Smith (New York: Holt, Rinehart, & Winston, 1966), p. 429.
[2]See Henry Allen, "Phrases To Die for. . .OK?" *The Detroit News*, June 6, 1979.

Figure 2.6

B.C.   By permission of Johnny Hart and Field Enterprises, Inc.

Some codes, like the legal ones, are elaborated verbally. With these types of codes the speaker must presume that the listener holds a less detailed set of experiences than he or she does. Some of these special codes and symbols are so restricted or so elaborate that they become a hybrid language or jargon. If you're not in on a code being used in a particular situation, the experience can be debilitating (see Figure 2.6).

Abstraction

We form *concepts* by combining words and images according to their common elements. After looking at a great many automobiles, we can typically abstract some common features: wheels, power plant, controls, general size. If we see a Lotus for the first time our abstract concepts of automobile should help us classify it as a car. Lower than others, engine in the middle, but it still has all the common features: *carness* or *automobileness*. You might also classify it as *sports* car, which suggests that our concepts are overlapping and seldom simple. Without the power to abstract we would have to form a new concept for every new phenomenon or experience, and thinking as we know it would be impossible. Intelligence is, in part, a measure of a person's ability to deal with abstractions.

Abstracting is a process of thinking in which we selectively leave out details about concrete or real things. This involves inference—that is, it goes beyond that which is observed or observable. The further we are from this thing—the *referent*—the more potential problems of specific meanings arise. For example, finding Fido in Figure 2.7 as a carnivore might be more difficult for some people than finding him as a Springer Spaniel dog. On the other hand, someone who knew nothing about dogs specifically might be able to classify Fido as a canine or of the family *canidae*.

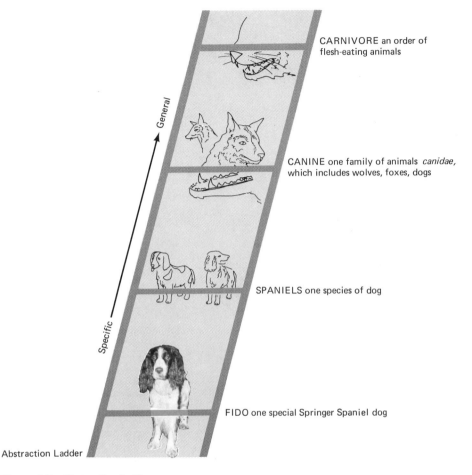

CARNIVORE an order of flesh-eating animals

CANINE one family of animals *canidae,* which includes wolves, foxes, dogs

SPANIELS one species of dog

FIDO one special Springer Spaniel dog

General

Specific

Abstraction Ladder

Figure 2.7   Abstraction ladder.

If we are told that the Rosses have a new *canine* of the family *canidae,* our high-school Latin (or experience with the Army K-9 corps) may help explain *canine.* "Why didn't they say that the Rosses had a new dog?" But wait, the dictionary says that a *canine* could also be a fox or a wolf. "Good grief, the Rosses have a pet wolf!?" What's happening here can be illustrated and explained as shown in Figure 2.8.

When we receive a symbol or sign, it travels to our *thought or reference* center. As in our communication model in Chapter 1, we consult our storehouse of experience to find the thing or *referent* to which the symbol may refer. Line A in Figure 2.8 indicates what a person ideally perceives as a *correct* symbol, in this case the word *canine.* Line B represents the cognitive selecting and sorting of knowledge and experience which ideally represent an *adequate* referent. The broken line C indicates that the *word canine* and a *real canine* are not the same, making very clear the crucial point that the symbol and its referent are not *directly*

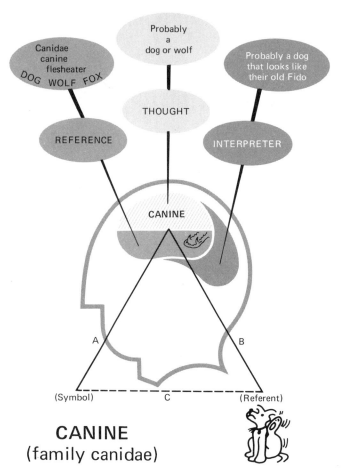

CANINE
(family canidae)

Figure 2.8
A model of meaning   Adapted from C. K. Ogden and I. A. Richards, *The Meaning of Meaning* (New York: Harcourt, Brace, 1936; London: Routledge & Kegan Paul, 1936), p. 11.

related. The word is not the thing! You cannot sit on the word *chair*, write with the word *pencil*, or hunt with the word *dog* or even the word *Fido*. Because the true referent (the dog pictured) is not a Springer Spaniel (like Fido), the interpretation shown in Figure 2.8 was only partly correct.

GENERAL SEMANTICS

Basic Premises

The term *general semantics* is credited to Alfred Korzybski and is amplified in his book *Science and Sanity*.[3] If semantics concerns mainly meaning and changes in meaning,[4] general semantics extends these concepts to include relationships between symbols and behavior. Korzybski was interested in a human's total response to his or her environment—in particular, how a person evaluates and uses language and how language affects his or her attitudes, feelings, and behavior.

[3]Alfred Korzybski, *Science and Sanity* (Lancaster, Pa.: Science Press, 1933).
[4]S. I. Hayakawa, *Language, Meaning, and Maturity* (New York: Harper & Row, 1954), p. 19; see also S. I. Hayakawa, *Language, Meaning, and Maturity* (New York: Fawcett Books Group, 1977).

Figure 2.9 Bloom County © 1981, The Washington Post Company. Reprinted with permission.

Korzybski believed that much of the misunderstanding in the world has been caused by too dogmatic an acceptance of the assumptions of basic Aristotelian logic, particularly in the human social realm. Since understanding and objective communication depend upon the relationship between language and reality, Korzybski believed that any system that was oversimplified "in the sense that words were confused with things" presented a threat to one's psychological and emotional flexibility, maturity, and sanity.[5]

The propositional nature of language can be a problem in some language systems. Even absurd statements can be grammatically correct. For example:

Figure 2.10

I'm your teacher's guide

[5]For an excellent discussion of semantics, see Hayakawa, *Language, Meaning, and Maturity*; see also S. I. Hayakawa, *Language in Thought and Action*, 4th ed. (New York: Harcourt, Brace, Jovanovich, 1978); and Stuart Chase, *The Tyranny of Words* (New York: Harcourt, Brace, 1959).

Because of the propositional nature of language, we may become too literal and too rigid in our evaluations of words. Such characteristics lead ultimately to poor logic, poor language habits, emotional imbalance, and misunderstanding. The principles of general semantics help combat such dangers by allowing a communicator to judge his or her own evaluative process through the following kinds of checks or rules:

NONIDENTITY OR THE *IS* PROBLEM

"This *is* where we are," said the tour guide, pointing to a map. Not really; after all, the map *is not* the territory. Try shooting with the word *gun*, or digging with the word *shovel*. It seems so obvious that language and thought are not identical, yet we often fall victims to our own abstracting. Every baseball fan knows what a foul ball is, but in Figure 2.11 we see an umpire who thinks a foul ball is a foul ball.

Figure 2.11   B.C.   By permission of Johnny Hart and Field Enterprises, Inc.

RULE: The word is not the thing, only an arbitrary symbol.

NONALLNESS OR THE *ET CETERA* PROBLEM

We learned in the discussion of abstracting that we always leave something out. The problem is that we sometimes forget even the unspoken et cetera. Even the best of maps can't include every bend in the road, every small trail, et cetera. One old professor used to hold up an apple and ask his class to say everything they could about it in five minutes. After twenty

Figure 2.12   Wizard of Id.   By permission of Johnny Hart and Field Enterprises, Inc.

minutes he stopped them. It was obvious that they could go on all day: Types mentioned included Jonathan, Northern Spy, crab; then uses mentioned included pies, juices, ciders, candies; then care mentioned included pruning, fertilizing, spraying, replanting. Add the hybridizing, the economics, the history, even Johnny Appleseed, and we can begin to comprehend the admonition: "One cannot say everything about anything—there is always more." Surely a catapult suggests more than a falling rock.

SELF-REFLEXIVENESS

This is the general semanticist's term for the dilemma of having to use language to talk about language. We're climbing up the abstraction ladder again; we really don't have any choice. Unless we occasionally remind ourselves of that fact, we may only be raising confusion to a higher level. Sydney Harris attempts to control self-reflexiveness in the following explanation (but he is forced to also illustrate "self-reflexiveness"):

If, for instance, I say that I have a "hankering" for cheese, there is no mistaking what I mean. A "hankering" is not a yearning or a deep longing or a burning desire; it has a small but definite range of meaning—and it has no exact synonym. No other word would do as well in its place.

But when I speak of "faith" in God or some doctrine, then I am immediately plunged into verbal chaos. How does "faith" differ from "belief"? And both of them from "conviction"?

When we say, in common speech, that we "believe" something, we could usually just as accurately say "think" or "assume" or "judge" or "guess" or "opine" or "estimate," or any other of a handful of other verbs of approximate meaning.[6]

Special Problems

In addition to the *is, et cetera,* and *self-reflexive* difficulties in understanding, we can add the special language problems of *indexing, dating,* and *either-or.*

The *index rule* relates to false generalization, overstatement, and overgeneralization. All Democrats are not alike, nor are all Republicans. This rule would have us *think* in terms of, if not actually index or catalog, Democrat 1, Democrat 2, Democrat 3, and so on. It is a warning against taking stereotypes seriously and failing to appreciate individual differences.

If a person driving into Detroit for the first time (1) witnessed a serious accident; (2) observed a truck exceeding the speed limit; and (3) had a fender dented at a busy intersection, he or she might be tempted to draw some strong conclusions and to speak in strong language about Detroit drivers. However, that person would have to examine comparative safety records, driver-education programs, and driver insurance rates before drawing any valid conclusions about all or most Detroit drivers. Even then, he or she might want to hedge any generalizations by noting that Detroit has more cars per person than any other city in the world.

[6]Sydney J. Harris, *Chicago Daily News,* December 18, 1963.

The irony and tyranny of overgeneralization is that it is usually not intended—it seems so obvious to the just-described driver that all Detroit drivers are crazy! When a person speaks from first-hand experience in a sincere and friendly voice without being aware of faulty abstracting or generalizing, that person is exhibiting a serious problem.

One of the most widespread communication faults is *false generalization*. People fall into this fault through selectively leaving out details and concluding after only superficial examinations that things are true beyond doubt. One practical solution is to qualify and *index* statements with great care.

Dating language is another form of indexing worthy of a special rule. The date of an event can significantly affect the meaning of an utterance. John Lennon's line "Come together, over me" has varying degrees of semantic clout depending on the date it is uttered: January, 1957 (no special significance); October, 1969 (Beatles' *Abbey Road* is released); April, 1970 (Paul McCartney announces he has left the Beatles); December, 1980 (John Lennon is shot).

The *either-or* response is a type of overgeneralization which usually indicates that an individual is concealing differences of degree. Absolute rulers and demagogues use the following devices: "You are either for me or against me." "It's right or it's wrong." When we routinely think and speak in "black-or-white," "true-or-false" terms we are guilty of concealing differences of degree and of false-to-fact language use. The person guilty of these exaggerations runs ethical and interpersonal risks often leading to resentment, particularly among sophisticated listeners.

GENERAL COMMUNICATION ASSUMPTIONS

Communication has Content and Relational Dimensions

"Eve, we've got a chance to get the *Detroit News* delivered way up here if enough of us subscribe—are you interested?"

"Oh we would *never* read the *Detroit News*."

"Well, thanks anyway. I guess you'll have to run to town everyday for a day-old *Detroit Free Press*."

The content dimension of this interaction was clear: a simple question about a newspaper. The response language and tone "We would *never*" suggests that Eve doesn't care for the *Detroit News*, but more, it suggests that anyone who does is rather stupid. That's the relational dimension. Had Eve responded in a pleasant tone, "No thanks, we don't mind going to town for our paper," the relational communication would have been different. Whether the perceived rudeness was intentional or just a stray, flip remark remains a nagging question. Did Eve simply mean that one paper (*Detroit Free Press*) was all they had time to read? These nonverbals help define relationships, sometimes in ways not really intended by either person.

I recently stood on a corner in Hamilton, Bermuda, focusing my camera and hoping to take the classic travel-poster picture of the police officer holding an open umbrella, and directing traffic from a raised platform. I said to a pleasant-looking chap attempting the same shot, "It's too bad the cop isn't in the box." The man completely ignored me. Did I affront him? Fortunately another person approached him speaking German. My "chap" didn't speak a word of English. When I spoke to him in his native German we related in a very warm manner. Content and relationship dimensions are present in almost all communication interactions.

Communication has Digital and Analogic Dimensions

The meaning you're decoding from these words is mostly *digital* and abstract. The pictures and diagrams are mostly *analogic* conveyers of meaning. The content dimension is more apt to be digital, the relationship dimension, analogic. In oral language the nonverbals, especially voice, carry the analogic message. Fido, the dog, understands you when you talk to him but not digitally except for some word conditioning. He understands you from your tone of voice and your hand signals—that is, analogically. The digital dimension is typically arbitrary: yes-no or true-false. An analogy would be a toggle switch that can be either off or on. The analogic dimension is more equivalent to the degrees of control found in a dimmer switch. In human communication these two dimensions interact and often depend upon each other to capture and convey meanings. The digital is necessary for some analogic communication to make known whether it is positive or negative. A whining dog may be expressing happiness or injury and it can't tell you which (at least orally). A crying human can explain whether his or hers are tears of joy or tears of sorrow. Watzlawick, Beavin, and Jackson put this concept clearly, if pedantically, as follows:

> Digital language has a highly complex and powerful logical syntax but lacks adequate semantics in the field of relationship, while analogic language possesses the semantics but has no adequate syntax for the unambiguous definition of the nature of relationships.[7]

Communication has Behavioral Dimensions

We can be "uncommunicative"; we can make it clear that we'd really rather not talk or interact. But how do we do that? By looking away, closing our eyes, remaining silent—all signs by which we *communicate* that we don't want to communicate. Perhaps we don't communicate when we're asleep, but depending upon the situation or context, even sleeping may communicate something. Suppose you

[7]Paul Watzlawick, Janet Beavin, and Don D. Jackson, *Pragmatics of Human Communication* (New York: W. W. Norton, 1967), p. 66.

fall asleep in a theatre or at school. Is it from boredom? Fatigue? Illness? Even the simple act of not writing a letter is often decoded as uncaring or insensitive.

Of course, many of these messages are not intended, but they are messages nevertheless. There is some truth in the old adage, "If you're concerned about making a fool of yourself, better to remain silent than to open your mouth and remove all doubt." However, there *are* times when your silence or inaction is decoded very harshly and it is better to take a chance. Perhaps the letter you sent or the letter of response was lost in the mail. Perhaps your feelings of embarrassment or being put down are based on a misinterpretation of the message intended.

One can simply not talk, but one cannot simply not behave, and behavior communicates.

USING RULES TO COORDINATE MEANINGS

All language and all interaction are governed by some kind of rules. We can't even talk to one another if we don't know how to employ rudimentary grammatical rules. We have to put a noun and a verb together to make a sentence. The *syntactical* part of language, they way we put words together to form phrases and sentences, is the most rule governed. If we never really get in tune with these rules, it has been suggested that our thinking processes and our perceptions of reality may be impaired. This theory is known as the Saper-Whorf hypothesis.[8]

> The real purpose of language is to talk about the world you can't see: the past, the future, the world of the mind. If we fail to master the tool, then difficult, important ideas go out of public discourse. We live meager, pinched lives, all of us, because we speak and write such meager, pinched language.[9]
>
> Grammarian Richard Mitchell

The *semantical*[10] part of language discussed earlier is concerned with rules about how symbols denote objects. Even though words are not things, they are agreed upon (mostly) referents. If "bad" means good and "bomb" means junker-car (for very long), we are headed toward misunderstanding.

We have seen that there are also shared rules that govern relationships. The major functional unit of human communication is the attribution of meanings to language, voice, and action. We are able to attribute meanings based on the *content, contexts given,* and the *relationships defined.* Human communication is largely a process whereby rule-governed symbols are shared and exchanged. As

[8]See Benjamin L. Whorf, "The Relation of Habitual Thought and Behavior to Language," in *Language, Thought, and Reality,* ed. John B. Carroll (Cambridge, Mass.: M.I.T. Press, 1956), pp. 134–59.

[9]From "American Scene," *Time,* January 29, 1979, p. 5.

[10]Not to be confused with general semantics, a *broader* concept of language, thinking, and attitude.

receivers we try to decode and give meanings to the symbols we receive. A review of our original model (Figure 1.10) in Chapter 1 illustrates this basic process.

This approach can be summarized under three premises:[11]

1. Humans act toward things based on meanings they have for them.
2. The meanings people have for things grow out of their social interactions with others.
3. Meanings are modified, contextualized, and generally manipulated through an interpretive language process used by the individual

We create, modify, interpret, and coordinate meanings essentially through the use of rules. To the extent that we share common interpretive rules in making sense of symbols, we *coordinate* our meanings.[12] The relationship rule systems we all employ are composed of at least two general types: regulative rules and constitutive rules.

Regulative rules guide us through context and relationship interpretations. They help us determine whether the analogic dimension is positive or negative. A happy party greeting of "you old S.O.B." typically has a different content or digital meaning than it might in another context. If you know the rule you are not offended (or perhaps not as much). You are able to better judge intent. Good manners help regulate our communications. A loud and constant interrupter is viewed as rude; a monologuer as overbearing if we agree on those rules and if we perceive them as pertinent to the context.

Constitutive rules help us determine how content or digital meanings may vary. The word "thanks" is clear enough on a strict, content-dimension rule: an expression of gratitude. However, we have a rule that says a sarcastic tone reverses the meaning; if "thanks" is said in such a tone, it then denotes ingratitude. We learn to apply these rules and to coordinate them with people and situations.

Some self-centered, rules-be-damned language habits suggest a hard-headed personality. Humpty Dumpty only cares what words mean to him:

> Humpty Dumpty said: "There's glory for you."
> "I don't know what you mean by 'glory,'" Alice said.
> Humpty Dumpty smiled contemptuously. "Of course you don't—till I tell you.". . .
> "But 'glory' doesn't mean 'a nice knock-down argument,'" Alice objected.
> "When I use a word," Humpty Dumpty said in a rather scornful tone, "It means just what I choose it to mean, neither more nor less."[13]

[11]Herbert Blumer, "Symbolic Interaction: An Approach to Human Communication," in *Approaches to Human Communication*, eds. Richard W. Budd and Brent D. Ruben (Rochelle Park, N.J.: Spartan Books, 1972), p. 401.

[12]W. Barnett Pearce, "The Coordinated Management of Meaning: A Rules-Based Theory of Interpersonal Communication," in *Explorations in Interpersonal Communication*, ed. Gerald Miller (Beverly Hills, Calif.: Sage, 1976), p. 25.

[13]Lewis Carroll, *Through the Looking Glass* (Cleveland: World Publishing, 1946), p. 245.

An extremely irritating form of this habit is what we might call *arrogant dismissal.* Irving Lee illustrates this most clearly in the following pattern of disagreement:

> The mood of dismissal [is that] in which a man makes it clear that he wishes to go no farther, to talk no more about something which is to him impossible, unthinkable, wrong, unnecessary, or just plain out of the question. He has spoken and there is little use in trying to make him see otherwise. If he has his way there will be no more discussion on the matter. "It won't work and that's all there is to it. . . . I refuse to listen to any more of this nonsense. . . . Anybody who comes to such a conclusion has something wrong with him. . . . We've never worked that way before and we aren't going to start."[14]

Those who consistently engage in this kind of behavior are considered to have relational "problems." Simplistic language usually reflects simplistic thinking. When we operate even temporarily with no rules or with different constitutive rules—for example, when we interact with people from other cultures—the confusion can be considerable. A belch at the dinner table is rude in one culture, a sign of appreciation in another.

IMPROVING OUR LANGUAGE HABITS

Almost any good course in speech, whatever its context, puts a high premium on language habits. The instructor will criticize you diligently, knowing that proper language habits will make it easier for you to adjust to the demands of life in college and beyond.

Reading and listening will help improve your language behavior. In both, you are receiving and decoding rule-based communication. Good listening and reading habits have been an important base in the training of almost all successful communicators.

Remember the problems of abstraction and the rules of codes and words; apply the *is, et cetera, indexing, dating,* and *either-or* rules of general semantics.

Consider the communication assumptions to be *rules*—especially "communication has content and relational dimensions." Think before you speak! When you read or listen try to determine what the words mean to the sender. How might the timing of the communication, when it is said—morning, evening, happy time, and so forth—alter the meaning? Consider in listening all the communication signals and cues; the nonword signals, the gestures, visual aids, vocal emphasis, and others, are part of the message. The way that an idea is stated cannot be separated from the idea itself. In listening or reading, you should be aware of your own beliefs, prejudices, or lack of knowledge. What we believe can seriously interfere with our abilities to decode. This is not to suggest that we should not believe anything. Were this the case, we might never make necessary decisions. The point is

[14]Irving J. Lee, *How to Talk with People* (New York: Harper & Row, 1952), p. 46.

Figure 2.13 Peanuts © 1967 United Feature Syndicate, Inc.

simply that we should know more precisely *what* we believe and be aware of its role in our listening and reading habits.

When you speak, try to think like your listeners; try to understand your subject and position from *their* point of view. Knowing your audience is critical; so too is knowing what you think. If you do not care what the audience thinks and are not very sure of your word meanings, you are in for a difficult time. Remember that the meaning, after all, is really in the mind of the receivers and that you must use your language to help the receivers select meanings from their experiences that agree with your purpose.

Learn the syntactical and grammatical rules of language; they seriously affect how you are understood by others. Recall that language habits and thinking habits are thought to be related. If your language is based on loose and variable rules, your communication may be colorful, but over time it will be confusing and impaired.

Even the phonological rules (sounds) become critical when they interact with the grammatical system. Rule breakers here "may encounter significant *difficulty with reading.*"[15]

Consider the semantical aspect also as rules based. Try to use words as precisely as possible. Do you say "disinterested" when you mean "uninterested"; "masterful" when you mean "masterly"; "jiving" when you mean "rapping"; "shucking" when you mean "griping"? Does "incredible" mean "unbelievable" or "fabulous"? Does "fabulous" mean "false" (like it once did) or does it mean "sensational"? If you tell the doctor in the hospital emergency room that your face has "gone numb," do you mean that it is paralyzed? That it has no feeling? If your paralyzed face can sensate feeling (like a nail scratch), it is *not* numb. The difference can change the diagnosis from a stroke to the less serious Bell's Palsy.

"Every idle word that men shall speak they shall give account thereof in the day of judgment" (Matthew 12:36).

SUMMARY

A word is a kind of symbol, and it is a generally accepted representation of a thing. There are obviously more things and concepts in the world than there are words, so a word may be thought of as a representation or generalization with a meaning in accordance with its context.

[15]Rita C. Naremore, "Language Variation in a Multicultural Society," in Thomas J. Hixon, Lawrence D. Shriberg, and John H. Saxman, *Introduction to Communication Disorders* (Englewood Cliffs, N.J.: Prentice-Hall, 1980), p. 191.

Different types of social systems tend to generate different speech systems, ways of talking, or language codes. Generally, the closer we are to people (common experience), the more restricted our language codes become. With elaborated codes the speaker must presume that the listener holds a set of experiences different from his or her own. Sensitive interpersonal communication should be elaborative when appropriate.

Abstracting is a process of thinking in which we selectively leave out details about concrete or real things. Abstraction occurs at different levels. As we move from lower to higher we tend to consider fewer and fewer details of the specific, original object: Fido, Springer Spaniel, dog.

Semantics may be defined as the study of the laws and conditions under which signs and symbols may be said to be meaningful. It is the study of the relationship between words and things and, further, of how human action is influenced by words. Semantics principally concerns meaning and changes in meaning.

Three assumptions important to understanding meaning are: (1) communication has content and relational dimensions; (2) communication has digital and analogic dimensions; (3) communication has behavioral dimensions.

Good communication depends on people's being able to coordinate their meanings. This hinges upon their abilities to infer meanings from contexts, signs, and symbols, and then to encode and transmit in such a way that they mesh with the receiver's meanings.

All communication interaction is governed by rules. A conflation of rules is a combination or a sharing of rules between people. To the extent that people share common interpretive rules, they are able to coordinate their meanings. An individual's use of syntactical and grammatical rules seriously affects how he or she is understood by others.

STUDY PROJECTS

1. Collect two examples of context confusion that caused language to mean different things to different individuals.
2. List five words or short language segments that annoy you (almost regardless of context), and try to explain why.
3. In a small group, prepare and perform a skit and introduction that illustrate one of the following:

   A. Digital versus analogic communication;
   B. Content versus relational communication;
   C. Behavioral communication;
   D. Syntactical and semantical rules.

4. Find an advertisement or commercial that you feel is racially, sexually, or culturally debasing (linguistically), and explain your choice.

3

Nonverbal communication

General learning outcomes

- We should learn four basic functions of nonverbals: (1) expressing emotion; (2) conveying attitudes; (3) self-presentation; and (4) managing turn taking.

- We should learn that much nonverbal communication is unconscious.

- We should understand five hallmarks of nonverbal communication: (1) they communicate; (2) they tend to be believed; (3) they are situation bound; (4) they are seldom isolated; and (5) they affect our relationships.

- We should learn about the major types of nonverbal communication: (1) kinesics; (2) paralanguage; (3) objects; (4) proxemics; and (5) chronemics.

THE IMPORTANCE OF NONVERBAL COMMUNICATION

THE NONVERBAL DEMAGOGUE

There is a story told of a deaf-mute who instigated a rebellion in India by inflaming a mob on the basis of nonverbals alone. Never underestimate the power of nonverbal communication.

Figure 3.1

Functions Performed

Consider the picture in Figure 3.2. There is no verbal message, no sound, yet we get a message. From the picture alone we sense that *emotion* is being ex-

Figure 3.2
Wide World Photos.

pressed, that there seems to be a difference of opinion, and that attitudes are being conveyed.

Two of the main functions or "uses" of nonverbal behavior are *expressing emotion* and *conveying attitudes*.[1] The young man in the picture appears to be fulfilling these functions. So does the police officer!

A third function of nonverbal communication is a kind of *self-presentation*—revealing one's personality, as it were. Uniforms, like those shown in Figures 3.2 and 3.3, also contribute to our attributions about what kind of person is communicating.

Figure 3.3   Wide World Photos.

[1]Michael Argyle, *Bodily Communication* (New York: International Universities Press, 1975); see also Michael Argyle, *The Psychology of Interpersonal Behavior*, 2nd ed. (New York: Penguin Books, 1972), p. 47.

The more we know about the people in the pictures, or the circumstances in which they are pictured, the more attributions about their *presentations* we are apt to make.

The fourth function of nonverbal communication involves the less dramatic, but important nonverbal behaviors that usually accompany our verbal messages. We view this function as essentially that of *managing turn taking*—that is, learning how to indicate when one wants to interrupt another; when one doesn't want to be interrupted oneself; when one wants feedback, more attention, and so on.

These, then, are four basic functions or uses of nonverbal communication: (1) expressing emotion, (2) conveying attitudes, (3) self-presentation, and (4) managing turn taking.

Unconscious Communication

Mark Knapp tells the delightful and true story of "Clever Hans," a celebrated trick horse that, responding only by tapping his front foot, could tell time, use a calendar, and make all manner of arithmetic calculations. A commission of horse experts tested and retested Clever Hans and concluded that he was for real.

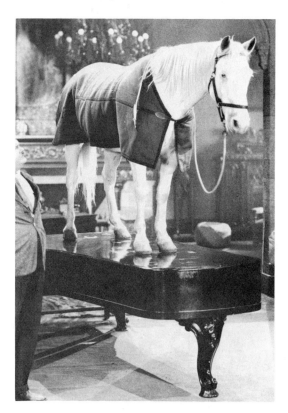

Figure 3.4

Finally one experimenter discovered that Hans could only answer a question if someone in his visual field knew the answer. Knapp explains, "When Hans was given the question, the onlookers assumed an expectant posture and increased their body tension. When Hans reached the correct number of taps, the onlookers would relax and make a slight movement of the head—which was Hans' clue to stop tapping."[2] Hans had no real verbal ability, but an uncanny special ability to respond to very subtle nonverbal cues given off by those around him. Knapp comments cleverly:

> It is not unlike that perceptiveness or sensitivity to nonverbal cues exhibited by a Clever Carl, Charles, Frank, or Harold when picking up a woman, closing a business deal, giving an industrious image to a professor, knowing when to leave a party, and in a multitude of other common situations.[3]

Once again we should not underestimate the power and importance of nonverbal communication.

What made Hans' ability so believable was the fact that the audiences were totally unaware that they were tipping him off. These unconscious (as well as conscious) nonverbals are a definite part of our communication system. The way a person walks or sits at a given moment may demonstrate that person's mood more adequately than his or her words do. When we try to avoid looking awkward, it usually communicates even more awkwardness and looks unnatural and ridiculous.

In the case of Clever Hans, one might say that his audiences *empathized* with him. They projected their concerns and desires (nonverbally) to him. This projection is the basis of empathy. Empathy includes a muscular reaction; to an extent, an audience imitates the actions of the speaker. When a speaker appears mortally afraid and tense, the audience dies a little. When the speaker acts tired, the audience feels tired or bored. When a person paces the floor like a caged lion, the audience usually tires before the speaker does.

Apparently, in the long run we cannot avoid acting nonverbally, and, therefore, we cannot avoid communicating. That our nonverbal behaviors may be unintentionally contrary to our verbal messages is cause for concern. We express our attitudes through our body actions, our voices and articulation patterns, the objects we wear or own, our uses of time and space, our language, and, of course, our verbal messages. Interpersonal communication, then, includes an almost countless number of channels.

The *context* in which the communication episode takes place also conditions the nonverbals. I once arrived at the wrong party in formal clothes. Everyone else was in ski clothes; it mattered little what I said verbally—I felt ridiculous.

[2]Mark L. Knapp, *Nonverbal Communication in Human Interaction* (New York: Holt, Rinehart & Winston, 1978), p. 2; see also O. Pfungst, *Clever Hans, The Horse of Mr. Von Osten* (New York: Holt, Rinehart & Winston, 1911).
[3]Knapp, *Nonverbal Communication*, p. 2.

When I arrived at the right party a block away, I looked like everybody else. Some emotional contexts (fear, love, hate) aren't as humorous as my party story. People display quite different nonverbal responses to various emotional situations. One study found that some people are more sensitive than others to these nonverbal signals and that such individuals tend to function better socially and intellectually. The same study also found that young people are less sensitive to nonverbal signals than are older people.[4]

It has been said that only 35 percent of our total communication is verbal. When we speak face to face with a person, that person may be receiving 65 percent of our message by means other than the words we use—by our tones of voice, our gestures, even by the way we stand or sit and are dressed.[5] No wonder that in some contexts our voices and our actions speak so loudly that our words are often unheard or are not considered important.

Hallmarks of Nonverbal Communication

Our nonverbals of whatever kind, conscious or unconscious, may be characterized as follows:

1. They always communicate something.
2. They are believed.
3. They are bound to the situation.
4. They are seldom isolated.
5. They affect our relationships.

1. THEY ALWAYS COMMUNICATE SOMETHING. Assuming some kind of human interaction, one cannot *not* behave, and since behavior is nonverbal communication, *one is always communicating something.* A blank stare communicates something to the decoder, even if it is just confusion. This is not always appreciated by less sensitive personalities. These behaviors may be consciously or unconsciously conveyed, but one way or another they communicate. They communicate emotion and attitudes, they communicate who we are, and they help us manage interpersonal interactions.

There is little doubt as to the roles involved in Figure 3.5. Object language (clothes) clearly helps with identification. The look of concern is written in the child's eyes, face, and posture. Emotion and attitudes are being conveyed here. The doctor's self-presentation may be stereotyped, but it does illustrate how nonverbals achieve that function.

[4]Robert Rosenthal and others, "Body Talk and Tone of Voice—the Language without Words," *Psychology Today,* September 1974, pp. 64–68.

[5]Randall Harrison, "Nonverbal Communication: Exploration into Time, Space, Action, and Object," in *Dimensions in Communication,* eds. James H. Campbell and Hal W. Hepler (Belmont, Calif.: Wadsworth, 1965), p. 101. For another view see Timothy G. Hegstrom, "Message Impact: What Percentage Is Nonverbal?" *The Western Journal of Speech Communication,* 43, no. 2 (Spring 1979), 134–42.

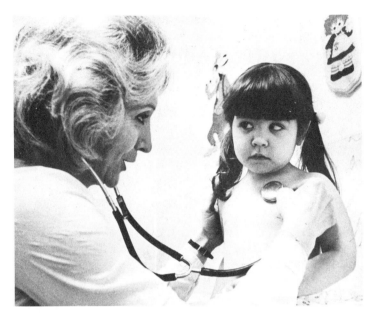

Figure 3.5
Beaumonitor, William Beaumont Hospital System, Royal Oak, Michigan, Spring 1981. Photo by Tom Treuter.

2. **THEY ARE BELIEVED.** Perhaps nonverbals should not be believed, but this tendency exists. Con artists have always taken advantage of this fact. Nonverbals may be hard to fake for most of us, but not for good actors. When what you *say* disagrees with how you *look* or *sound,* people tend to believe the nonverbals. Consider this example: Would you buy a used car from these men (Figure 3.6) Neither is believable as the salesperson of the year.

Figure 3.6

When it comes to basic emotions, the face is thought to be the most believable. Two distinguished scholars insist it is, even across cultures and even where there is no television to teach the stereotypes.[6] Cartoonists capture these believable stereotypes with great regularity:

ANGER   FEAR   HAPPINESS   SADNESS

Figure 3.7

3. THEY ARE BOUND TO THE SITUATION. The context or situation makes a lot of difference. A baby's smile might indicate pleasure in one situation or gas in another. A thumb in the air might mean A-OK on the launch pad or a request for a ride on the highway. When the context or situation is not appreciated or considered, nonverbals can be confusing indeed. When it is obvious, our nonverbals are most clear. Is there any doubt, after looking at Figure 3.8, about how the Florida Senate voted on ERA?

Figure 3.8
Wide World Photos.

4. THEY ARE SELDOM ISOLATED. It is very difficult for most of us to be boiling mad and yet control our actions and voices so that we appear calm. A glisten of perspiration, a faster eyeblink, a slight tremble, a dryness in the voice—these and more signs give us away. Even when we are laughing on the outside (and crying on the inside), the character of our laughter probably gives us away.

[6]Paul Ekman and Wallace V. Friesen, *Unmasking the Face* (Englewood Cliffs, N.J.: Prentice-Hall, 1975), p. 23.

These other nonverbals tend to be related, consistent, and supportive of one another. When they are not, suspicions about intent are raised. Except in pictures or audiotapes, nonverbals are difficult to isolate.

For all the importance of the nonverbal messages, the lesson here should be clear: Don't ignore the verbal; it's still the major part of most interpersonal interactions. To concentrate on only one isolated movement, expression, or tone is a poor way to infer meanings.

5. THEY AFFECT OUR RELATIONSHIPS. We decide three important things about people largely on the basis of nonverbal communication. These are: (1) our personal liking of or attraction to them; (2) their power status, influence, or clout; and (3) our feelings about the responses we get from them.

Let's review each of these as nonverbal codes:

1. Sometimes, by nonverbal cues alone, we might feel attracted toward another. That person seems to be a "likeable sort," "a good person," and easy to be with. That the opposite can be the case is all too clear.

2. A power assessment is our evaluation of another person's status, influence, or clout. Nonverbal cues become important in judging these, particularly in the absence of verbal information.

3. Another nonverbal area of interpersonal decision making relates to our perceptions of responsive listeners, people who can and will appreciate our positions or our problems.

These three nonverbal decisions about people lead us in and out of a lot of communication trouble.

Figure 3.9
Detroit Free Press Photo by Alan Kamuda.

Figure 3.10 The University of Michigan Information Services. Photo by Bob Kalmbach.

Benjamin Franklin
as recreated by Ralph Archbold.

TYPES OF NONVERBAL SIGNALS

Kinesics (Language of the Body and Face)

Kinesics can perform all of the communication functions: expressing emotion, conveying attitudes, self-presentation, and managing turn taking. Figure 3.11 captures all of these functions with the exception, perhaps, of managing turn taking.

Posture, gestures, and walking are some of the specific ways the body communicates. The proximity or closeness of the body, as shown by the baseball manager in Figure 3.11, also communicates. Space and distance factors are discussed shortly under *proxemics*.

POSTURE. Your posture is an important part of the general impression you make. It affects the empathy of the listeners and what they conclude from your signals. The prize-winning photo in Figure 3.12 is a good example of how posture affects impressions.

The way you carry yourself tends to show whether or not you have confidence in yourself. Whether you slouch and cower or whether you stand with military bearing affects your outlook and sense of power and your control over yourself. Is there any doubt that the little "Feller" in Figure 3.13 is a "mean" pitcher?

Figure 3.11
Detroit Free Press Photo by Alan Kamuda.

Figure 3.12 Photo by Andrew Hosie, *Glasgow Daily Record*, Scotland.

Figure 3.13
By permission of Sears, Roebuck and Co.

Posture is an important part of self-presentation: Along with your face, it affects empathy and what people conclude from your signals. When you are the speaker, good posture involves distributing your body weight in a comfortable and poised way consistent with the impression you wish to make. You should be erect without looking stiff, comfortable without appearing limp. Your bearing should be alert, self-possessed, and communicative. Good posture and poise reflect a kind of cool unconcern. The great danger, as with all stylized body action, is appearing artificial, overly noticeable, or out of place.

GESTURES. Your gestures reveal more than you might think. Observe the gestures of people you know well and see if their actions reveal to you their real personalities.

Nervous gestures are often annoying to others. Wringing hands is often a sign of nervousness or indecision. Drumming on the table or kicking the chair are messages that may indicate boredom or impatience.

In discussing gestures, we are concerned mostly with the hands and arms, but always keep in mind that you gesture with your entire body and personality. In a very general sense, we all use gestures for two rhetorical purposes—to reinforce an idea or to help describe something.

Reinforcing gestures, such as clenching a fist or pounding on the table, help convey attitudes or strong feelings of some kind. Such actions usually emphasize one's words.

In disagreeing verbally one might routinely turn the palms down or out. In appealing one might naturally turn the palms up or in. These types of gestures reinforce through emphasis. Other gestures reinforce through a kind of suggestion. In communicating a scolding attitude, we might wag a finger in much the same stereotyped way that the teacher does. No two persons use these reinforcing gestures exactly alike, but the stereotype is usually recognized. These also are called "emblems."[7] They are usually translated rather directly; examples would be the hitchhike or A-OK signs.

Figure 3.14

[7]Paul Ekman and Wallace V. Friesen, "The Repertoire of Nonverbal Behavior: Categories, Origins, Usage, and Coding," *Semiotica*, 1 (1969), 49–98.

Description is an obvious function of gestures. All descriptive gestures are also partly reinforcing. The person describing a blind date with gestures communicates more than just size and shape; a listener might, for example, quickly pick up a message of approval or disapproval. Ekman and Friesen refer to such gestures as "illustrators."

The use of some of the gestures just discussed can develop a consistency approaching a grammar. The early American Indians had an elaborate retinue of nonverbal signs which for them was an important language. The deaf have a system of hand signals called signing that carries an amazing amount of meaning. Other special groups besides the deaf have special signs—for example, athletes, secret societies, and racial and ethnic subcultures. When we find that a gesture that means "come here" in America means "go away" in Italy, we begin to sense the problem.

WALKING. Walking is not usually a large part of interpersonal communication; however, in conflict interactions, in storytelling, at cocktail parties, and during public speaking, walking may be a telling part of self-presentation.

Actors have long known the importance of walk to express various moods and degrees of emphasis. The *femme fatale* has a walk that clearly communicates her role; the sneaky villain also has a stylized walk. The child about to be spanked walks quite differently from the child on the way to the movies. In public speaking walking may serve as a form of physical punctuation. Transitions and pauses may be strengthened by a few steps to the side, emphasis by a step forward. Like the actor, the speaker wishes to appear natural, not awkward. If your walking is ungraceful or mechanical, it will distract from its intended purpose; if it is random, it will distract from the general purpose of your speech. In short, the way you walk tells a lot about you. It can show energy, enthusiasm, sloppiness, indifference, fatigue—or any number of other things about you.

FACIAL EXPRESSIONS. Two scholars who have spent a lifetime studying the recognition of emotions from facial expressions insist that Darwin was correct in claiming that there are universal facial expressions of emotion. Ekman and Friesen identify the following: *happiness, sadness, surprise, fear, anger,* and *disgust.*[8] Can you identify the emotions depicted in the following?

Figure 3.15

[8]Eckman and Friesen, *Unmasking the Face,* pp. 22–25.

Most facial expressions of emotion, especially in the presence of others, are still somewhat culture-bound. Eckman and Friesen comment cogently on the pragmatic effects of acculturation as follows:

> Although the appearance of the face for each of the primary emotions is common to all peoples, facial expressions do vary across cultures in at least two respects. What elicits or calls forth an emotion will usually differ: people may become disgusted or afraid in response to different things in different cultures. Also cultures differ in the conventions people follow in attempting to control or manage the appearance of their faces in given social situations. People in two different cultures may feel sadness at the death of a loved one but one culture may prescribe that the chief mourners mask their facial expression with a mildly happy countenance.[9]

They also report evidence from a study of Japanese and American college students that we tend to communicate nonverbally more stereotypically when we are not alone.[10] A graduate student at Wayne State University recently found the same results in our culture.[11] Of course, we are interested in situations in which we are with others. If, in moments of stress or anxiety, we regress, then perhaps these reversions appear universally as well. Since acculturation is akin to social acting, we may find the culture-bound and stereotypical behavior more useful than the true basic portrayals. We cry when we're happy; we cry when we're sad. In a study in which emotions of the face were posed and photographed, viewers correctly identified the emotions.[12] We are quite good at stereotypes if they are a part of our culture.

A more recent study by Williams and Tolch[13] indicated that there are two elements in the perception of acted facial expressions, *general evaluation* and *dynamism*. By general evaluation they mean a viewer's evaluation of those characteristics of an expression which reveal such ethical qualities as goodness, gratefulness, kindness, and the like. Dynamism is an evaluation of qualities such as active or passive, fast or slow, interesting or boring, and so on. Acted facial expressions based on only these two elements were differentiated successfully by viewers. However, an acted "no message—neutral" expression introduced into the study was usually seen as having both *evaluative* and *dynamic* qualities.

[9]Ibid., pp. 27–28.

[10]Ibid., p. 23.

[11]William Kennedy, "The Communication of Affect via Facial Expression" (unpublished doctoral dissertation, Wayne State University, 1978).

[12]Henry E. Garrett, *Great Experiments in Psychology* (New York: Appleton-Century-Crofts, 1941), p. 330; see also J. Frois Wittman, "The Judgment of Facial Expression," *Journal of Experimental Psychology*, 13 (1930), 113–51; and Delwin Dusenbury and Franklin H. Knower, "Experimental Studies of the Symbolism of Action and Voice—I: A Study of the Specificity of Meaning in Facial Expression," *Quarterly Journal of Speech*, 24, no. 3 (1938), 435.

[13]Frederick Williams and John Tolch, "Communication by Facial Expression," *Journal of Communication*, 15, no. 1 (March 1965), 17; see also J. Tolch, "The Problem of Language and Accuracy in Identification of Facial Expression," *Central States Speech Journal*, 14 (February 1963), 12–16.

Figure 3.16
Irish eyes are glaring. John McNamara was so mad his eyes were popping as he glared at umpire Nick Colosi. Wide World Photos.

Schlosberry suggests that facial expression can be evaluated in terms of what he calls pleasantness or unpleasantness, sleep or tension, and rejection or attention.[14]

The eyes and especially *eye contact* are considered valuable sources of information as well as conveyors of attitude.

Yasin, a student from Kuwait, admits to being an eye watcher which is why he stands so close. He tells us that all Arabs watch eyes, and specifically, the pupils. According to Yasin, we can detect truth, deceit, surprise, satisfaction, and the like if the total context is kept in mind. There is support for Yasin's statement. Evidence indicates that a man's pupils double in size when shown a picture of a nude woman. Good card players and magicians have an advantage because they know that an opponent's pupils will involuntarily widen when dealt a good card.[15]

Eye contact at close range is needed for this kind of pupil analysis. A longer range attitude analysis of this notion of eye contact also exists. Teachers of public speaking have been advising it for years: "Be more direct; establish eye contact."

On the interpersonal level, a person enamored with another person may spend more time staring at the person than listening to him or her. One researcher has concluded:

> If the usual short, intermittent gazes during conversation are replaced by gazes of longer duration, the target interprets this as meaning that the task is less important than the personal relation between the two persons.[16]

Argyle makes several other points about eye contact that suggest the conveying of attitudes:

1. A looker may invite interaction by staring at another person who is on the other side of a room. The target's studied return of the gaze is generally

[14]Harold Schlosbery, "Three Dimensions of Emotion," *Psychological Review*, 61 (1954), 81–88.
[15]Eckhard H. Hess, *The Tell-Tale Eye* (New York: Van Nostrand Reinhold, 1975), p. 15; see also E. Hess, "Attitude and Pupil Size," *Scientific American*, 212 (April 1965), 46.
[16]Argyle, *The Psychology of Interpersonal Behavior*, pp. 105–16.

interpreted as acceptance of the invitation, while averting the eyes is a rejection of the looker's request.

2. There is more mutual eye contact between friends than others, and a looker's frank gaze is widely interpreted as positive regard.

3. Persons who seek eye contact while speaking are regarded not only as exceptionally well-disposed by their target, but also as more believable and earnest.[17]

Paralanguage (Voice and Articulation)

Can we express emotions through the voice alone? You bet we can. Consider a piercing scream—"Help, murder, rape!" Even without the words we get the emotional message of *fear.* "YUCK, what a gruesome sight," we hear as someone observes the picture in Figure 3.17. *Disgust* is in the voice.

What do you *hear?* Fear, disgust? The voice clearly expresses emotions. It is so effective at conveying attitudes that often we don't need the language. Tone, pitch, and inflection say it all. As a matter of fact, when the voice contradicts the words—"She said *NO,* but there was *YES* in her voice"—we tend to believe the voice. The voice is thought to be a harder signal to fake yet the old radio actors were great fakers. This suggests that voice has a lot to do with self-presentation, and that you can do something about it. As in pantomime, there are certain long-standing stereotypes that we take for granted in the use of the voice. We recognize certain radio roles as voice stereotypes: the mean character, the hero, the sissy, the dunce. The very great danger in using voice stereotypes is that one might take on an artificial voice permanently. Of course, we all occasionally fail to match the voice we "put on" with the situation in which we find ourselves. Listen to yourself on occasion. If you sound "arty" when talking about fertilizer, your voice habits may be altering your personality in ways that will seriously affect your communication.

Figure 3.17

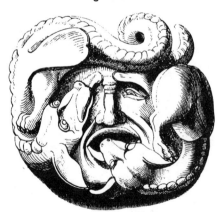

[17]Ibid.

The voice contributes much to self-presentation. It may be the single most important code we use. Studies of voice and social status indicate the importance and the communication potential of this nonverbal code. There is evidence that one's social status can be determined in large part by the signals we receive from the voice alone, apart from language.[18] There is also evidence that Americans tend to downgrade a person who speaks with a foreign accent.[19]

Managing turn taking is another very important function of paralanguage. Your hand signals as you seek the floor are probably coordinated with a louder voice. Mark Knapp captures some standard voice (as well as kinesic) behaviors as someone tries to get the floor:

> When the speaker and listener are well synchronized, the listener will anticipate the speaker's juncture for yielding and will prepare accordingly—getting the rhythm before the other person has stopped talking, much like a musician tapping a foot preceding his or her solo performance. If the requestor's *rhythm* does not fit the speaker's, we might observe some stutter starts, for example, "I . . . I . . . I . . . wa . . ." Sometimes the turn-requesting mechanism will consist of efforts to speed up the speaker, realizing that the sooner the speaker has his or her say, the sooner you'll get yours. . . . The most common method for encouraging the other person to finish quickly is the use of rapid head nods, often accompanied by verbalizations of pseudoagreement, such as "yeah," "mm-hmm," and the like. The requestor hopes the speaker will perceive that these comments are given much too often and do not logically follow ideas expressed to be genuine signs of reinforcement.[20]

You have considerable control over certain characteristics of your voice. You can change your *rate* of speaking; you can adjust your *loudness* almost as you would that of a radio; you can speak at different *pitch* levels; and you can alter the overtones or partial tones of your voice, which represent a kind of *quality* control often called *timbre* or *vocal color*. Along with *intonation*, sounding the vowels, these characteristics are the nonverbal signals that help a listener determine the structure and meaning of what you say.[21] They are known as vocal qualifiers.

RATE. Test passages have been devised for measuring verbal speed in wpm (words per minute). In general, a rate of more than 185 wpm is considered too rapid for a normal public-speaking situation, and a rate of less than 140 wpm

[18]James D. Moe, "Listener Judgments of Status Cues in Speech: A Replication and Extension," *Speech Monographs*, 39, no. 2 (1972), 144–47.

[19]Anthony Mulac, Theodore D. Hanley, and Diane Y. Prigge, "Effects of Phonological Speech Foreignness upon Three Dimensions of Attitude of Selected American Listeners," *Quarterly Journal of Speech*, 60, no. 4 (December 1974), 411–20.

[20]Mark L. Knapp, *Essentials of Nonverbal Communication* (New York: Holt, Rinehart & Winston, 1980), p. 133.

[21]Arthur Wingfield, "Acoustic Redundancy and the Perception of Time-Compressed Speech," *Journal of Speech and Hearing Research*, 18, no. 1 (1975), 96–104.

is considered too slow.[22] The problem of measurement is confounded by interpersonal interactions in which situations, moods, and contexts are considerably more variable than in public-speaking settings.

Interpersonally, certain communications may take place at a very rapid verbal rate and others at a slow or mixed rate. A further problem associated with verbal rate is that words are not really separately formed units but tend to flow from one sound to another; this affects both articulation and pronunciation. Take the phrase, "Did you eat?" If really speeded up, it becomes "Jeet?" This process is called *assimilation*. The length of sounds or tones is also a factor in verbal rate, as are pauses, phrasing, and general rhythm patterns.

The *duration* of sounds and words normally varies with our moods. We generally use tones of relatively short duration when expressing anger and more prolonged tones for expressing love.

Your use of *pauses*[23] and phrases is a factor in your rate of speaking. The "pregnant pause" is no idle jest; it has much to do with communication. A phrase is a group of words that forms a thought unit. Pauses occur between words and between phrases, and the number and duration of pauses seriously alter the meaning of what you say. The complexity and nature of your speech material should also affect your decisions regarding the use of phrases and pauses. If you were to use a long pause after a phrase for emphasis, fine, but if the phrase were relatively silly you might appear ridiculous. If you were to use long pauses in a random manner not related to meaning (not an uncommon error), you would then *confuse* your listener. Short pauses generally indicate that there is more to come. If you routinely use a rather intermediate-length pause without consistently relating it to what you are saying, you run the added danger of *monotony*, a tiresome lack of variation.

When we increase our rates in normal conversation, that alone carries a message. In addition, our pitch goes up, articulation suffers, and pauses take on less significance or are lost altogether. It becomes, in large part, a question of self-presentation. If your fast rate is done rhetorically with full awareness of the *relationship* risks, that's one thing. If it's done simply as a bad habit, the risk is that it may be construed by others as compensatory or tactless.

LOUDNESS. Loudness is a measure of the total signal. You may think of loudness generally as volume, but speech science indicates that volume is related so intimately to pitch that the term loudness may be misleading. Your volume is easier to raise as your pitch goes up. Furthermore, it is possible to speak with more force or intensity without altering your volume proportionately.

[22]Grant Fairbanks, *Voice and Articulation Drillbook* (New York: Harper & Row, 1960), p. 115. Some authorities argue that since listening rates may range from 400 to 800 wpm, a public-speaking rate of 200 wpm is not unrealistic.

[23]Norman J. Lass and Marcia Paffenberger, "A Comparative Study of Rate Evaluations of Experienced and Inexperienced Listeners," *Quarterly Journal of Speech*, 57, no. 1 (1971), 89–93.

Figure 3.18

Extreme loudness has strong *relationship* ramifications for most people. We reserve it for emergencies or issues of great concern—and sometimes for interpersonal conflicts that "get away from us." As Chief illustrates in Figure 3.18, loudness also expresses emotion.[24]

There is another side to this loudness question. Sometimes we speak very softly. Among the psychological reasons for a lack of voice projection is a form of avoidance of the speech situation. People tend to *withdraw* from threatening situations. It is almost as if speaking with a soft, barely heard voice is the next best thing to not being in the situation at all.

Your receivers will help you adjust your loudness. Look at them for feedback signs. Are they straining to hear? Are they withdrawing?

Much of what we call *vocal variety* is related to loudness. The force with which you utter certain phrases or words is a form of oral punctuation and can add much to another's understanding of what you say. The manner in which you apply force to what you say is also a factor in vocal variety. An audible whisper can be a powerful nonverbal as well as verbal emphasis in some interactions.

PITCH. We can pretty accurately determine sex and, to a point, age through pitch alone.[25] Normal pitch changes as we move from childhood to adolescence to adulthood, and these pitches are generally recognizable as belonging to the appropriate age groups.

Interestingly, men's voices reach their lowest pitch during middle age and then rise slightly with age.[26] It appears that the same may not be true of women; pitch remains more constant during their adult years.[27]

---

[24]However, accuracy of perceived emotions on voice cues alone varies. See J. R. Davitz and L. Davitz, "The Communication of Feelings by Content-Free Speech," *Journal of Communication*, 9 (1959), 6–13; see also J. R. Davitz, *The Communication of Emotional Meaning* (New York: McGraw-Hill, 1964).

[25]N. J. Lass, K. R. Hughes, M. D. Bowyer, L. T. Waters, and V. T. Broune, "Speaker Sex Identification from Voiced, Whispered and Filtered Isolated Vowels," *Journal of the Acoustical Society of America*, 59 (1976), 675–78.

[26]E. D. Mysak, "Pitch and Duration Characteristics of Older Males," *Journal of Speech and Hearing Research*, 2 (1959), 46–54.

[27]R. E. McGlone and H. Hollien, "Vocal Pitch Characteristics of Aged Women," *Journal of Speech and Hearing Research*, 6 (1963), 164–70.

A drop in pitch at the end of a statement frequently indicates that a person is ready to yield the floor. If you are maintaining the floor in part through rapid rate, your pitch rises. When we speak, we use a variety of pitches which are normally distributed in terms of amount of usage. If we were to plot the number of occurrences of the different pitches we use, we would find a central pitch around which the others vary in relatively predictable amounts.

For most people, optimum pitch should be the habitual or central pitch. Often, our optimum pitch is found a little below the habitual or normally used pitch because of tensions that restrict the vocal apparatus.

QUALITY. Voice quality results from the modification frequency modulation of the vocal-cord tone by the resonators. It is that attribute of tone and sound waves that enables us to distinguish between two sounds that are alike in pitch, duration, and loudness.

Other things being equal, we can easily distinguish the overly nasal, breathy, or harsh voice. In addition, we are able to make nonverbal distinctions of a much more subtle nature. For example, we recognize the voice of a person who is sincerely touched by a tribute or the voice of a person who is suppressing anger. Emotional moods affect voice quality and may have profound effects upon emphasis and meaning. In this context, voice quality is often referred to as *timbre*.

Voice quality is a problem when one's voice contains consistent deviations that detract from the message or its meaning. Certain organic disorders, such as a cleft palate or nasal obstructions, can cause unusual voice quality. Emotional moods may also result in temporary deviations from voice quality. In addition, voice quality may be affected by the strictly temporary physical problems caused by head colds, sore throats, and the like.

An expert in voice and diction training once said, "Bluntly stated, one may have a dull, uninteresting, or unpleasant voice because his voice is defective or improperly used; but he may also have such a voice because he is a dull, uninteresting, or unpleasant person." Vocal training, like all speech training, cannot take place in a vacuum; rather it is intimately related to the whole personality. Just as personality affects voice, voice improvement may affect personality.

ARTICULATION CONTROL. This refers to your diction and pronunciation, especially the way you form or "articulate" the consonants. It greatly affects the quality of your total expression. Saying *dese, dem,* and *dose* for *these, them,* and *those* indicates something about the sender apart from the verbal message. What it says may vary considerably with the context. Hollywood spends much time and money working on the articulation (and dialects) of attractive, Brooklyn-born, future stars, whose pronunciations affect their self-presentations. Ironically, a standard American dialect may have to be roughened to achieve a self-presentation for a particular role.

To some extent, we adapt our articulation in groups and situations in which a different dialect is spoken, particularly if we are part of such a group. Many students have developed two dialects in order to communicate more easily. Sometimes, the use of a second dialect has social and practical advantages.[28] Saying "Ax me a question" may enhance your self-presentation in one group and diminish it in another. Pronunciation is related. In old Milwaukee the word *theatre* was typically pronounced "the-*ay*-ter," a compromised carryover from the German pronunciation of "das Theater" ("tay-*ah*-ter"). In Detroit we hear "th-*uh*-ter." People in some localities may say "drammer" for "drama." The extremely valuable dictionary is a little awkward on some pronunciations because there are three generally accepted dialects in the United States (eastern, southern, and standard American). The most widespread dialect is standard American, and our dictionaries and national mass media are geared to this dialect.

Writing pronunciations of words is awkward. One way to do this is to agree upon symbols based strictly upon sound. Thus, the International Phonetic Alphabet was born. It has one symbol for every different sound in the language. The news services use a system of *respelling* similar to what was used in the previous paragraph. Dictionaries use diacritical marks to show pronunciation. Accent or stress is indicated as primary (′) or secondary (,). A guide to pronounciation and to the particular diacritical system used is carefully explained in the introduction to any good dictionary.[29] It is well worth your reading.

Table 3.1   Examples of Pronouncing Systems

WORD	DIACRITICAL SYSTEM	INTERNATIONAL PHONETIC SYSTEM	RESPELLING SYSTEM
chaotic	/kā-ˈät-ik/	[keˈɑtɪk]	kay-otic
theatre	/ˈthē-ət-ər/	[ˈθiətɚ]	the-uh-ter
nativity	/nə-ˈtiv-ət-ē/	[neˈtɪvɑti]	nay-tiv-ity

Some of the more common pronunciation errors are a result of improper stress, errors in spelling-phonetics (that is, pronouncing words as they are spelled), sound substitutions, additions, reversals, and subtractions.

Objects (Clothes and Things)

Dear Mr. Molloy: I am second in command of a large management consulting firm. We send our people all over the world to consult in highly technical fields. They are mostly engineers, and the majority have several graduate degrees.

[28]Mildred C. Matlock, "Teaching Standard English to Black Dialect Speakers," *Michigan Speech and Hearing Association Journal*, 10, no. 2 (1974), 91–99. See also Geneva Smitherman, *Talkin and Testifyin: Language of Black America* (New York: Houghton Mifflin, 1977); Thomas J. Hixon, Lawrence D. Shriberg, and John H. Saxman, *Introduction to Communication Disorders* (Englewood Cliffs, N.J.: Prentice-Hall, 1980), pp. 191–93.

[29]See especially *Webster's New Collegiate Dictionary* (Springfield, Mass.: G. & C. Merriam, 1980), p. 32A.

For the last few years, we've had our annual convention in Arizona, where we have found a hotel that everyone likes. The problem is, every time we show up, we each get the same gift: a free cowboy hat and a big belt buckle with the year's motto on it. Now the fellows have taken to wearing these belt buckles to work. I don't think it does much damage here in California, but I suspect that when they go East or to Europe and Japan, it gives off the wrong message. —*D.J., San Diego*

Dear D.J.: You're absolutely right. If your men are wearing these cowboy belt buckles with conservative suits, they may come across as untrustworthy. If, on the other hand, they're wearing the type of suits that go with these belt buckles, they are sending an even stronger negative message. The "cowboy look" does not travel well. In most other sections of the world, it says "rube," and its says it very loudly in Japan and Europe. I suggest you tell the fellows to leave their belt buckles back on the ranch.[30]

Right or wrong, many stereotypes are associated with "clothes and things." Research helps us define even these. Persons who wear bizarre clothes are considered more radical, activist, and more likely to experiment with drugs. People who wear more conventional dress are associated with everyday jobs and "traditional fun."[31] The problem is in knowing what kind of "clothes and things" are conventional, in style, or expected of us. This happens to be the problem of all

Figure 3.19 Judith Waters, "The Cinderella Syndrome: A Study of the Relationship between Physical Appearance, Level of Skill, and Salary." *Fairleigh Dickinson University Magazine*, Feb., 1980, pp. 11–15.

Would you hire this woman as she appears to the left? Not if you reacted to her photo like a group of employers questioned, who gave her zero ratings. However, proving that appearances do count, the employers said they would hire the same woman (right) with the same resume, after she spruced up with a new hairdo and makeup.

[30]*Detroit Free Press*, July 20, 1980, p. 2.
[31]For more on these matters, see Mark L. Knapp, *Essentials of Nonverbal Communication*, pp. 113–19.

communication, whether nonverbal or verbal, public or interpersonal. The point is that the nonverbals of clothes and things make a big difference in the way we are seen *totally*—that is, socially, vocationally, sexually, and so on.

Proxemics (Space and Distance)

Each of us carries a kind of space bubble around us to mark off our personal territories which varies in size from person to person and according to the culture from which we come. Most hostile people are thought to have larger bubbles. They are more easily angered and upset because it is easier to bruise their larger bubbles. People also have different bubbles for different situations. We "occupy" a certain room of the house: my room, Dad's den, and Mom's living room are rather special at times. Invading another's room can make us quite unpopular. Attitudes are being conveyed here; burst a bubble and you'll find emotions being expressed.

Cultural influence is considerable. Latin Americans and Arabs tend to stand close together when they talk. Most North Americans like to talk at arm's length. What is normal distance for Latin Americans and Arabs is considered intimate by most of us. The possibility of poor or at least confused interpersonal communication is obvious. Within our own culture these appropriate distances change according to the message and how well we know the listeners.[32] We tend to stand farther away from strangers than from friends. Of course, we are apt to stand closer when saying "I love you" than when saying "Hello there." We also use our voices differently according to distance, message, and mood. Edward Hall has proposed a scale that helps identify the relationships (see Figure 3.20 on p. 78). Figure 3.21 depicts the various speech situations which a person might encounter.

Chronemics (Time)

Most Americans are serious if not neurotic about being *on* time. We also take leaving time very seriously and are quick to attribute messages and attitudes to "time" behaviors. Some Americans have more casual attitudes about time than others. Some students are routinely late for all their classes and their reasons probably have nothing to do with their regard for the other students, the professor, or the course. However, people do tend to read lateness as some kind of negative attitude.

Cultural differences point up the importance of time as nonverbal communication. Navajo Indians have great interest in immediate or *now* time, but little in future time. Their language has no words for "future" or "late." Iranians have less interest in *now* time, but great interest in past time.[33] An appointment in our

---

[32]For an interesting discussion of these matters, see Judee K. Burgoon and L. Aho, "Three Field Experiments of the Effects of Violations of Conversational Distance," *Communication Monographs*, 49, no. 2 (June 1982), pp. 71–88.

[33]For more on cultural differences see Hall, *The Silent Language*.

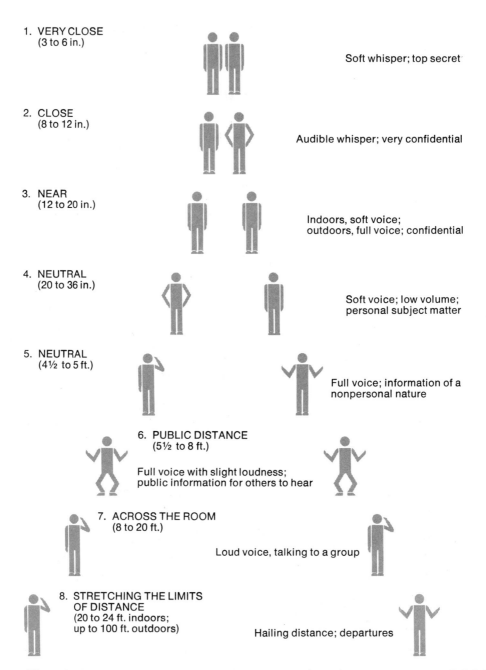

1. VERY CLOSE
   (3 to 6 in.)

   Soft whisper; top secret

2. CLOSE
   (8 to 12 in.)

   Audible whisper; very confidential

3. NEAR
   (12 to 20 in.)

   Indoors, soft voice;
   outdoors, full voice; confidential

4. NEUTRAL
   (20 to 36 in.)

   Soft voice; low volume;
   personal subject matter

5. NEUTRAL
   (4½ to 5 ft.)

   Full voice; information of a
   nonpersonal nature

6. PUBLIC DISTANCE
   (5½ to 8 ft.)

   Full voice with slight loudness;
   public information for others to hear

7. ACROSS THE ROOM
   (8 to 20 ft.)

   Loud voice, talking to a group

8. STRETCHING THE LIMITS
   OF DISTANCE
   (20 to 24 ft. indoors;
   up to 100 ft. outdoors)

   Hailing distance; departures

Figure 3.20 Adapting the voice to distance, message and mood. Adapted from Edward T. Hall, *The Silent Language* (Garden City, N.Y.: Doubleday, 1959), pp. 208–9.

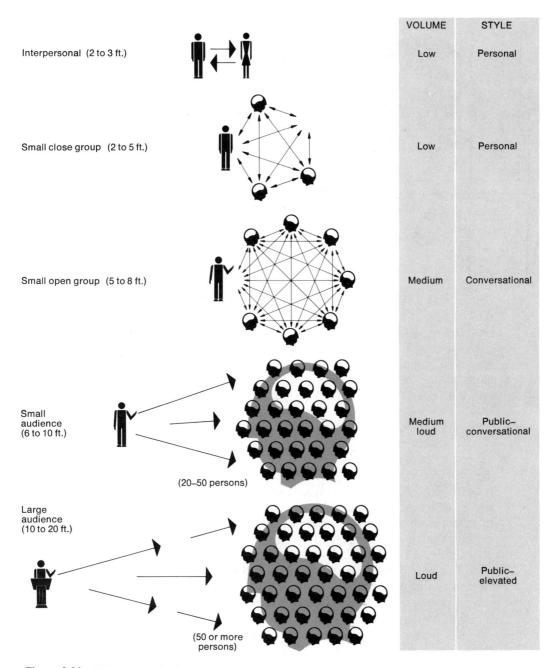

		VOLUME	STYLE
Interpersonal (2 to 3 ft.)		Low	Personal
Small close group (2 to 5 ft.)		Low	Personal
Small open group (5 to 8 ft.)		Medium	Conversational
Small audience (6 to 10 ft.)	(20–50 persons)	Medium loud	Public–conversational
Large audience (10 to 20 ft.)	(50 or more persons)	Loud	Public–elevated

Figure 3.21   © Raymond S. Ross.

Figure 3.22
Juror jailed for a night in Canton, Ohio, because she overslept and was two hours late for jury duty in a rape trial—1981.

culture for 10:00 A.M. on Tuesday means just that (give or take five or ten minutes). However, the Navajo might hear only Tuesday; South Americans might hear any time between 10:00 A.M. and 11:00 A.M. Of course, even these cultures have succumbed to more technical time demands such as airline departures, radio and television programming, timed laboratory experiments, and the like. In our culture, an invitation to drop by *any time* (rather than a specific day and time) is usually interpreted as "don't bother," unless there is a very close personal relationship which allows predictions of *appropriate* time. The same general invitation in another culture may literally mean that *any* time is appropriate.

In our culture we are more time specific and when we don't follow the general rules, we are perceived as sending a message. Others will attribute meanings to our deviant behavior. A long-distance phone call in the middle of the night typically has a different urgency than one during the day. Being thirty minutes late for a forty-five minute job interview invites all kinds of negative inferences from the waiting person. Seldom are we in trouble for being early, but we may get into trouble for being late! Almost every interview form includes an evaluation of the subject's dependability, which often translates into his or her attitude toward being on time. Our general culture tends to stress promptness. Television viewers complain by the thousands when a scheduled program is delayed by a news special or by a game that runs into overtime.

Lateness suggests low regard for the sender, the situation, or the message. The late person who remains silent runs some interpersonal risks. If one has no really good reason for being late, and no one really cares, perhaps it doesn't matter. Students say that about some large lecture classes (400 students) with no attendance requirement. However, in small classes in which relationships are more personal, a routinely late person (fifteen to twenty minutes) is inviting negative attributions about such behavior.

Even if an explanation for unusual tardiness is weak or nobody's business, some apology is in order. "I'm sorry; I can't explain right now." It cuts down the number of negative attributions possible and keeps the communication door ajar. We can often save strained interpersonal relations by giving good reasons when we are late.

Staying time in a classroom situation is defined by the bell at the end of a class. However, in less formal business and social settings, there is more leeway.

Other Signal Systems

The study of touch or tactile communication is called *haptics.* Except for social and legal dimensions we don't really know much about how this basic code works. Some cultures are more touch oriented than others. Observations of interacting couples in cafes provided these interesting differences in contacts per hour:

San Juan, Puerto Rico	180
Paris, France	110
Gainesville, Florida	2
London, England	0[34]

Figure 3.23

The legal problem ranges from suggesting touching to physical abuse. Modern labor contracts are often quite specific about not striking (hitting) one another. In one instance a supervisor was vigorously scolding an employee while at the same time shaking his finger under the employee's nose. The supervisor insisted he never hit the employee, but a grievance was filed. At the hearing the supervisor conceded that he might have inadvertently "touched" the employee. The arbitrator ruled against the company. Most supervisory development courses instruct managers to *never* touch an employee for any reason. A handshake is acceptable, but that's about all. A pat on the back, especially if it's a little low, may

[34]Sidney M. Jourard, "An Exploratory Study of Body-Accessibility," *British Journal of Social and Clinical Psychology,* 5 (1966), 221–31.

be construed as sexual harassment. Taboos against striking an officer in the military or a civilian police officer are other examples of how we are conditioned to reserve touching for very special family and intimate situations.

The study of smell or olfactory communication is called *aromatics*. There is evidence that sweat and various odors are related to our emotional states. It is the basis for the Palmer sweat and galvanic skin devices. Animals perceive sex odors and it is thought that the human animal can do likewise. However, Americans spend most of their time stamping out, rubbing out, and spraying out body odors. Socially, natural body odors are negative signals; conversely, we try to communicate sexuality, masculinity, sweetness, and so on, with artificial smells from perfume bottles, aftershave lotions, tobacco, gum, and cologne. Someone even attempted to develop a new car smell that could be sprayed inside of used cars.

There are many other nonverbal codes, too many to discuss here. However, the simple but important one of silence should be mentioned. The ultimate nonverbal insult is often simply to be ignored. ("Look at me when I speak to you!") Silence can be a powerful message. The "blind date who never called" has sent quite a message to the other person. Sometimes people remain silent simply because they are confused, tired, embarrassed, or honestly did not hear. Remember this when you are ignored (or think you are) and try one more time.

SUMMARY

The four basic functions of nonverbal communication are: (1) expressing emotion; (2) conveying attitudes; (3) self-presentation; and (4) managing turn taking.

It has been said that only 35 percent of our communication is verbal; 65 percent of our messages may be given by means other than the words we use: by our tones of voice, our gestures, the way we stand, sit, and dress.

Empathy, the projection of oneself into the situation of another, includes a muscular reaction; the audience imitates, in part, the actions of the speaker. Speakers should adapt their body actions to the empathy of the audience. Constant pacing, for example, should be avoided, because it will probably wear out the audience before it does the speaker.

Our nonverbals of whatever kind, conscious or unconscious, may be characterized as follows: (1) they always communicate something; (2) they are believed; (3) they are situation-bound; (4) they are seldom isolated; and (5) they affect our relationships.

Types of nonverbal communication include: kinesics (language of the face and body); paralanguage (language of the voice); and those utilizing the environmental dimensions of objects, space, and time. There are universal facial expressions of emotion: happiness, sadness, surprise, fear, anger, and disgust.

However, most facial expressions, especially in the presence of others, are still somewhat culture-bound. Facial expressions can be evaluated in terms of pleasantness or unpleasantness, sleep or tension, and rejection or attention. The eyes are considered valuable sources of information as well as conveyors of attitude.

Voice may be the single most important nonverbal code we use. It is often so effective at conveying emotions and attitudes that we don't need verbal language. Tone, pitch, and inflection say it all. Vocal qualifiers over which you have some control are: (1) rate; (2) loudness; (3) pitch; (4) quality; and (5) articulation.

Object language uses the influence and display of material things. It includes the clothes we wear, and the jewelry, cosmetics, and so forth, that make a statement. The key word is appropriate.

Space and distance (proxemics) relationships refer to the personal space or territory we deem acceptable. Our preferences are culture-bound. Appropriate space and distance are closely related to the message, situation, and mood. We adapt our voices in rather set ways to these aspects. E. T. Hall suggests an eight-point scale from three inches to 100 feet. Another scale suggesting proper volume and style according to type of communication (interpersonal, small group, audience) was shown in this chapter.

People in our culture tend to read lateness as some kind of negative attitude. Other nonverbal signals include: haptics (touch), aromatics (smell), and silence.

STUDY PROJECTS

1. Take turns trying to communicate the following messages through body action language:

    a. Don't blame me.
    b. I'm the piano tuner.
    c. She (he) is really something!
    d. Will you walk with me?
    e. Oh, Ed (Eunice), let's park here.
    f. Oh, Ed (Eunice), let's not park here.

2. Prepare a two- to four-minute descriptive speech that requires considerable body action (for instance, a speech on shooting the rapids, water skiing, ski jumping, the big game, the close race, the big storm, a frightening episode, a close call, an embarrassing moment).

3. Prepare a one-minute pantomime in which you use body action to provoke an empathic response (for example, walking and fatigue, lifting and strain, falling and pain, taste and ecstasy, and so forth).

4. Do a nonverbal analysis of a television drama or comedy. Define a number of situational contexts and show how emotions or attitudes were expressed nonverbally by the actors.

5. Try an experiment in object language. Wear something unusual (for you) and interact with some family or friends. Write a one-page report of what happened to the communication. Discuss it in class.

6. Try a space and distance experiment. Sit in someone's favorite chair or place, or stand closer to people than you usually do. Write a one-page report of what happened in the ensuing communication. Discuss it in class.

4

Listening behavior

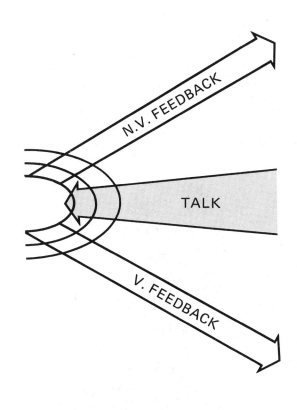

General learning outcomes

- We should learn the importance of listening to human communication and understanding.

- We should learn to apply a four-step listening model: sensation, interpretation, comprehension, and response.

- We should learn the filters of and the barriers to effective listening so that we may improve our own listening and speaking behavior.

- We should learn the behavioral response ladder (REDDAL) to help us concentrate on the sender.

Most of us have perfectly good ears.

So why, then, are we such perfectly awful listeners—listening on the average at a 25% level of efficiency.

The fact is, there's a lot more to listening than hearing.

After we hear something we must interpret it. Evaluate it. And finally, respond to it. That's listening.

And it's during this complex process that we run into all kinds of trouble.

For example: We prejudge—sometimes even disregard—a speaker based on delivery or appearance.

We let personal ideas, emotions or prejudices distort what a person has to say. We tune-out subjects we consider too difficult or uninteresting.

And because the brain works four times faster than most people speak, we too often wander into distraction.

Figure 4.1
Knowing how to listen takes more than two good ears.   Used with permission of Sperry Corporation.

Yet as difficult as listening really is, it's the one communication skill we're never really taught.

Well, as a corporation with more than 87,000 employees, we at Sperry are making sure we use our ears to full advantage.

We've set up expanded listening programs that Sperry personnel from our five divisions worldwide can attend. Sales representatives. Sperry Univac computer engineers. Even the Chairman of the Board.

We're convinced that effective listening adds a special dimension to what we can do for our customers. And when you speak to someone from Sperry we think you'll be equally convinced.

It's amazing what more than two good ears can do.

We understand how important it is to listen.[1]

Figure 4.2   Wizard of ID.   By permission of Johnny Hart and Field Enterprises, Inc.

THE IMPORTANCE OF LISTENING

Hal Boyle agrees that no one is willing to listen anymore and that there is a tremendous market for good listeners. He humorously offers to rent his ears as follows:

> Whenever anyone grabs me by the lapels and starts wagging his jawbone, I'll silently hand him a printed folder which says:
>
> "You are speaking to a man who earns his living by listening. So, please button your mouth unless you are willing to pay my rates, which are as follows:
>
> "Listening to comments on the weather, baseball and politics: 50 cents an hour.
>
> "Listening to husbands complain about their wives: 75 cents an hour.
>
> "Listening to wives complain about their husbands: Ditto.

[1]Sperry is Sperry Univac computers, Sperry New Holland farm equipment, Sperry Vickers fluid power systems, and guidance and control equipment from Sperry division and Sperry Flight Systems. Do you have more than two good ears? Write to Sperry, Dept. 4D, 1290 Avenue of the Americas, New York, New York 10019 for a listening quiz that's both fun and a little surprising.

"Listening to campaign speeches and periodically breaking into loud cheers: $1 an hour.

"Listening at cocktail parties: $2 an hour before midnight, $4 after midnight, plus two free drinks for the road.

"Listening to views on Vietnam and other international problems: $5 for 15 minutes.

"Listening to gossip: No charge—if it's about anyone I know. Otherwise $1 an hour.

"Listening over the telephone: Double usual rates, payable in advance.

"Listening to your troubles: $15 a morning, money to be refunded if you spend all afternoon listening to my troubles.

"Standby rate for waiting while you make up your mind what you want to talk about: 10 cents a minute.

"Pay up or shut up!"

What do you think of the idea? What, you didn't hear a word I said? See what I mean?

Nobody listens.[2]

Sometimes we listen in groups or audiences, as we do in the classroom; sometimes we listen to just one other person. Students spend 46 percent of an average school day listening; 66 percent of this time is spent in classrooms listening to teachers. The principles, models, and advice that follow make sense in all of these settings, but there are some important differences in emphasis.[3] Our motivation to listen may be stronger in the one-on-one situation, *but not always*. We are usually more interested in the topic or content in an audience situation, rather than the relational aspects of the speaker, *but not always*. We typically find it easier to respond and ask questions in an interpersonal setting, if only because we don't have to compete with so many others.

The "but not always" refers in part to the various *reasons* why we listen in the first place. We may be listening to another for the sheer joy of it; a good story teller, a pleasant voice. We may be listening out of stark terror as we contemplate failing organic chemistry. We also listen to evaluate, to remember, and to learn. Our motivations can be quite different.

Sometimes we are more interested in our relationship to the other person than to the actual message. When asking information of a stranger, we are probably more interested in the content. However, if we are strangers in a foreign country we may have more or at least equal interest in the relationship our listening behavior communicates. We might otherwise appear brash or even ugly-American. How we respond as listeners affects the sender and therefore conditions, to some

---

[2]Reprinted from "Nobody Listens Any More" by Hal Boyle in *Boston Traveler*, August 17, 1966. © 1966 The Associated Press. Used by permission of The Associated Press.

[3]See especially Robert N. Bostrom and Enid S. Waldhart, "Components in Listening Behavior: The Role of Short-Term Memory," *Human Communication Research*, 6, no. 3 (Spring 1980), 221–27.

extent, what messages follow. In some emotionally charged situations listening serves a cathartic or empathic purpose. During the Blitz of London in World War II the government recruited listening squads—people who would visit bomb victims who had lost families and homes and just listen. This proved to be very hard work. The listeners were exhausted after only a few hours' involvement. Some even resorted to acting roles in which they looked like they were listening, but they were, in fact, tuning out once they had established that the story was as terrible as many they had heard before. A need or request for listening is not always a request for help; it may also be just a need or request for a sympathetic and understanding presence.

Listening is the other half of talking. If people stop listening, talking becomes useless—a point not always appreciated by talkers.

Are we any good at listening? Stuart Chase thinks not:

> Americans are not good listeners. In general they talk more than they listen. Competition in our culture puts a premium on self-expression, even if the individual has nothing to express. What he lacks in knowledge he tries to make up for by talking fast or pounding the table. And many of us, while ostensibly listening, are inwardly preparing a statement to stun the company when we get the floor.[4]

There is hope! We have evidence that listening can be improved through understanding the process and acquiring better attitudes about social interaction and listening itself. Listening training improved the listening ability among elementary students.[5] College students improved their listening comprehension through a program first designed for industry.[6] Oral reading seems to help.[7] There is even evidence that improving our listening skills may improve our reading skills.[8]

Good listening habits are important. William Work, who synthesized much of the research just cited, reminds us that to a large extent, *we are what we listen to.*

> Nutritionists tell us that we—quite literally—*are* what we eat (and drink and breathe). In terms of our physical being, this is true. In terms of our psychic selves, we—quite literally—*are* what we hear and read and view.

[4]Stuart Chase, "Are You Listening?" *Reader's Digest*, December 1962, 80.

[5]Susan Fleming Blackburn, "The Construction, the Implementation, and the Evaluation of a Title I Primary Grade Listening Program," "Eric Report," *Communication Education,* 27, no. 2 (March 1978), 150.

[6]Deane Ford Schubach, "An Experimental Evaluation of a Program for Improvement of Listening Comprehension of College Students," "Eric Report," *Communication Education,* p. 151.

[7]Margaret Weidner, "Reading Achievement of Grade Four Students," "Eric Report," *Communication Education,* p. 150.

[8]Robert Lee Lemons, Jr., "The Effects of Passive Listening and Direct Training in Listening upon the Reading and Listening Skills of a Group of Black Fourth Graders," "Eric Report," *Communication Education,* p. 149; Thomas G. Sticht and others, "Auding and Reading: A Developmental Model," "Eric Report," *Communication Education,* p. 149.

As our social structures and systems become more complex, each individual becomes more dependent on the ability to process information effectively. Competence in listening and speaking is central to the achievement of that end. Being a good listener will not guarantee "success" or happiness or the securing of one's life goals, but, for most, poor listening will stand in the way of their attainment.[9]

LISTENING MODEL

If we can become better listeners by understanding the listening process, the following four-step model may help. Listening is perception, and you will recall that perception was defined as having two broad components: sensation and interpretation. One has to bring one's past experience, attitudes, and emotions to bear on the sensations of which one is aware to make any sense or interpretation of them. One's interpretation can, of course, be wrong, or at least unlike the one intended by the sender. The third step in listening, comprehension, involves understanding, appreciation, and evaluation. Response to the sender and to one's own understanding is the fourth step.[10]

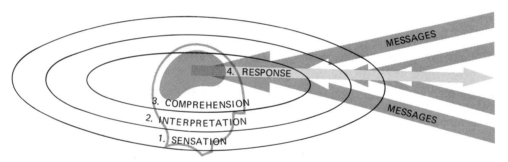

Figure 4.3 Ross listening model.

The oral messages entering the model in Figure 4.3 illustrate that some messages are never heard because they never reach the sensation circle or level. Other messages may only reach the interpretation circle and may perhaps never be totally understood. Even the messages that penetrate the comprehension circle

[9]William Work, "Eric Report," *Communication Education*, p. 152.

[10]Two other excellent models of the listening process are: Wolvin-Coakley (RECEIVING, ATTENDING, ASSIGNING MEANING, RESPONDING), see Andrew D. Wolvin and Carolyn Gwynn Coakley, *Listening* (Dubuque, Iowa: Wm. C. Brown, 1982), p. 51, and Sier (SENSING, INTERPRETATION, EVALUATION, REACTION), see "Your Personal Listening Profile" © 1980 Sperry Corporation, p. 4; see also Raymond S. Ross and Mark G. Ross, *Relating and Interacting* (Englewood Cliffs, N.J.: Prentice-Hall, 1982), pp. 214–16; see also Lyman K. Steil, Larry L. Barker and Kittie W. Watson, *Effective Listening* (Reading, Mass.: Addison Wesley, 1983).

may not be totally understood. The arrows also remind us that many times we are dealing with several messages simultaneously or at least in very close succession. They may compete with and distort one another. Because of their complexity or perhaps emotionality some of these messages may need more time to go through the steps and overcome the specific barriers found at one or more of them. Your response, step four, may help or hinder your listening comprehension. "Oh shove it." "I don't think I heard you." "What did you call me?" "That's heavy: Run it by me again."

It seems clear that all of the steps can be operating at the same time and with more than one message. It is no surprise that we often have tragic listening breakdowns. There is good evidence that poor listening contributed to several of our recent airline disasters.

In step 1, *sensation,* we are really talking about hearing. Of course our perceptions are related, and hearing is frequently affected by our other senses. We see as well as hear another person. The hearing barriers include:

HEARING BARRIERS, STEP 1: SENSATION

1. Noise;
2. Hearing impairment;
3. Fatigue;
4. Sensory distraction;
5. Sender deficiency.

These are reasonably obvious. If someone is operating a jack hammer or beating a drum you may lose a verbal signal in sheer noise. Universities still give audiometric screenings (hearing tests) to new students, and find young people with hearing losses of which they are not aware. We all have learned that we hear poorly when we are tired. Sensory distraction could be competing noises or other verbal

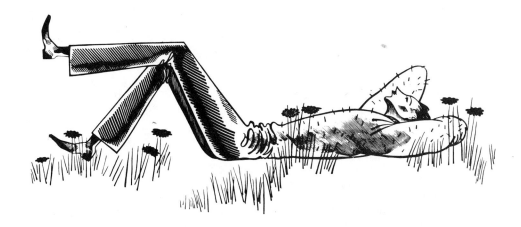

messages. It could also be distraction by the other senses. A really foul smell, temperature extremes, an attractive face—any of these can be barriers to hearing. Sender deficiency refers to a really poor speaker, one who lacks volume, projection, or is so dull as to make hearing actually difficult.

We may think of step 1 as mainly auditory sensation, keeping in mind that all of our other senses also contribute to what we finally decode. Listening, then, is dependent upon our senses of hearing and our abilities to hear despite the barriers. Assuming we have overcome the barriers and are willing to stay attentive, we are finally *auding* (or hearing) but not yet seriously listening.

In step 2, *interpretation,* we are talking about the beginning of *listening,* which is assigning meaning to what we hear. We may never fully comprehend or understand the message, but we are receiving part of it. Our decoding may be quite different from what the sender intended. Our past experiences serve as listening filters which unconsciously affect the interpretations of what we hear. Consider some of the following in Figure 4.4:

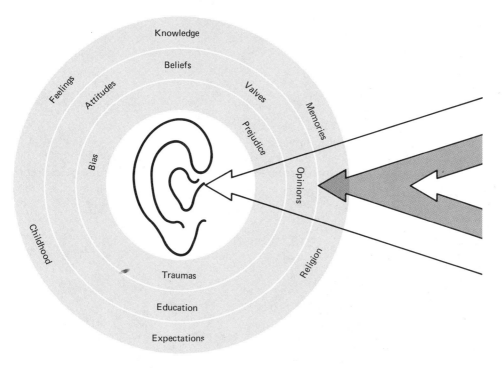

Figure 4.4   Listening filters.

This leads us to the interesting problem of *listening barriers.* All of the *hearing* barriers of step 1 also affect step 2. Listening barriers can best be expressed as bad listening habits. Much of the reason behind poor listening is explained by these bad habits.

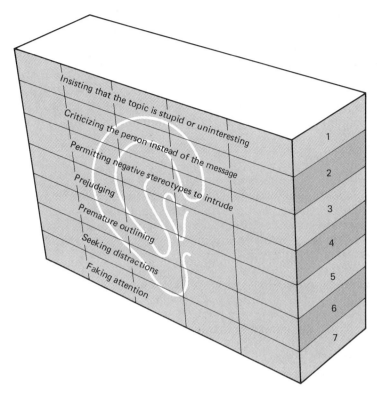

Figure 4.5
Listening Barriers, Step 2: Interpretation[11]

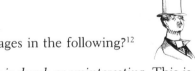

Can you think of a person who engages in the following?[12]

1. *Insisting the topic is dumb or uninteresting.* This is a great way to duck listening. After all, it takes hard work to relate the topic to something you do like or do find interesting. Some topics are by their nature difficult and complex—insisting they're boring will only help you avoid making an effort.

2. *Criticizing the person instead of the message.* Try to dismiss a person's appearance or speech mannerisms when they offer you an excuse for not listening to the message. This often takes real effort!

[11]For a programmed approach to overcoming the barriers see (and hear) Ella A. Erway, *Listening: A Programmed Approach* (New York: McGraw-Hill, 1979).

[12]These bad habits are adapted from Ralph G. Nichols and Leonard A. Stevens, *Are You Listening?* (New York: McGraw-Hill, 1957), pp. 104–12 and Larry Barker, *Listening Behavior* (Englewood Cliffs, N.J.: Prentice-Hall, 1971), pp. 61–66.

3. *Permitting negative stereotypes to get in the way.* If we hear something that opposes our most deeply rooted prejudices, our brains may become overstimulated in a way that leads to bad listening. We mentally plan a rebuttal to what we hear, develop a question designed to embarrass the talker, or perhaps simply turn to thoughts that support our own feelings on the subject at hand. Closing our minds may cause us to tune out, yawn, or get so upset that we confuse or miss the message. When we let emotionally loaded words distract us we are also exhibiting this trait.

4. *Prejudging,* or jumping to the conclusion that we understand the other person's meaning before he or she has fully expressed it. Worse yet, we often find ourselves mentally preparing and rehearsing answers to questions or points before fully understanding them. This all-too-common bad habit can make us appear stupid or rude.

5. *Premature outlining.* What you're listening to may not always be outlineable. Listen for a while and find out. Jot down the key concepts and let them grow to an outline. Being too quick to outline may interfere with listening.

6. *Seeking distractions.* A dandy way to avoid listening is to actively seek out distractions: Look out the window for something, anything, that might be more interesting; concentrate on another person who intrigues you; daydream, or actually cause a distraction.

7. *Faking attention,* also called sleeping with your eyes open. You only pretend to listen and your act gets pretty good. You smile, nod, and blink; you may even fool the speaker. That's why this bad habit is so mean—you may be fooling (and cheating) both yourself and the speaker.

In step 3, *comprehension,* we are talking about *understanding and* appreciation of what you are listening to. Comprehension also includes critical evaluation. You not only understand the message intended (or most of it) but you are also aware of your own reactions. All of the barriers and bad listening habits pertain here, but there are additional ones over which you may not always have as much control as those previously discussed.

Ralph Nichols has listed the factors he believes are most important to listening comprehension.[13] All of them are also critical to helping you better analyze *your* listeners in order to adapt to them.

[13]Ralph G. Nichols, "Factors in Listening Comprehension," *Speech Monographs,* 15, no. 2 (1948), 161–62.

Intelligence

Reading comprehension

Recognition of correct English usage

Size of the listener's vocabulary

Ability to make inferences

Ability to structuralize a speech (that is, to see the organizational plan and the connection of the main points)

Listening for main ideas, not merely for specific facts

Use of special techniques while listening to improve concentration

Real interest in the subject discussed

Emotional adjustment to the speaker's thesis

Curiosity about the subject discussed

Physical fatigue of the listener

Audibility of the speaker

Speaker effectiveness

Admiration for the speaker

Respect for listening as a method of learning

Susceptibility to distraction

Room ventilation and temperature

Use of only the English language at home

High-school scholastic achievement

High-school speech training

Experience in listening to difficult expository material

In step 4, *response,* we are talking about the things you do and say *while* you are listening (or right after). Responding is a form of feedback which is both verbal and nonverbal.

We can probably do a better job of responding if we remember why we are listening. We are not always involved in deep, evaluative listening, or even in informational listening. We often listen for fun and recreation—for enjoyment. We can be poor listeners and poor conversationalists as well, if we push all social discourse into content analysis. Sometimes people talk just for the sheer joy of it, and that, not the words, is the real message. Good listeners must be sensitive to this kind of communication behavior. Does "How are ya?" from a person you pass on the street call for a ten-minute response—or is it simply a form of recognition? How about "Nice day." "Like heck it is! What do you mean by that?" Consider Lucy's reaction to "Happy New Year" in Figure 4.6.

Figure 4.6   Peanuts. 1962 © United Feature Syndicate, Inc.

John:	"Mr. Jones, I have a problem to . . ."
Mr. Jones:	"John we all have problems; get to it."
John:	"I guess it can keep. . ."
Mr. Jones:	"Now what the hell is that supposed to mean!?"
John:	"Our department is being audited and . . ."
Mr. Jones:	"My God, why didn't you say so?"
John:	". . . what's happened so far is . . ."
Mr. Jones:	"Save it John, we need a meeting."

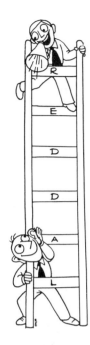

Responsively listen.

Express emotion with control.

Don't change the subject.

Don't interrupt.

Ask questions.

Look at the other person.

Figure 4.7
Illustration by Ric Estrada. Reprinted by permission of the publisher, from LISTENING MADE EASY, by Robert L. Montgomery, p. 78 © 1981 by AMACOM, a division of American Management Associations, New York. All rights reserved.

I have personally found that people respond positively to empathetic listeners as people have a deep need to be listened to, and effective listeners also know how to obtain the information and results they seek.[14]

Madelyn Burley-Allen,
President, Dynamics of Human Behavior

In interactive listening, illustrated in the preceding dialogue, there is more opportunity for response. Robert L. Montgomery suggests a ladder of steps that will help a listener concentrate on the sender.[15]

In addition to these, always consider the context and situation. Word meanings change, tempers change. . . . After a terrible budget meeting, Ross emerges:

Bernie: "I'd like you to look at this new. . ."
Ross: (angrily) "What the hell is wrong now?"
Bernie: "Is this a bad time?"
Ross: "I'm sorry Bernie, it really is, can we. . ."

[14]Madelyn Burley-Allen, *Listening: The Forgotten Skill* (New York: John Wiley, 1982), p. iii.
[15]Robert L. Montgomery, *Listening Made Easy* (New York: Amacom, 1981), p. 78.

Ross responded honestly and Bernie wisely tested the waters to see if Ross was in a listening mood. Sometimes we try to avoid difficult listening situations by not responding at all.

After silently listening to an emotional and unfair railing about a fellow teacher, Professor Frey stares at the floor. . .

Railer: "Thank you, Professor Frey. I'm glad you agree with me."
 Frey: (startled) "Hold on—where did you get that idea?"

Had Frey not had the second opportunity to respond clearly he could have been grossly misunderstood by the "railer" and perhaps his fellow teachers as well.

Perhaps there are times when we should interrupt or at least reflect the message back to the talker:

"Let me ask you this . . . "
"Do I hear you saying . . .?"
"Are you assuming that I . . .?"

A responsive listener tries to be a participant-observer. Most of us, in our interpersonal endeavors, have no problem being participants. It's being *observers* too that creates problems. Being able to participate-observe allows us in a sense to review our previous behaviors. Being able to see our behaviors as an interaction sequence gives us clearer pictures of our intentions and purposes in the interactions. Early awareness of our intentions within interpersonal communication settings puts us on more stable communicative ground in the management and coordination of our behaviors.

SUMMARY

Listening is an integral part of the processes of communication and perception and is the most used of the communication skills. It may be defined as a conscious cognitive effort using mainly the sense of hearing (reinforced by other senses), which in turn leads to interpretation and understanding.

The importance of listening is reflected by surveys that indicate people may spend as much as 60 to 75 percent of their time listening. Americans are not thought to be good listeners. There is evidence that we can improve our listening habits through understanding the listening process and through developing better attitudes toward the task of listening.

A four-step listening model is discussed: (1) sensation; (2) interpretation; (3) comprehension; and (4) response. The *hearing barriers* to step 1, sensation, are: noise, hearing impairment, fatigue, sensory distraction, and sender deficiency. The *listening barriers* to step 2, interpretation, are: insisting the topic is stupid or un-interesting, criticizing the person instead of the message, permitting negative stereotypes to intrude, prejudging, premature outlining, seeking distractions, and faking attention. Some of the barriers to step 3, comprehension, are: intelligence, reading ability, vocabulary, thinking ability, and experience.

A key fourth step to improving our listening habits is response—that is, making listening an active process. Here are some ways: (1) look at the other person; (2) ask questions; (3) don't interrupt; (4) don't change the subject; and (5) express emotion with control.

Failure to listen adequately has relational implications. We can uninten-tionally put someone down by our failure to listen. The key to communicative competence and good listening is in being a participant-observer—that is, observ-ing our own behaviors as well as others' while at the same time being active par-ticipants.

STUDY PROJECTS

1. Develop your own verbal-pictorial model of the listening process. (See models in the chapter.)
2. Create a seven- or eight-word message and whisper it to one class member who in turn whispers it to the next person. Have the last class member repeat the message aloud and compare it to the original. Discuss the results.
3. Apply the Ross four-step model to a specific communication incident you have observed or were part of and evaluate the listening behavior. Report verbally and/or pictorially what lessons this exercise yielded. Pay special attention to the bad listening habits.
4. For the next five days make daily entries in your communication log (Chapter 1 project) that illustrate one or more of the bad listening habits discussed in this chapter.
5. Try really listening to a speaker the next time you have an opportunity. Report in 100 words or less what you have learned about your listening habits.
6. Rogerian feedback exercise. Divide into groups of three. Have two people con-verse and the third serve as a reporter-observer. After each short communica-tion, have the listener attempt to paraphrase the message to the satisfaction of the sender. For example:

   Sender: "One of every four persons has been sexually abused."
   Listener: I heard, "One of every four women has suffered wife abuse."
   Sender: "No, not quite. Let me try again. . ." (and so on, until the sender is satisfied with the paraphrase).

The reporter should explain what he or she observed.

7. Check yourself on the following bad listening habits.[16] Then compare your list with those of other classmates. Discuss. Think of a specific person whom you feel is a bad listener. Check the inventory in a way that best describes that person's behavior. Discuss.

		FREQUENCY			
	Almost Always	*Usually*	*Some-times*	*Seldom*	*Almost Never*
1. Routinely calling the subject uninteresting	☐	☐	☐	☐	☐
2. Criticizing the speaker personally	☐	☐	☐	☐	☐
3. Being overstimulated by some point within the speech	☐	☐	☐	☐	☐
4. Listening primarily for facts instead of ideas	☐	☐	☐	☐	☐
5. Trying to outline everything	☐	☐	☐	☐	☐
6. Faking attentiveness to the speaker	☐	☐	☐	☐	☐
7. Tolerating or creating distractions	☐	☐	☐	☐	☐
8. Paying little attention to difficult material	☐	☐	☐	☐	☐
9. Letting emotional words arouse anger	☐	☐	☐	☐	☐
10. Daydreaming	☐	☐	☐	☐	☐

[16]Adapted from Nichols and Stevens, *Are You Listening?*, cited earlier in this chapter.

5

Relating and interacting

General learning outcomes

- We should learn how to improve our attribution process in impression formation.

- We should understand the interpersonal needs of inclusion, control, and affection.

- We should learn how we infer our own personal attributes and selves.

- We should learn the major influences of self-concept: significant others, sense of competence, perceived role, group memberships, and special situations.

- We should learn the three parts of managing impressions (self-presentation): front, dramatic realization, and mystification.

- We should learn that self-disclosure can hurt as well as help interpersonal relations.

- We should learn five factors of interpersonal attraction: nearness, similarity, status, physical characteristics, and rhetorical sensitivity.

ON NEEDING OTHERS

Physical isolation can be a terrible thing. Solitary confinement in prison may indeed be the most sadistic of all punishments. We do know from experimental research and real-life episodes that real isolation makes us more anxious, less cogent, more suggestible, and prone to hallucinations.

Some of the same results accrue to people who are *not* on life rafts or stranded like Robinson Crusoe. A form of social isolation may afflict all of us if we feel "left out" or in one way or another separated from others.

It is clear that life is no good alone—we need others. We need people for love, reassurance, approval, a sense of reality, and, most critically, communication, even if it be simply a nonverbal presence.

In a busy, complex world of superficial acquaintances and many strangers we are forced to form impressions, sometimes very quickly, sometimes very inaccurately. It is through these impressions that we organize our perceptions of others, that we get a "handle" on them. This leads us to make decisions about liking and possible future interaction.

We may sometimes form global impressions of a person on the basis of a single attribute such as height, weight, pipe smoker, and so forth. Some attributes are not trivial but may still lead our impressions astray. Status, position, titles, and even names are all important in impression formation, yet numerous researchers tell us that any of these, especially in isolation, can mislead us.

Even the most subtle of cues figure in our awareness and impressions of

WOMEN TALK
BUT MEN CUT IN

Wanda: Did you see here that two sociologists have just proved that men interrupt women all the time? They—
Ralph: Who says?
Wanda: Candace West of Florida State and Don Zimmerman of the University of California at Santa Barbara. They taped a bunch of private conversations, and guess what they found. When two men or two women are talking, interruptions are about equal. But when a man talks to a woman, he makes 96% of the interruptions. They think it's a dominance trick men aren't even aware of. But—
Ralph: These people have nothing better to do than eavesdrop on interruptions?
Wanda: —but women make "retrievals" about one-third of the time. You know, they pick up where they left off after the man—
Ralph: Surely not all men are like that, Wanda.
Wanda: —cuts in on what they were saying. Doesn't that—
Ralph: Speaking as a staunch supporter of feminism, I deplore it, Wanda.
Wanda: (sigh) I know, dear.

Figure 5.1   Reprinted by permission from TIME, The Weekly News Magazine, September 25, 1978. Copyright, Time, Inc., 1978.

others—a perfume, grooming, the color of a tie, an interruption. The most important point is that these impressions have behavioral consequences.

First impressions are, then, very important interpersonally. Even when we are aware of the risks we really have little choice in many interactions if we are to meet our overwhelming need to make sense (often nonsense) of the very complex social world in which we live.

This tendency leads us to draw conclusions about people's motives, traits, and personality characteristics often after only minimal observation. We attribute *causes*, as it were. Attribution theorists suggest several ways in which we can improve this process. We should, for example, spend less time on inferred dispositions (he or she is lazy, sadistic, etc.) and more time on actual observation of specific actions. Attribute qualities only after taking the context and consequences of a person's behavior into account. Also, consider differences between conscious, direct observations and those based on feelings and indirect observations. Nonverbals can be important here. Also important are the following factors: Is the person under pressure? Does the person have free choice? What do others, better informed than yourself, say about the person observed?

It is so easy to be wrong. Mark Twain captures the problem of quick personality attributions: "In all matters of opinion our adversaries are insane."

INTERPERSONAL NEEDS

If you were attracted to a new group, a new organization, or just some new friends, it has been theorized that you would ask yourself three specific kinds of questions. The kinds of interpersonal questions with which you would probably struggle are shown in Figure 5.2. The struggle is *intra*personal—that is, your thinking is a kind of talking to yourself.

Assuming that all of us have some need for affiliation and association, it seems reasonable to contemplate questions of *inclusion* in your chosen group. Your need to both give and receive direction (and this varies with the person and the circumstances) prompts you to contemplate questions of *control*. Your interpersonal need to belong and to be liked generates questions of *affection*.

According to William Schutz these three—*inclusion, control,* and *affection*—are our primary social needs and they go a long way toward determining how we behave and relate to others.[1]

Inclusion deals with such things as attention, acknowledgment, recognition, prominence, identity, and participation.[2] Other terms thought to connote positive or negative feelings of inclusion are associate, together, and involved (positive) and outcast, detached, and ignored (negative).

Control is communicated by behaviors expressing leadership, power, accomplishment, and intellectual superiority (among others). When control is perceived as repressive, oppressive, or unfair—"The leaders are slavedrivers"—then

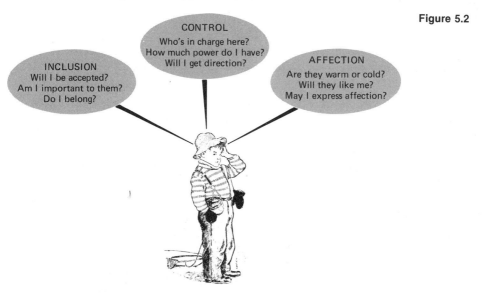

Figure 5.2

CONTROL
Who's in charge here?
How much power do I have?
Will I get direction?

INCLUSION
Will I be accepted?
Am I important to them?
Do I belong?

AFFECTION
Are they warm or cold?
Will they like me?
May I express affection?

[1]William Schutz, *Firo: A Three Dimensional Theory of Interpersonal Behavior* (New York: Holt, Rinehart & Winston, 1958), p. 13.
[2]Ibid., p. 22.

this side of the control need is typified by behaviors expressing rebellion, resistance, and, in some cases, submission.[3]

When we perceive appropriate direction and some decision making over our small part of any group, we approach a kind of optimal fulfillment of this powerful interpersonal need. This state of affairs is thought to enhance, or at least preserve, our feelings of self-respect.

The flavor of affection is embodied in "situations of love, emotional closeness, personal confidences and intimacy. Negative affection is characterized by hate, hostility, and emotional rejection."[4]

It is possible, of course, to be high on affection and inclusion and low on control. You like the people, but hate the boss. Ideally we will find some optimal fulfillment, not only within each need, but also across all the needs.

Our success and comfort with this balancing act is thought to have much to do with our relating and interacting.

SELF-CONCEPT

We have learned of our need for others; now we learn that we need others to discover and know who *we* are. Some social psychologists tell us that the process of inferring attributes about ourselves is much the same as inferring attributes about others.

We also learned about the tricky business of perceiving events and things in Chapter 1. Now we look specifically at how we go about perceiving ourselves and how this knowledge can help us make better perceptions of and inferences about others. Getting to know ourselves and determining our personal attributes is what self-perception and self-concept are about. Attribution theory involves not only our personal attributes, but also how we infer the personal attributes of others.

How we perceive ourselves is important because it helps us *intra*personally control our actions. It partially determines how we will behave and then how we will perceive and evaluate that behavior.

Self-concept has been defined as "the sum total of the view which an individual has of himself. Self-concept is a unique set of perceptions, ideas, and attitudes which an individual has of himself."[5] It is both conscious and unconscious, and it changes with our most recent experiences and self-perceptions. We use words such as *self-percept, self-concept,* and *self-identity* to talk about one's notion of oneself.[6] Words such as *self-esteem, self-valuation,* and *self-regard* are of a slightly different order. We tend to think of these as positive or negative traits.

[3]Ibid., p. 23.
[4]Ibid., p. 24.
[5]Donald W. Felker, *Building Positive Self-Concepts* (Minneapolis: Burgess, 1974), p. 2.
[6]John J. Sherwood, "Self Identity and Referent Others," *Sociometry,* 28 (1965), 66–81.

A related term is *self-acceptance*. A person with high self-acceptance exhibits a willingness to accept both positive and negative notions as a part of his or her total self-concept.

A discussion of some of the major influences of self-perception and self-concept follows.

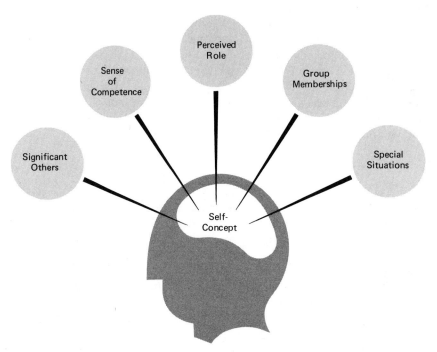

Figure 5.3 Self-concept influences

A large portion of each of our self-concepts is shaped by comparisons to and interactions with others whom we consider *significant* to us. We develop concepts of our physical, emotional, and social selves, and we tend to perceive, respond, act, and communicate to a considerable extent using these complex self-images.

How others feel about us, or at least how we think they feel about us—particularly if they are significant "others," whether reference groups, respected friends, or even those whose roles are ill defined—is probably the most important part of self-concept. What these others expect of us, how they react to us, and how socially realistic we are in evaluating these expectations and reactions form a large part of our self-concept.

Our sense of *competence* is also related to our self-concept. "Competence means capacity, fitness, or ability. The competence of a living organism means its fitness or ability to carry on those transactions with the environment which result

"I hope you don't mind my joining you—I've reached the chapter in my book where I'm to start showing a genuine interest in people."

Figure 5.4
The Girls by Franklin Folger.

in its maintaining itself, growing and flourishing."[7] A self- concept that includes a feeling of incompetence may leave us in a state of helplessness and inertia and may promote a sense of inferiority. We must build realistic confidence as well as competence into our self-concept. Persistent challenge to our sense of personal competence is a prime mover toward frustration and, not infrequently, aggression. Our sense of competence is important to our interactions and communication with others.

Group memberships are an important influence on us. Our self-concepts reflect the society in which we live. Our families, schools, churches, and temples are all thought to greatly influence our self-concept and personality in general. This is not to suggest that we are all carbon copies of those having backgrounds similar to our own. Even the culture in which we live determines only what we learn as a member of a group, not what we learn as individuals. This explains in part why humans alter their behavior in what seem to be most inconsistent ways. Living in a society requires one to meet certain standards or to fit into certain patterns roughly agreed on by the members of that group. Much nonstandard individual behavior is *sublimated*—expressed in constructive, socially acceptable forms in deference to these group codes. The *valuation, regard,* and *acceptance*

[7]Robert W. White assisted by Katherine F. Bruner, eds., *The Study of Lives* (New York: Atherton, 1966), p. 74.

Figure 5.5 Peanuts. © 1958 United Feature Syndicate, Inc.

individuals have of their total group—and their conceptions of the group's valuation, regard, and acceptance of them—are critical to the development of their self-concepts.

Role pertains, in part, to a more specific aspect of group membership and is also thought to have a strong influence on our self-concept. Some roles are cast upon us by society because of our age, our sex, even our size, and, unfortunately, sometimes our race. Some roles we assign ourselves on the basis of our life goals, and some are really disguises of our private personalities, disguises that we create in order to be accepted by certain groups. In its most important sense a role is that part we cast for ourselves on the stage of life. We may portray many roles to the world, but each of us determines, with the aid of society and its subgroups, what our particular roles will be. Our self-concepts are influenced by these decisions.

Figure 5.6 The Wizard of Id. By permission of Johnny Hart and Field Enterprises, Inc.

The *situational* influences upon our self-concepts and our total personalities include those exceptional, unpredictable, and often accidental events that happen to all of us. These are events that can alter our lives, and cast us into roles that may profoundly affect our self-concepts—jail sentences, lost loves, scholarships, riots, wars, demonstrations, insights or perspectives suddenly and never before achieved.

A really good teacher probably alters the lives and careers of many unsuspecting students. An unexpected failing grade or a hard-won A from such a teacher can be self-concept shaker and/or maker!

Figure 5.7   Photo by Marc Anderson.

Research suggests that an unreasonable or unrealistic self-concept, particularly one low in self-esteem, may contribute to failure, thereby acting as a kind of self-fulfilling prophecy. George who will not even discuss a math course because his self-concept tells him he is mathematically illiterate is not apt to do well in a math course. This is tragic when *only* a student's poor opinion of himself stands in the way of success. However, suppose a student really has little or no math aptitude. Were he to develop an unrealistically positive conception of his mathematical ability, he would obviously be headed for frustration and ultimately an even poorer self-concept than the original one.

The point is that our self-concepts, whether good or bad, high or low, should be within the realm of physical or social reality. Knowing what is *realistic* as well as what is exceptional is, of course, the eternal problem. For the most part we try to be consistent in our self-images. When we are extremely frustrated, perhaps by too positive or too negative self-images, we may resort to various unrelated behaviors to compensate for our frustration. (For example, we may become over-talkative when insecure.) A realistic self-image can be a critical part of communication and perception as well as of motivation generally. Every person is the center of his or her own field of experience, and the way one perceives and responds to that field is one's own reality.

Human communication is affected by self-concept in several interesting ways. In general, we can expect others to perceive and react to us and the rest of the world in ways that are as consistent with their self-concepts as possible. Trying to "see" and understand others by understanding what their self-concepts are thus becomes a characteristic of sensitive human communication. We should all occasionally reevaluate our *own* self-concepts in terms of physical and social reality. Sometimes we downgrade or take ourselves too seriously. If the *self-regard* part of our self-concepts is unusually negative, we might very well become difficult, negative, or even sullen communicators. Unrealistically positive *self-valuations* can, of course, make us different but equally painful communicators. Healthy, reality-centered, positive self-concepts should, other things being equal, make us better and more confident communicators. Most important, we should also exhibit some willingness to accommodate change.

In review, a good self-concept is objective, realistic, positive, and yet self-accepting; it can live with negative notions too. A healthy self-concept should include some willingness to change, a tolerance for confusion, patience with disagreement, and empathy for other self-concepts. If you are a "significant other" for someone, if only for a moment, you have a special communication responsibility, for we are reasonably sure that individuals' significant others are keys to the development of their self-concepts.

Self-concept is a major part of one's personality. We may consider personality to be the sum of a person's knowledge, motives, values, beliefs, and goal-seeking patterns.

SELF-PRESENTATION

Managing Impressions

The creative sociologist Erving Goffman suggests that in our efforts to present our best and most persuasive selves, we try to give appropriate performances on the stage of life. Consider a college senior preparing for an employment interview. Our student may attempt an impression of maturity, self-confidence, knowledgeability, and dependability. This can be done in the following general ways:

Presenting an appropriate front.[8]   An appropriate front is general behavior which is designed (or natural) to better define (persuasively, we hope) who you are. Parts of your personal front include such things as appearance and manner. It also includes things over which you have only limited control, such as sex, age, and size. Your clothes, posture, gestures, facial expressions, and language patterns are more modifiable dimensions of your front. Should our hero appear in dirty shorts, with unbrushed hair, and profanely using the English language, he or she would present quite a different front than if he or she were neatly dressed, well coiffed, and polite.

Dramatic realization.[9]   According to Goffman, we must clearly realize the roles expected of us and work them into our performances. We may have to be talented actors to hide our lack of confidence. If the role calls for attentiveness, we had better give such an impression. We may be paying attention, but perhaps we are not perceived that way; this constitutes unfortunate impression management. A flip physician who writes a fast prescription, however accurate the quick diagnosis, may be viewed suspiciously by the patient.

[8]Erving Goffman, *The Presentation of Self in Everyday Life* (Garden City, N.Y.: Doubleday, 1959), p. 22.
[9]Ibid., p. 30.

Mystification.[10]   This notion of impression management refers to perceptions of social distances between the actor and the audience. Our previously mentioned physician is more apt to be concerned with this kind of impression than our interviewee. That is, the physician must not become too folksy lest he or she lose some of the mystery of the medical role. Our college student, however, must accommodate the real or fancied social-distance factors in the theatre in which he or she is operating.

Consider your own impressions of *front, dramatic realization,* and *mystification* from the two following pictures.

Figure 5.8   Photography by Guy Morrison, Bloomfield Hills, Michigan.

[10]Ibid., p. 67.

Self-Disclosure

All interpersonal communication starts (or ought to) with at least some *guesstimate* of where the other person is coming from. It would be convenient if everyone in whom we were interested simply disclosed everything about themselves—or would it? A first or second date might be a little less exciting without any surprises. It has been suggested that too much self-disclosure, even among married couples, causes some difficulty.[11]

Apparently a transparent openness can hurt as well as help interpersonal relations. Without any disclosure it's almost impossible to really communicate, much less get to know someone. Some creative studies suggest a *reciprocity* in this matter—that is, we tend to trade information:[12] "The more you tell me, the more I'll tell you"—to a point! Appropriateness is more important than amount of reciprocity.[13] As always, so much depends on the content, the situation, the people, and the climate of trust.

There is, then, a *compensatory* dimension to self-disclosure. Sometimes after a difficult or frustrating experience we may withdraw and remain silent to avoid further personal hurt, but we might also pour out our problems to the first unsuspecting ear we find.[14] Good bartenders are nonthreatening listeners to lots of compensatory self-disclosure. Such compensation is not always unhealthy, but when it strains important relationships it may be on the verge of being so. Some demanding interpersonal encounters have been described as a "tyranny of openness" by some social psychologists.[15]

What is a healthy openness? So very much depends upon the relationship you have with the other person involved. Some types of relationships may be described as *necessary*, others as *discretionary*. If you have a job, it is *necessary* to relate to your boss in at least some pragmatic, job-related way. It is not necessary that you relate in matters of a more personal nature, such as your politics and your feelings toward others. You have, of course, some *discretion* here (as does your boss). Knowing when to exercise that discretion, on what topics, how much disclosure, and so forth, are cornerstones of interpersonal relations.

Figure 5.9 shows how to attempt to get a perspective on an appropriate amount of openness and disclosure for relationships ranging from superficial to intimate, either necessary or discretionary.

Healthy relating and reacting should primarily be related to the people,

[11]Georg Simmel, "The Secret and the Secret Society," in *The Sociology of Georg Simmel*, ed. K. Wolff (New York: Free Press, 1964), p. 329.

[12]Zick Rubin, "Disclosing Oneself to a Stranger: Reciprocity and its Limits," *Journal of Experimental Social Psychology*, 11, 1975, 233–60.

[13]Lawrence A. Hosman and Charles H. Tardy, "Self-Disclosure and Reciprocity in Short- and Long-Term Relationships: An Experimental Study of Evaluational and Attributional Consequences," *Communication Quarterly*, 38, no. 1 (Winter 1980), 20–30.

[14]L. Rosenfeld, "Self-Disclosure Avoidance: Why I am Afraid to Tell You Who I Am," *Communication Monographs*, 46, no. 1 (March 1979), 63–74.

[15]Irwin Altman and Dalmas A. Taylor, *Social Penetration* (New York: Holt, Rinehart & Winston, 1973).

Disclosure ↑

Openness ↑

DISCLOSURE MUCH

SOME

LITTLE

1   2   3   4   5

Superficial Relationship   Disclosure Curve   Intimate Relationship

Figure 5.9
Disclosure curve.

the situation, and the context. Your relationship analysis should direct the appropriate interactional openness and self-disclosure.[16] Nevertheless, some people seem to be more open across a great many situations and contexts. Others are more secretive. Personality attributions without a great many observations can be spurious.

Here are some useful questions to ask in making disclosure decisions:

1. *Is it a "necessary" or a "discretionary" disclosure?* This is not always easy to answer because of the content or situation. An intimate disclosure about your estranged wife is surely discretionary unless you're involved in therapy or counseling, in which case it may be necessary. Disclosing your income, investments, and bills is necessary disclosure when dealing with the IRS, but discretionary for most other contexts. The important thing is to sense the difference.

2. *Is it a long- or short-term relationship?* In some new encounters you may not really know. The guideline is that the amount of openness and disclosure usually increases as the relationship becomes more intimate. A good way to keep a short-term relationship short term is to disclose nothing; another way is to disclose too much intimate information too soon.

3. *What are the risks?* The risks are not only to yourself and the relationship, but to the other person or persons. Is there trust? Does the disclosure end here or have you told the world? Does it matter? Are you being pressured? "I've disclosed to you, now you've got to disclose." Is your disclosure compensatory? Are you apt to be sorry later? Have you disclosed enough?

[16]Jesse Delia, "Some Tentative Thoughts Concerning the Study of Interpersonal Relationships and their Development," *Western Journal of Speech Communication,* 44, no. 2 (Spring 1980), 101.

4. *What is the message/relationship importance?* Do you value the message disclosed the same as the relationship involved, or in some cases is the relationship more important than the message? Forthright discussions of necessary differences of opinions are to be applauded. However, if they preclude further discussions by destroying a relationship, you have need to pause. Prudence is a virtue!

INTERPERSONAL ATTRACTION

Our need to create and sustain relationships is one of the great stimulations of human interaction. When we talk to some individuals, nothing really significant or important happens. With others we may form positive first impressions, and then after a few months or perhaps even days we may sense that the relationship is going sour. Another possibility, of course, is that a very negative first impression may not remain negative. These possibilities are all aspects of *interpersonal attraction.*

Before discussing the *factors of interpersonal attraction,* we should remind ourselves that our perceptions—the way we see the world—are essential to each factor and that these perceptions include both our feelings and our beliefs. In other words, what we know and how we feel about things will lead us to infer the unknown from the known. Our beliefs about a person usually relate to obvious physical observations—good looks, overweight, dark complexion; our feelings usually affect our attributions about the individual's personality—nervous, peculiar, warm. Recall, however, that our perceptions are often inaccurate, as was demonstrated in Chapter 1.

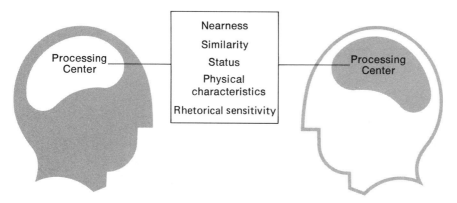

Figure 5.10 Factors of attraction.

How accurate are our interpersonal perceptions? What factors are part of these perceptions? There are some answers[17]: One is *age*. We get better as we get older—generally. Another is *intelligence*. Smarter people are usually more accurate. *Sex* is a third factor. There is no hard evidence, but there seems to be a tendency for women to be more accurate perceivers than men. Beyond these, very few personality characteristics stand out. Good and bad interpersonal judges are found among a wide variety of personalities. That some people are better judges of people than others (most of the time) seems obvious. Some behavior extremes, found to be blocks to happy perceptions of social adjustment, are discussed shortly in the section *Rhetorical Sensitivity*.

Numerous experiments have attempted to discover whether there are any systematic bases for our attraction to others. These studies have attempted to analyze the results of communication encounters. They suggest that our attractions to others are not haphazard, but rather that they are shaped and strengthened by at least five factors: *(1)nearness; (2) similarity; (3) status and recognition; (4) physical characteristics;* and *(5)* a social sensitivity we discuss as *rhetorical sensitivity*. The explanation breaks down a bit when two or more conflicting factors are operating at the same time. For instance, forced nearness to someone of widely dissimilar attitudes does not typically lead to attraction—perhaps better understanding if we are lucky.

Nearness

The first factor is the most obvious. Other things being equal, we tend to develop ties to those who live near us, work with us, go to church or temple with us, or who are in some way physically near us. After initial attraction has been established, separation or a lack of proximity will usually weaken the relationship unless other factors are strong and positive.

Persons who are both active as communicators and physically near the action—a student government scene, a political convention, or whatever—appear

[17]See Mark Cook, *Interpersonal Perception* (Baltimore: Penguin Books, 1971).

to have a potential advantage in terms of attraction.[18] Unless the person is a real boor, this is not surprising. This finding does suggest that we form attractions more readily to those near us, providing the other factors are not in gross conflict and providing there is opportunity for communication.

Similarity

We speak here not so much of physical similarities, but of similarities of attitudes toward questions and issues important to us. Momentary feelings of anxiety that are perceived as similar, even among total strangers, often trigger a fellowship tendency. We find it attractive to seek company, especially company of like mind or like situation. Similar personalities as well as attitudes—exceptions and old sayings to the contrary—do attract, and familiarity, other things being equal, breeds attraction, not contempt.

We tend to find others more attractive when we perceive them as holding attitudes similar to our own. This presents an opportunity for deceit: Unscrupulous persuaders may lead us to believe they hold attitudes similar to ours (when in fact they do not) for the purpose of selling an object or gaining a vote. This interesting fact of interpersonal attraction also suggests that each of us should be more open and objective when we listen to individuals who have attitudes differing from our own; such an occasion may be a good time for us to reexamine our own attitudes and the reasons behind them.

The point is that if you have really strong opinions about controversial issues such as abortion, aid to parochial schools, and God, then the attitudes you perceive in others toward these issues will affect their attractiveness to you (and your attractiveness to them). Our personal attraction, even to an old friend, may be strained if the friend suddenly discovers an attitude we hold toward race, cheating, or drugs that is quite different from his or her own. This is often true of lighter topics and attitudes as well. If you like sports trivia, movies, Chinese food, or skiing, you may be attracted to someone who has these same preferences.

Although there is some evidence that racial similarity leads to attraction, it is more accurate to say that the amount of perceived prejudice leads a person to like or dislike another.[19]

Status and Recognition

We are usually attracted to and enjoy being with people of high status and social standing because they offer us some reflected recognition. "Arnold Palmer was seated at the next table," we report as if he were an old friend. "I shook hands with the President," we say with pride. However, when critical issues override, as may be the case with some high-ranking politicians, we may have some conflict.

Some status and position is earned through special skills such as athletes

[18]See Mark Abrahamson, *Interpersonal Accommodation* (Princeton, N.J.: D. Van Nostrand, 1966).

[19]Gardner Lindzey and Elliot Aronson, eds., *The Handbook of Social Psychology*, 2nd ed., vol. 2 (Reading, Mass.: Addison-Wesley, 1968), pp. 498–500.

and actors possess; some through unusual achievement whether in sports, the arts, or business; some through super competence, whatever the endeavor or situation. Even though in general we find people with these attributes attractive, there are moments of ambivalence that sometimes cross our minds. This is especially true of the super achiever and the extremely competent. If you perceive yourself in any kind of competition with such a person your admiration may be tempered with some jealousy, envy, or even inferiority. If after great effort you've achieved a B average, your attractive roommate may lose some luster as he or she reports his or her usual A+ grades with only average effort.

This factor of attraction also includes more direct rewards, not in a monetary sense necessarily, but in terms of "He makes me happy, she makes me laugh, he is very helpful, she has all the answers." We tend to enjoy being with people who provide us with status, praise, and recognition—the teacher who laughs at our jokes, the person who begs us to tell a certain story, the friend who flatters us for some quality. Because of the anticipated or expected rewards they contain, all of these events contribute to the attraction we may feel toward someone. This category of attraction is mainly a result of verbal communication, although nonverbal messages obviously may help.

Those who would play games with this factor of interpersonal attraction can fail miserably if their praise or flattery is found to be unwarranted or phony. Honesty with a measure of prudence is still the best policy. The status of the person praising or blaming us also influences this dimension of attraction. As was indicated in the interaction model, a person's self-concept is also part of this complex equation.

Sometimes, status and recognition can be translated better as a person's offering a helping or supportive relationship. An anticipated reward of a sympathetic ear is often a strong reason for interpersonal attraction. Good listeners are attractive people, perhaps because they are so rare.

Physical Characteristics

When we first see other people, we are affected by what we see, even before we communicate orally. Large, fat, sloppy, handsome, cool, or whatever—each characteristic will attract or repel us. Physical characteristics are more than just physical attractiveness, although in an initial meeting we often have little else to judge.

By *physical characteristics* we mean the total physical makeup of an individual. This includes environmental causes of appearance, such as diet, drugs, and climate, as well as hereditary factors. People vary physically in their reaction times, energy levels, and rates of learning. They also vary in hearing, sight, color, size, shape, and so on—all of which add up to and influence total personality as well as physical attractiveness. After all, beauty is skin deep only in the superficial sense. However, there are sharp cultural differences of opinion about what constitutes physical beauty. Male students from the Middle East consider lean model stereotypes as less attractive than their chunkier sisters. There are also *individual* differences of opinion about these matters in all cultures. The feedback we decode from society about our physical makeups and the way we accommodate that feedback probably affect our attractiveness more than our superficial physical characteristics do.

Other things being equal, well-adjusted, smart young people are perceived as more attractive than those who are not as smart. There is some evidence that physical attractiveness is more important between than within the sexes. That is, girls tend to care more about what their boyfriends look like than what their girlfriends look like (and vice versa). The role of clothing, cosmetics, calorie counting, surgery, and other possible means of improving our appearances becomes critical when added to what nature gave us.

Rhetorical Sensitivity

"Rhetorical sensitivity is a particular attitude toward encoding spoken messages. It represents a way of thinking about what should be said and then a way of deciding how to say it."[20] It is, according to Hart and Burks, ". . . that type of . . . sensitivity which . . . makes effective social interaction manifestly possible."[21]

In this text's view rhetorically sensitive (RS) people are interpersonally attractive. They judge encounters carefully before taking stands on issues, they distinguish between "content" and "relational" communication, and they know when to "speak up" or "shut up." They deal with conflict forthrightly *and* with sensitivity.[22]

Figure 5.11

[20]Roderick P. Hart, Robert E. Carlson, and William F. Eadie, "Attitudes toward Communication and the Assessment of Rhetorical Sensitivity," *Communication Monographs,* 47, no. 1 (March 1980), 2.

[21]Roderick P. Hart and Don M. Burks, "Rhetorical Sensitivity and Social Interaction," *Speech Monographs,* 39, no. 2 (June 1972), 75.

[22]For more on applications to interpersonal communication, see especially Steven A. Ward, Dale L. Bluman, and Arthur F. Dauria, "Rhetorical Sensitivity Recast: Theoretical Assumptions of an Informal Interpersonal Rhetoric," *Communication Quarterly,* 30, no. 3 (Summer 1982), 189–95.

People not rhetorically sensitive have been described as "noble selves" (NS) and "rhetorical reflectors" (RR). Noble selves have been characterized as persons who see "any variation from their personal norms as hypocritical, as a denial of integrity, as a cardinal sin."[23]

Rhetorical reflectors have been described as persons who "have no self to call their own. For each person and for each situation they present a new self."[24] They empathize with (or at least appear to empathize with) and reflect each situation in which they find themselves.

Figure 5.12

The rhetorically sensitive persons seek to moderate these extremes. They are not braggarts but neither are they chameleon like, fearfully reflecting and hiding in each encounter. The continuum of sensitivity might be scaled as shown in Figure 5.13.

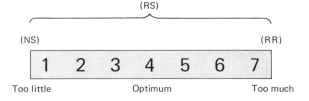

Figure 5.13
Sensitivity toward most interactions: (NS) noble self; (RR) rhetorical reflector; (RS) rhetorically sensitive

Rhetorical sensitivity, then, is an effective matching of message sending to the requirements of the receivers *and* to the situation and context. It is a measure of a person's audience-analysis efforts and willingness to carefully consider

[23]Donald Darnell and Wayne Brockriede, *Persons Communicating* (Englewood Cliffs, N.J.: Prentice-Hall, 1976), p. 176.
[24]Ibid., p. 178.

the psychological environment before encoding messages. It is the ability to accurately judge public and interpersonal encounters and to sense when to be a reflector and when to be a noble self.

SUMMARY

Isolation is a terrible thing. Life is no good alone; we need others. We need people, even simply a nonverbal presence, for love, reassurance, approval, a sense of reality, and, most critically, communication.

First-impression decisions about people are very important. Even when aware of the risks, we really have little choice in many interactions if we are to meet our overwhelming need to make sense of the very complex social world in which we live. This need leads us to speculate about people's traits and attributes. These constructions help us decide all kinds of appropriate behaviors. This tendency to organize and synthesize cues leads us to draw conclusions about people, often after only minimal observation. Attribution theorists suggest that we should spend less time on inferred dispositions and more time on specific observation of actions, contexts, and consequences. Life is full of interdependent relationships. It is through coordination, patience, and communication that we may achieve action.

Inclusion, control, and *affection* are our primary social needs; they go a long way toward determining how we behave and relate to others. Inclusion deals with such things as attention, acknowledgment, recognition, prominence, identity, and participation. Control is communicated by behaviors expressing leadership, power, accomplishment, and intellectual superiority. The flavor of affection is embodied in "situations of love, emotional closeness, personal confidences, and intimacy."[25]

The process of inferring attributes about ourselves is much the same as inferring attributes about others. Self-concept is the sum total of the view which we have of ourselves. It affects not only our attitudes, but also our achievements and performance. Competence means capacity, fitness, or ability. Sense of competence is related to self-concept. Also related are significant others, group memberships, social roles we play, and the situations in which we find ourselves.

The three parts to one's impression management are: (1) an appropriate front; (2) dramatic realization; and (3) a sense of mystification.

Openness is related to relationships, some of which are necessary, others of which are discretionary. We need some disclosure to have any kind of relationship, even a necessary one. How much openness depends on whether we are building a relationship, just maintaining one, or perhaps easing out of one.

Attraction is shaped and strengthened by at least five factors: (1) nearness; (2) similarity; (3) status and recognition; (4) physical characteristics; and (5) rhetorical sensitivity.

[25]Schutz, *Firo: A Three Dimensional Theory,* p. 24.

STUDY PROJECTS

1. Analyze one of your interpersonal communication relationships in terms of the interpersonal needs the relationship fulfills. Analyze the relationship in terms of the inclusion, affection, and control needs the relationship serves.

2. Write a short essay explaining how you think your self-concept was formed by any or all of the five factors discussed.

3. "All the world's a stage, and all the men and women are merely players" (Shakespeare). We all attempt to manage others' impressions of us. Analyze your instructor's impression management in terms of his or her front, dramatic realization, and mystification.

4. In a small group, explore your feelings about self-disclosure. How much? Under what circumstances? When? In what kinds of relationships? Advantages? Disadvantages? You may want to consider the *disclosure* curve and the five "useful questions" discussed.

5. Select a person who attracts you, and assess your evaluation of that person in terms of the factors of attraction discussed in this chapter. (Or do the same for a person whom you find unattractive.) Be prepared to discuss your evaluation in class.

6. Read Appendix B, *The Employment Interview,* and prepare to discuss the reasons behind such unusual interpersonal behavior.

6

Managing conflict

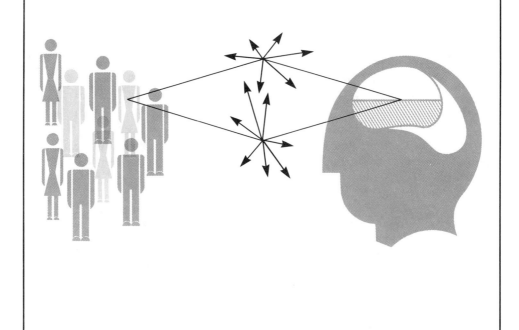

General learning outcomes

- We should learn that interpersonal conflict involves perceptions of incompatible goals and/or threats to a relationship, and that communication is the heart of the matter.
- We should learn the attributes of a rhetorically sensitive personality.
- We should learn the characteristics of "unfair fighting."
- We should learn how to confront conflict with perspective.
- We should learn how to evaluate our communication styles.
- We should learn how to apply a conflict agenda.

ON DEFINING CONFLICT

Sometimes conflict is dumped in your lap. You arrive at the office and an act of nature has cut off all of the power and heat. That's not an interpersonal conflict. However, if you are in a leadership role, it can quickly become one if people feel that you should have anticipated such a calamity and had auxiliary power and heat available. Interpersonal conflicts are sometimes like that too. They catch us by surprise, but perhaps they shouldn't as often as they do. "I didn't know she was unhappy." "I had no idea I was being unkind." "He just up and left me." All of these are familiar lines to marriage counselors.

Conflict is inevitable but, as we see in this chapter, not always the end of the world. So much depends on how we manage it. Some experts even think conflict is an integral part of real intimacy.[1] What causes close relationships to fall apart is an unwillingness to face conflicts constructively—and a tendency to face them destructively or simply to avoid them as long as possible.

Conflict almost always involves perceptions of incompatible goals and/or threats to a relationship. That communication is at the heart of the matter is clearly stated by Simons:

> Communication . . . is the means by which conflicts get socially defined, the instrument through which influence in conflicts is exercised, and the vehicle by which partisans or third parties may prevent, manage, or resolve conflicts.[2]

[1]Andrew M. Greeley, *Sexual Intimacy* (New York: Seabury Press, 1973); see also Irwin Altman and Dalmas A. Taylor, *Social Penetration: The Development of Interpersonal Relationships* (New York: Holt, Rinehart & Winston, 1973); Mark L. Knapp, *Social Intercourse: From Greeting to Goodby* (Boston: Allyn & Bacon, 1978).

[2]Gerald R. Miller and Herbert S. Simons, eds., *Perspectives on Communication in Social Conflict* (Englewood Cliffs, N.J.: Prentice-Hall, 1974), p. 3.

The message content might concern an issue or goal of varying importance to you and the receiver. Perhaps you've used strong language on an issue of only minor concern to you but of major concern to the receiver. "Well, if *that's* how you feel about dogs . . ." "Oh, I'm sorry, I didn't know you were into pets that much . . ." You sense that a relationship may be put in jeopardy over an issue which, for you at least, was not very important.

To blurt out your strong political feelings to a dorm acquaintance is one thing. To do the same with an employer of a different persuasion (but with whom you have a satisfactory relationship) might be quite another matter. Much depends on the employer. Some people seem to have a greater tolerance for differences of opinion and conflict. So much depends upon the situation. Are you blurting out your feelings on or off the job? Are they job relevant or recreational?

A very large part of *interpersonal* conflict involves your concern for the *relationship* with another person. Will the message or content part of your interaction threaten the relationship?

COPING BEHAVIORS

It is our position that a rhetorically sensitive person will have more interpersonally satisfactory experiences. The specific attributes of such a person should be especially valuable in heading off unnecessary interpersonal conflicts or in coping with them when necessary.

The first suggestion is to take a general intrapersonal and interpersonal perspective of being rhetorically sensitive.

Rhetorical Sensitivity

ADAPTING TO SPECIFIC AUDIENCES, RECEIVERS, CONTEXTS, AND SITUATIONS. The rhetorically sensitive person appreciates that his or her self-concept is understood by others through interaction with others in contexts and situations that are meaningful to them. Rhetorically sensitive (RS) people know that "talk is not everywhere valued equally."[3] To adapt is to be an appropriate social actor, one who can live with reasonable role taking.

EVALUATING MESSAGE RELEVANCE.   The RS evaluates the *purpose* of his or her information in any interaction. If the interaction has little rhetorical purpose and threatens the relationship, the RS will consider silence. The RS assesses when to speak up and when to shut up. The RS does not run from a fight, but considers whether the issue is relevant and worth the effort. If so, the RS works diligently to couch the interaction prudently and persuasively.

CONSIDERING CONTENT AND RELATIONAL DIMENSIONS.   The RS is aware that *how* you say something is sometimes more important than *what* you say. The RS is not opposed to "straight talk" but is opposed to "letting it all hang out." The RS is opposed to manipulation, but not to ethical strategies that enhance an interaction. In the words of Hart and Burks:

> Is it inappropriate to choose carefully among alternate strategies so that my words will have the greatest social impact possible? Or is it really so wrong to stop a moment, to sift through the myriad verbalizations that can make social an idea, and to choose those rhetorical forms that appear best suited to the situation at hand?[4]

Figure 6.1   WILLY'N ETHEL by Joe Martin. © 1982 Field Enterprises, Inc. Courtesy of Field Newspaper Syndicate.

[3]Gerry Philipsen, "Speaking 'Like a Man' in Teamsterville: Culture Patterns of Role Enactment in an Urban Neighborhood," *Quarterly Journal of Speech*, 61, no. 1 (February 1975), 13–22.

[4]Roderick P. Hart and Don M. Burks, "Rhetorical Sensitivity and Social Interaction," *Speech Monographs*, 39, no. 2 (June 1972), 90. For a detailed discussion of five constituent parts of a rhetorically sensitive attitude, see Roderick P. Hart, Robert E. Carlson, and William F. Eadie, "Attitudes toward Communication and the Assessment of Rhetorical Sensitivity," *Communication Monographs*, 47, no. 1 (March 1980), 2.

Fair Fighting

It's easy to be unfair, unkind, and unobjective. We expect some tolerance from others when we temporarily "lose it," and we usually *intend* to extend it to others. The problem is that we don't always take the time, or have the time, to painstakingly analyze every interpersonal interaction or every hidden hang-up, real or fancied, that confronts us.

We need not ignore all rationalizations, compensations, regressions, and so forth. We cannot and, as we see, sometimes should not. Nevertheless, an objective and sensitive analysis often calls for considerable discounting since the message may have been more ventilation than substance.

If communication is the means by which conflicts become socially defined, then it is imperative that we don't let normal adjustment tendencies misdefine the real conflicts. This coping perspective ideally includes the ability to know when to take a person *literally* and when not to. The situation often helps locate the tolerance line. The political arena seems to allow more adjustive shouting than other situations.

Being tolerant of adjustive behavior even when it provokes anger is perhaps what Christ meant by turning the other check or what the old adage of "counting to ten" means.

One way to know what is fair fighting is to discuss what is unfair. In their book, *The Intimate Enemy: How to Fight Fair in Love and Marriage,* psychotherapist George Bach and colleague Peter Wyden review a great many dirty-fighting techniques or "crazy-makers."[5] Several are relevant to the kinds of interpersonal conflict about which we're talking. Even after appropriate excuses for special situations, these are really unfair.

Kitchen sinking throws every argument into the fight but the kitchen sink. It includes the sort of sick insult exchanges made famous in Edward Albee's *Who's Afraid of Virginia Woolf?* or Neil Simon's *California Suite.*

Hannah:	I never liked San Francisco. I was always afraid I'd fall out of bed and roll down one of those hills.
Billy:	Not you, Hannah, you roll *up* hills.
Hannah:	Oh, good, you're bantering. The flight out wasn't a total loss. . . . Aren't you going to sit down, Bill? Or do they call you Billy out here. Yes, they do. Jenny told me. Everybody calls you Billy.
Billy:	(shrugs) That's me, Billy.
Hannah:	It's adorable. A forty-five-year-old Billy. Standing there in his cute little sneakers and sweater. Please, sit down, Billy, I'm beginning to feel like your math teacher.[6]

[5]Dr. George R. Bach and Peter Wyden, *The Intimate Enemy: How to Fight Fair in Love and Marriage* (New York: William Morrow, 1969), p. 135.

[6]From *California Suite* by Neil Simon. Copyright © 1977 by Neil Simon. Reprinted by permission of Random House, Inc.

Gunny sacking saves up all manner of grievances and complaints which are "toted along quietly in a gunny sack . . . (till) they make a dreadful mess when the sack finally bursts." Bach and Wyden catch this crazy-maker with the following episode:

HE: Why were you late?
SHE: I tried my best.
HE: Yeah? You and who else? Your mother is never on time either.
SHE: That's got nothing to do with it.
HE: The hell it doesn't. You're just as sloppy as she is.
SHE: (*getting louder*) You don't say! Who's picking whose dirty underwear off the floor every morning?
HE: (*shouting*) I happen to go to work. What have you got to do all day?
SHE: (*shouting*) I'm trying to get along on the money you don't make, that's what.
HE: (*turning away from her*) Why should I knock myself out for an ungrateful bitch like you?[7]

Some conflict in the preceding example was legitimate; she was late. But check the gunny sacking and some kitchen sinking: the mother-in-law complaint, the masculinity grievance, the money complaint.

Belt lining, as in boxing, strikes a blow at or below the belt line—a foul in some cases, painful at best. We all have a psychological belt line or tolerance level for *some* interpersonal pain. Communications can be more prudently transmitted when we know where those belt lines are. If a boxer had his trunks up around his neck, we'd think it an unfair fight, yet some people face conflict situations in much the same way, making low blows out of the mildest of admonitions. For some the trunks are around the ankles, masochistically inviting low blows. Striking low blows is a fairly sure way to become embroiled in dirty fights (or to be ignored).

All of us need to check the belt lines of others and perhaps to adjust our own from year to year and situation to situation. In dealing with intimates and friends we are advised to give some clues indicating where our belt lines are so we do not deceive others.

Monologuing is incessant talking, a verbosity which tolerates no real feedback. In discussing the "Language of Maladjustment" Wendell Johnson describes an extreme case:

One of the most striking cases I have ever known is that of a lady who seems to have no terminal facilities whatever. It is quite probable that she could talk all day; I have never felt up to making the experiment. An interesting thing about her speech is that a little of it is not unpleasant. Listening to her talk is somewhat like watching a six-day bicycle race; the first few laps are even a little exciting, perhaps. It is the five-hundredth lap that gets you. She seems to be motivated by a profound sense of frus-

[7]Bach and Wyden, *The Intimate Enemy*, p. 3.

tration in her social and professional activities; in any prolonged mono-
logue she eventually settles down to a steady outpouring of criticism and
pained astonishment concerning her real and imagined rivals. In common
parlance, she is a "cat." Her denunciations of other people, given usually
in confidential tones, seem to serve as a crutch with which she supports
her own tottering self-esteem.[8]

According to Bach and Wyden, monologuers are enormously resented.
They have only limited constructive advice for victims of monologuing: Walk out,
cover your ears, hold up your hand, reward acknowledgments.[9] They have found
that the best training for monologuers is to let them see and hear themselves and
their victims on television. This is one way to get them to absorb feedback.

Sandbagging sets up or traps someone into saying something that is later
held against him or her. It is often a phony plea for openness. For example, suppose you comply to a specific request by laying out the administrative heads in
your organization and are subsequently attacked by the sandbagger who supports
Uncle Lou and the administration. Sometimes sandbagging can be more subtle: a
con artist might listen patiently and attentively until you put your foot in your
mouth or buy the swamp land and essentially sandbag yourself. Was Ethel set up
in the following exchange?

Figure 6.2   WILLY'N ETHEL by Joe Martin. © 1982 Field Enterprises, Inc. Courtesy of
Field Newspaper Syndicate.

CONFRONTING CONFLICT

Perspective Taking

If you feel that you must confront, then an intrapersonal consideration of
the following general questions should give you perspective and help you prepare
for such encounters:

[8]Wendell Johnson, *People in Quandaries* (New York: Harper & Brothers, 1946), pp. 245–46.
[9]Bach and Wyden, *The Intimate Enemy*, p. 142.

How critical is the conflict? Must it be confronted immediately? Should it be? Has your irritation magnified the problem? Is it really your business? Have you "looked again"? Irving Lee found that when we are emotional and angry, three out of every four times a "look again" proves we were wrong or at least not totally justified in our anger.[10]

Is the conflict primarily relational or content oriented? All interpersonal conflicts are in part relational, but some are entirely so. Other conflicts, in which issues are the primary causes, may have some relational consequences. An argument over twin or double beds may be "content oriented" for some, but lovers would, we're sure, find it "relational" as well. In fact, the beds themselves may have been a secondary issue from the start. Assigning weights to content and relational matters is not always easy but we should try. If a friend is constantly monologuing using the same tired issues, it is probably relational. Perhaps you have taken the issues too seriously and your friend hasn't; perhaps you need some new friends.

Is the receiver aware of the conflict? The marriage counselor examples earlier illustrate this point of awareness: "I had no idea she was unhappy." We may be very aware of another's behavior if it is bothersome and frustrating to us, but if, thanks to the silence of others and ourselves, that person is unaware of a problem, we have a conflict with a very special twist—a twist that we must consider *before* engaging in systematic confrontation. Your approach to this type of encounter should vary depending on whether the other person is an intimate, a casual friend, a superior, a subordinate—in short, depending on the way in which the relationship is important to you.

Is there a role difference? In Utopia all people are equal and their roles in society make no difference. Presidents and kings are viewed in the same way as the rank and file. In reality such equality is a cruel illusion. Many needless conflicts are spawned by innocents who confuse "equal under the law" with "equal in all ways." Without even discussing intelligence, we can note that some people have better reaction times, retention skills, and abilities to abstract complicated data than others. These variations can make for role differences, but so can the existence of easier assigned or elected roles. In the military it is clear that RHIP, Rank Has Its Privileges. That's why we have NCO (noncommissioned officers) Clubs and Officers' Clubs. That's why the president of a major corporation or government agency has a chauffeured car and others do not. Like it or not, role difference makes a difference. You must address this issue pragmatically as you assess the criticality of the conflict and the approach or strategy you will use in confronting it.

Am I prepared to lose? A really mean question! You should, after all, think positively and have faith that after honest discussion people will see things your way, or if not *your* way, surely some other way mutually acceptable to all. After sitting in on arbitration cases it became obvious to me that some conflicts don't get resolved at all, and that third parties sometimes simply hand down resolutions

[10]Irving J. Lee, *How to Talk with People* (New York: Harper & Row, 1952), pp. 113–20.

and decisions. There are winners, there are losers, and there are times when we're not sure whether we've won or lost.

Calculate your risks in these matters. If I lose, will my relationship suffer? How will I maintain contact? Will I be able to confront this conflict again perhaps with more success next time? Am I destroyed? Does a loss mean my job? Can I live with it?

Coping with conflict is serious business and calls for thoughtfulness, awareness, and a willingness to confront with perspective. A discussion of appropriate style and an encounter agenda follow.

Your Communication Style

Earlier we discussed your concern for the content versus the relationship in a conflict. This dichotomy could also be stated as your concern for your personal goals in the conflict versus your concern for the relationship (in any given conflict).

Borrowing from Blake and Mouton[11] and the Jay Hall revision[12] we get a characterization of the styles available. The horizontal scale shown in Figure 6.3 allows you to assess just how important your personal goals are in any given conflict. The vertical scale allows you to assess just how important the relationship is to you in any given conflict. There are eighty-one intersections, but the four styles

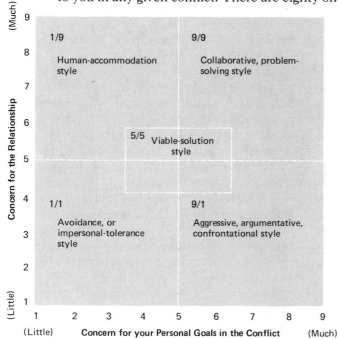

Figure 6.3

[11]Robert R. Blake and Jane S. Mouton, *The Managerial Grid* (Houston: Gulf Publishing, 1964), p. 10.

[12]Jay Hall, *Conflict Management Survey* (Woodlands, Tex.: Teleometrics International, 1969).

typified by the corners plus a central compromise style are enough to make the point.

Your analysis of your specific conflict should help you choose an appropriate style. Ideally you should seek a 9/9 *collaborative, problem-solving style,* but some conflicts quickly call for backup styles when collaboration fails. Sometimes the time factor is enough. A conflict between two pilots on a damaged aircraft calls for quick assessment of what to do, but when time runs out, the senior officer turns to an *aggressive* 9/1 style: "We're going to abort. Prepare for an emergency landing." This happens despite the pilot's concern for the relationship between the pilot and the crew.

The 1/1 Avoidance or Impersonal-Tolerance Style. In this case you have little concern for the relationship and if the conflict impinges only slightly on your personal goals, your style might very well be a low-profile one.

The 9/1 Aggressive, Argumentative, Confrontational Style. With this approach you have much concern for the conflict and minimal concern for the relationship. The senior pilot in the earlier example was backed into this one. His argument was a short one given the emergency.

The 5/5 Viable-Solution Style. This is a compromise style in which your concerns are typically low or mixed. The viable-solution style is not always an easy one and not always the best, long-term resolution of a conflict but it is sometimes a necessary step toward achieving a more collaborative, problem-solving style.

1/9 Human-Accommodation Style. In this situation the concern for the relationship is unusually high, and the concern for personal goals is either low to begin with or is surrendered for the sake of the relationship. This is a useful but tricky style . . . sometimes. Suppose you are smitten with an incredibly attractive person who literally takes your breath away. You discover that he or she has strong political leanings which are the opposite of yours. Unless your politics are truly at the 9 on the scale, you would probably use a style that accommodates the relationship and yields on the political conflict. Depending on how the relationship develops, you might move to any of the other styles. You might, of course, really change your politics, but you won't change the other person's if you stay at 1/9.

9/9 Collaborative, Problem-Solving Style. Here one has much concern for the relationship *and* much concern for personal goals. This is an enlightened style based on the assumptions that conflicts are natural in the human experience; conflicts are amenable to rational, cooperative problem solving; and a sensitive openness is the necessary first step. The problem with ideal styles is that situations, contexts, and circumstances are not always ideal. For example, the organization person is tied (or ought to be) by constitutions, bylaws, labor agreements, affirmative action, the IRS, and other laws of the land. In addition to requiring participation, the 9/9 style is usually very time consuming. Don't be in a hurry.

Part of your style decision should be based on the typical styles used by the other or others involved in the conflict. If you know you are going to have to interact with a confirmed 9/1—that is, an aggressive, "tell it like it is" approach to conflict resolution—your starting point may be a little (or a lot) short of 9/9.

Figure 6.4 *An Encounter Agenda*

Conflict: Praparation and Practice

I. Preparation Perspectives
   A. How critical is the conflict?
   B. Is it primarily relational or content oriented?
   C. Is the receiver aware of the conflict?
   D. Is there a role difference?
   E. Am I prepared to lose?

II. Preparation and Practice
   A. Agenda building
      1. Personally define the problem.
         a. Singularly.
         b. Specifically.
         c. Fairly.
      2. Analyze exactly how it affects you.
      3. Consider fair-fight, constructive techniques.
         a. Don't kitchen sink.
         b. Don't gunny sack.
         c. Don't belt line.
         d. Don't monologue.
         e. Don't sandbag.
      4. Decide on an appropriate communication style.
         a. 1/1, avoidance or impersonal tolerance.
         b. 9/1, aggressive, argumentative, confrontational.
         c. 5/5, viable solution of the moment.
         d. 1/9, human accommodation.
         e. 9/9, collaboration, problem solving.
      5. Review positive attitudes about conflict.
         a. Conflict is serious business, but a natural
            hazard of living.
         b. When conflict is resolved effectively, with
            rhetorical sensitivity, such an experience can
            preserve or enhance a relationship.
         c. A positive, rhetorically sensitive openness is
            usually the first step toward conflict resolution.
         d. "When angry look again." If your anger is justified,
            it is human to admit it and to seek feedback from
            the appropriate respondent.
      6. Try it on a friend.
   B. Make an appointment (IMPORTANT)
      1. A mutually convenient time.
      2. A psychologically constructive time.

III. Confronting the Conflict (the actual encounter).
   A. State the conflict singularly, specifically, fairly.
   B. Seek agreement on the statement.
      1. Control emotions.
      2. Stay on the topic.
      3. Don't sandbag.
   C. Allow response time (or delay).
      1. Don't monologue.
      2. Solicit feedback.
      3. Keep analysis rational.
      4. Be open, positive, and rhetorically sensitive.
   D. If resolved or partially so, review your joint understanding.

THANKS

SUMMARY

Conflict is a hazard of living. A large part of interpersonal conflict involves your concern for the relationship with the other person. Will the message or content part of your interaction threaten the relationship? Communication is the means by which conflicts are prevented, managed, or resolved. Name calling, threats, deception, and sarcasm are destructive and elicit reactions of hurt, fear, confusion, and distrust. Constructive conflict is open, but it is relationship as well as issue centered, and it seeks an atmosphere of trust. It seeks a forthright but supportive, rational, problem-solving kind of issue confrontation.

"Rhetorical sensitivity is a particular attitude toward encoding spoken messages. It represents a way of thinking about what should be said and then a way of deciding how to say it."[13] It is a type of sensitivity which makes effective social interaction possible. Rhetorically sensitive people judge encounters carefully before taking stands on issues. They distinguish between content and relational communication and they know when to speak up or shut up.

Unfair fighting techniques include kitchen sinking, gunny sacking, belt lining, monologuing, and sandbagging. Assessing a conflict situation should include the following questions: (1) How critical is the conflict? (2) Is the conflict primarily relational or content oriented? (3) Is the receiver aware of the conflict? (4) Is there a role difference? (5) Am I prepared to lose?

Preparation behavior for conflict situations should include the following steps: (1) Define the issue or behavior that bothers you and state the conflict specifically. (2) Decide your communication style. (3) Review positive attitudes about conflict. (4) Make an appointment. (5) Confront the conflict systematically.

STUDY PROJECTS

1. Describe a conflict situation in which rhetorical sensitivity might have "saved the day."

2. Locate a good example (it can be a short one) of unfair fighting and prepare to share it with the class:

   Kitchen sinking
   Gunny sacking
   Belt lining
   Monologuing
   Sandbagging

3. Apply the working outline for conflict situations found at the end of this chapter to an old or current personal conflict and detail your plan for resolution (or, in the case of an old experience, what might have been).

[13]Hart, Carlson, and Eadie, "Attitudes toward Communication," p. 75.

4. Read Edward Albee's play *Who's Afraid of Virginia Woolf?* and locate one example of each of the unfair fighting types.

5. Discuss in two pages or less (or orally) an episode in which your communication style was inappropriate. Use the numbers from the chapter (e.g., 5/5).

6. After being assigned to a group of three to six, prepare a ten- to fifteen-minute panel discussion in which you try to apply the suggestions found in this chapter to the following case. What *might* have been done? What *can* be done at this point? What decisions should be made on grades and why? What would be an appropriate communication style (1/9, 9/1, 5/5, etc.)?
CASE: *You are a member of the Academic Fairness Committee.*

George is a junior majoring in theatre. The program in which he was enrolled included a large number of performance courses. In addition to getting practice in acting and technical work, however, George was also interested in good grades (he stated) because he was planning to go on for a Master's degree.

The grade that is being disputed is for a course in directing. The course required that each student direct six 20-minute video taped plays during the semester. Each of the directed scenes was critiqued by the instructor. The instructor, however, did not give the students any grades after the critiques. Since George, who has a 3.3 GPA, received favorable oral critiques from the instructor, he assumed that he would do well in the course.

The final grade given to George in the class was a D −. George went to the instructor and asked for a justification of the grade. The instructor told George that, even though he might have received a B or an A from any other instructor in the department, this work did not meet his own high standards. George took the tapes to another instructor, who testified that it was at least B − to A − work.

George appealed the D − because he felt that the instructor was too subjective and unfair in grading. This was the third complaint of this sort leveled against the instructor.[14]

Indicate your judgment on the following scales:

	Little	Great
Degree to which George is at fault for the grade	1 2 3 4 5 6 7	
Degree to which the instructor is at fault for the grade	1 2 3 4 5 6 7	
Grade you choose for George	F F+ D − D D+ C − C C+ B − B B+ A − A	

[14]Steven M. Alderton, research included in a published study, "A Processerol Analysis of Argumentation in Polarizing Groups," *Dimensions of Argument* (Salt Lake City: University of Utah Press, 1981), pp. 693–704.

7

Small-group communication

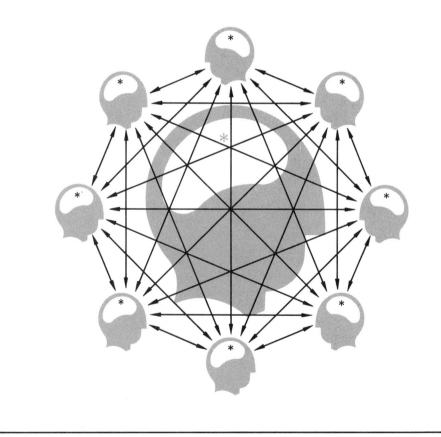

General learning outcomes

- We should learn the nature of dynamic, small-group discussion.
- We should learn that cooperative communication is essential to the success of a democratic society.
- We should learn the four characteristics of coacting groups.
- We should learn the contemporary forms of discussion and know when they are applicable.
- We should learn the phases and steps of group problem solving.
- We should learn about the reflective thinking process and its relationship to discussion agendas.
- We should learn of conformity dynamics and risks.

THE NATURE OF DISCUSSION

This chapter is concerned with systematic, cooperative decision making in small-group discussions. The term *discussion* is derived from the Latin *discussus*, to strike asunder, to pull apart, to separate and subordinate the elements and ideas that make up a question or topic. Discussion is not to be confused with debate. Debate is two-sided, discussion is many sided. Debate is competitive, discussion cooperative. If decision is impossible through discussion, then discussion may very well lead to debate. Debate may then lead to resolution. If it does not, the group very possibly will return to discussion. Premature or unnecessary debate has interfered in many group discussions. A discussion-debate continuum is illustrated in Figure 7.1.

Figure 7.1

According to communication theory, the unique aspect of discussion is that a participant is both sender and receiver at the same time—producing truly dynamic, interpersonal communication. Feedback and perception take on even greater significance in these circumstances.

The Nature of Small Groups

Most of our social interaction takes place in small groups. In this chapter, however, we are particularly interested in groups that are more than just small, casual gatherings. There must be some connecting link, some common purpose, intent, or problem that requires some modest interaction to make a "coacting" group. We might say the members of such a group share a kind of mutual identification. The small group is a dynamic collection as long as it has *cohesiveness*. *Cohesion* is the force that binds members of a group together. Our own senses of interpersonal responsibilities and behavior greatly affect our successful interactions. We must be sensitive to our own behavior as well as to the behavior of others. The feedback is often swift and to the point in small groups; audiences are usually slower to respond and are more formal in their patterns of response.

The small group differs from the larger audience in still other psychological ways. The audience is passive, the group usually active and dynamic. The group's size permits active verbal involvement and instant participation. Some members have greater desires to take charge than do others. The interacting group often develops a spirit or cohesiveness that resembles the "collective mind" of the mob. This phenomenon, called *social facilitation*, is usually considered in positive terms, but small groups have been known to run wild, something that audiences seldom do (except in panics).

The dyadic communication model can be adapted here to show the complex workings of the small, coacting group. If we consider interpersonal communication as feedback *loops*, with every pair within a larger group having its own loop, then we see quickly why three persons constitute something quite different interpersonally than two alone (see Figure 7.2). We suddenly have three times as many two-part loops to follow. The number of possible subgroups and relationships grows to seven. For example, in a group of three (A, B, and C) we can chart the following subgroups:

A—B—C   AB—C
A—B   AC—B
A—C   BC—A
B—C

The reason most small-group experts limit their research to groups of six or seven is clear if we look at a group of eight in terms of loops and subgroup relationships. (See Figure 7.3; single lines with arrows are substituted for loops in this figure.) We now find ourselves with twenty-eight two-part loops. Time is part of the equation. Perhaps over a period of days or weeks we could master that many

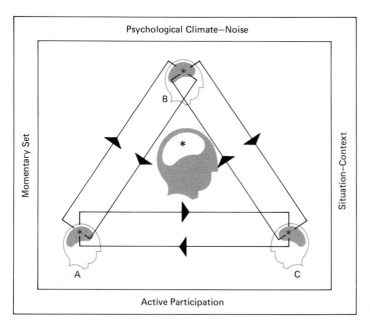

Figure 7.2
Model for a coacting group of three

Figure 7.3 Model for a coacting group of eight

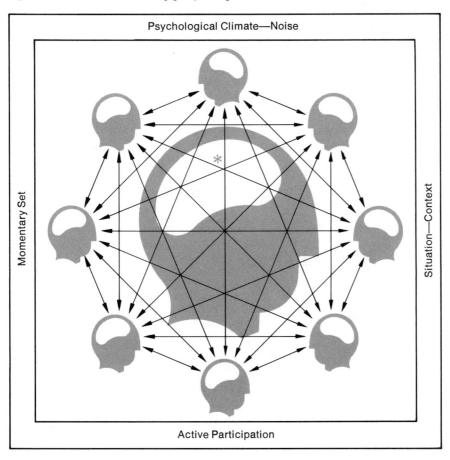

interactions. However, the total number of relationships and subgroups is quite astounding: 1009![1]

The small-group literature supports several *characteristics* pertinent to coacting groups.

1. *They share relevant common interests and engage in frequent interaction.*
2. *They (and others) define themselves as members and find that fact rewarding.*
3. *They identify with one another and share interlocking roles and goals.*
4. *They tend to act as a unit.[2]*

Certain *generalizations regarding the coacting small group* are also warranted from the research on such groups.[3]

1. Attitudes and behavior can be changed through group discussion.
2. On the average, small-group judgment tends to be better than individual judgment.
3. Small, agreeing groups develop more of a feeling of personal involvement and responsibility than do audiences.
4. Cooperative group communication can be improved through training.

In a broader sense, we might conclude that cooperative communication in small groups is essential to success in our society.[4]

Discussion Defined

The experts are in basic agreement about what we mean by group discussion.

Discussion is the process whereby two or more people exchange information or ideas in a face-to-face situation to achieve a goal.[5]

[1]The formula for predicting the total number of subgroup relationships may be expressed:

$$R = \sum d \frac{n!}{d!(n-d!)+1} \text{ where } d = s(n-1), (n-2)(n-3) \ldots (2).$$

[2]This list is a synthesis of ten small-group characteristics described by Dorwin Cartwright and Alvin Zander, *Group Dynamics: Research and Theory* (New York: Harper & Row, 1968), p. 48; see also John K. Brilhart, *Effective Group Discussion*, 4th ed. (Dubuque, Iowa: Wm. C. Brown, 1982), p. 9.

[3]See Jon Eisenson, J. Jeffrey Auer, and John V. Irwin, *The Psychology of Communication* (New York: Appleton-Century-Crofts, 1963), pp. 253–70; Bernard M. Bass, *Leadership, Psychology and Organizational Behavior* (New York: Harper & Row, 1973); A. Paul Hare, *Handbook of Small Group Research* (New York: Free Press, 1976); John W. Thibaut and Harold H. Kelley, *The Social Psychology of Groups* (New York: John Wiley, 1959); and Joseph E. McGrath and Irwin Altman, *Small Group Research* (New York: Holt, Rinehart & Winston, 1966).

[4]See Gerald M. Phillips and Eugene C. Erickson, *Interpersonal Dynamics in the Small Group* (New York: Random House, 1970).

[5]R. Victor Harnack, Thorrel B. Fest, and Barbara Schindler Jones, *Group Discussion Theory and Technique*, 2nd. ed. (Englewood Cliffs, N.J.: Prentice- Hall, 1977), p. 12.

[Discussion groups] consist of a number of persons who perceive each other as participants in a common activity, who interact dynamically with one another, and who communicate their responses chiefly through words.[6]

Discussion occurs when a group of persons assemble in a face-to-face situation and through oral interaction exchange information or attempt to reach a decision on shared problems.[7]

... an orderly process of cooperative deliberation designed to exchange, evaluate, and/or integrate knowledge and opinion on a given subject or to work toward solution of a common problem.[8]

... a number of persons who communicate with one another over a span of time, and who are few enough so that each person is able to communicate with all others, not at secondhand, through other people, but face-to-face.[9]

... a set of activities usually executed by a small group and directed toward determining appropriate answers to controversial questions of fact, conjecture, value, or policy.[10]

... a few people engaged in communication interaction over time, generally in face-to-face settings, who have common goals and norms, and have developed a communication pattern for meeting their goals in an interdependent fashion.[11]

Two other writers summed it up well when they said, "Discussion, then, is a means of thinking together through purposeful conversation."[12]

Assuming, then, that we have a real, interacting, face-to-face group—persons with some common goal, not just a loose collection of individuals—we might combine the preceding descriptions by saying that at its best *group discussion is a systematic and cooperative form of reflective thinking and communication.*

Contemporary Forms of Discussion

In this context, the word *form* refers to the type or format of discussion. In its most general sense, group discussion is a cooperative thinking effort, usually among twenty persons or less. The basic forms of group discussion are *dialogue,*

[6]Dean C. Barnlund and Franklyn S. Haiman, *The Dynamics of Discussion* (Boston: Houghton Mifflin, 1960), p. 20.

[7]Halbert Gulley, *Discussion, Conference, and Group Process,* 2nd. ed. (New York: Holt, Rinehart & Winston, 1968), p. 5; Halbert Gulley and Dale Leathers, *Communication and Group Process,* 3rd ed. (New York: Holt, Rinehart & Winston, 1977).

[8]Horace Rahskopf, *Basic Speech Improvement* (New York: Harper & Row, 1965), p. 348.

[9]George C. Homans, *The Human Group* (New York: Harcourt, Brace & World, 1950), p. 1.

[10]Dennis S. Gouran, *Discussion: The Process of Group Decision-Making* (New York: Harper & Row, 1974), p. 5; see also Dennis S. Gouran, *Making Decisions in Groups* (Glenview, Ill.: Scott, Foresman, 1982).

[11]John F. Cragan and David W. Wright, *Communication in Small Group Discussions* (St. Paul: West, 1980), p. 10.

[12]Wilhelmina G. Hedde and William N. Brigance, *American Speech* (Philadelphia: J. B. Lippincott, 1942), p. 40.

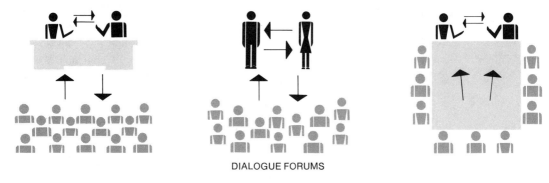

DIALOGUE FORUMS

Figure 7.4 Dialogue Forums

panel, and *symposium.* Three techniques that may be used with any of these forms are the *buzz group, role playing,* and *brainstorming.* A *forum,* that part of a discussion in which the audience may speak, can be and often is included in any of the discussion forms.[13]

A *dialogue* is a two-person interaction that may be simple conversation, an interview, or counseling. If a dialogue is held before an audience and the audience is invited to participate, the interaction becomes a dialogue forum. See Figure 7.4.[14]

The *panel* discussion is most often composed of three to seven persons pursuing a common goal in an informal climate that aids spontaneous interaction. An audience may or may not be present. A panel discussion generally calls for a procedural leader, one who plans, starts, and ends the meeting, and some *agenda* (discussed later in this chapter). See Figure 7.5.

Figure 7.5 Panel Forums

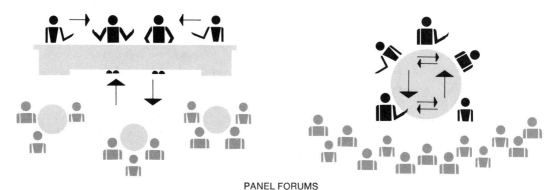

PANEL FORUMS

[13]See especially Kenneth G. Hance, ed., *Michigan Speech Association Curriculum Guide 3, Discussion and Argumentation-Debate in the Secondary School* (Skokie, Ill.: National Textbook Corporation, 1968).

[14]For an interesting discussion of physical arrangements, see Paul Bergevin, Dwight Morris, and Robert M. Smith, *Adult Education Procedures* (Greenwich, Conn.: Seabury Press, 1963); see also Robert Sommer, *Personal Space* (Englewood Cliffs, N.J.: Prentice-Hall, 1969), pp. 58–73.

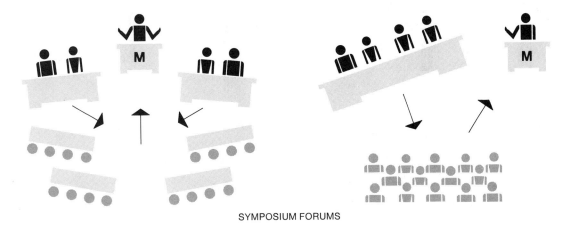

SYMPOSIUM FORUMS

Figure 7.6 Symposium Forums

A *symposium* is a small group (three to five) that has special knowledge of different aspects of a broad topic. Each individual makes uninterrupted speeches before an audience. A procedural leader controls the order of speakers and the time limits. A forum usually follows, except when an audience is not physically present (as with radio or TV broadcasts). Frequently, the symposium speakers then relate to one another more informally in a panel discussion. See Figure 7.6.

These forms of discussion may be used for information sharing, problem solving, or decision making, as well as for instructional purposes.

Examples of information-sharing groups are *staff meetings, study groups,* and *workshops.* The overlap among these groups is evident and probably unavoidable. A workshop, for example, may be thought of as a study group that has concentrated its work into a couple of days, or even a few hours.

Problem-solving groups include *committees, conferences,* and *governing boards* or *councils.* These discussion groups have the power of decision or at least the power to recommend actions based on their collective problem solving. Their group discussions are usually closed to nonmembers.

Instructional formats of discussion include case conferences, role playing, and to some extent all the forms and techniques of discussion. A *case conference* is a discussion of a real or hypothetical incident that is meant to have a learning outcome for the participants. It may or may not be conducted with an audience present. It can be evaluated according to participant interaction, leadership, agenda setting, and the solution.

Large groups in which wider forum participation is desired may be divided into subgroups of four to six persons for more intimate, informal discussion. This technique is known as *buzz,* "Phillips 66," or "Discussion 66." The numbers refer to subgroups of six who discuss a carefully worded question.[15] The results of the individual buzz sessions are reported to the larger group by a spokesperson. The

[15]Donald Phillips, "Report on Discussion," *Adult Education Journal,* 7 (October 1948), 181–82.

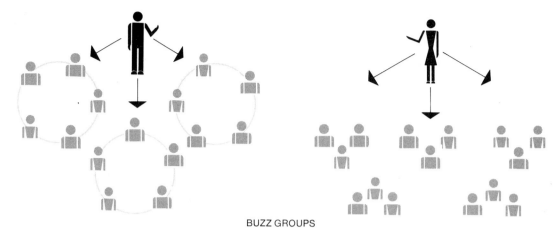

BUZZ GROUPS

Figure 7.7 Buzz Groups

number of people in the subgroups seems to be important: A person is more apt to speak up in a group of 6 than of 600. See Figure 7.7.

The extemporaneous acting out of assigned roles or dramatic parts in a group—often a case conference—is known as *role playing,* or what Hirschfeld has described as *extemporaction.*[16] As a technique, role playing is often a good preliminary to the other forms of discussion. See Figure 7.8.

Brainstorming is a technique that some speech-communication instructors use to show the effect of eliminating premature and discussion-inhibiting comments of an absolute or critical nature. This technique operates in an arbitrary psychological climate complete with penalties whose purpose is to prohibit immediate criticism of ideas. Brainstorming permits more creative ideas to come to light in a short period of time than does a more traditional climate.[17] This technique can also be combined with other forms and used for purposes other than instruction. It can be particularly useful when a great many ideas are wanted from

Figure 7.8 Role Playing

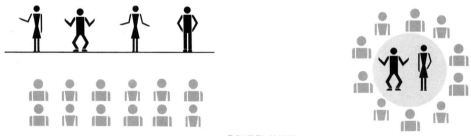

ROLE PLAYING

[16]From material supplied by Adeline Hirschfeld, Director of P.A.C.E. Project, "Creative and Sociodramatic Supplementary Educational and Cultural Enrichment Service," Title III, E.S.E.A., Oakland University, Rochester, Michigan, 1967.

[17]Alex F. Osborn, *Applied Imagination: Principles and Procedures of Creative Thinking* (New York: Charles Scribner's, 1963).

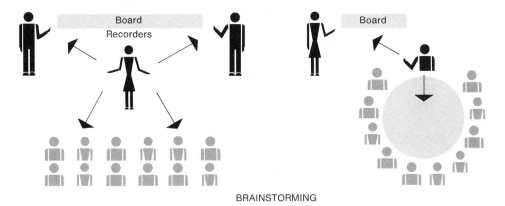

Figure 7.9 Brainstorming

a group in a short period of time. Brainstorming is a good technique for screening attitudes and opinions. Take the question, "What should this class use as a topic for a project discussion?" Under brainstorming rules, this question regularly produces sixty or seventy topics in ten minutes. No evaluative discussion of the topics is allowed until later.Using buzz groups to screen the list more systematically is a good followup. See Figure 7.9.

GROUP PROBLEM SOLVING

Phases

Bales and Strodtbeck divided problem-solving discussions into three phases on the basis of number of interactions. They found that in the first phase, the communications pertained to *orientation, information, repetition,* and *confirmation*; in the second phase, the interactions were for *analysis, evaluation,* and *seeking communications* or *giving opinions* and *feelings*; in phase three communications consisted chiefly of acts of *control,* and were about possible directions and ways of action.[18] Bales and Strodtbeck also indicate that as a group approaches the third phase, it experiences increasing strain on the members' solidarity and social-emotional relationships. Both positive and negative reactions tend to increase. The reduction of tension is apparent as differences are resolved and agreement is reached.

These same small-group experts found two major categories of behavior: one related to the more personal or social problems (social-emotional), and the other to the task or job that had to be done apart from personalities (task area).[19]

Tuckman devised a similar group-observation system and found the same

[18]Robert F. Bales and Fred L. Strodtbeck, "Phases in Group Problem-Solving," in *Group Dynamics: Research and Theory*, eds. Dorwin Cartwright and Alvin Zander (New York: Harper & Row, 1960), pp. 624–38.

[19]Robert F. Bales and Fred L. Strodtbeck, "Phases in Group Problem Solving," *Journal of Abnormal and Social Psychology*, 46 (1951), 485–95; see also Robert Bales, "A Set of Categories for the Analysis of Small Group Interaction," *American Sociological Review*, 15 (1950), 257–63.

two basic areas of social and task problems.[20] He felt there were four phases that could be observed:

PHASES	SOCIAL AND TASK EQUIVALENTS
1. Forming	a. Testing and independence
	b. Attempting to identify the task
2. Storming	a. Development of intragroup conflicts
	b. Emotional response to task demands
3. Norming	a. Development of group cohesion
	b. Expressions of opinions
4. Performing	a. Functional role-relatedness
	b. Emergence of solutions

A communication scholar's model involves four similar phases, but perhaps better explains how conflict is processed. Fisher suggests four phases of decision emergence:

1. Orientation
2. Conflict
3. Emergence
4. Reinforcement

The *emergence* phase is characterized by a form of modified dissent in which conflicting statements are softened through ambiguity. This is the most critical phase, according to Fisher. The *reinforcement* phase occurs when consensus is reaffirmed.[21]

The danger of oversimplifying so complicated a process is made clear by the research of Scheidel and Crowell, who suggest that the reflective thinking process as an agenda system is not a simple linear progression after all, but is rather a circular or spiraling course.[22] It's a little like a "Slinky" toy. The spirals of steel in the toy may be more compressed at the end of the spring in the same way as ideas are compressed when a group finally nears agreement. After studying idea development in ten discussions, Scheidel and Crowell concluded that members devoted one-fourth of their comments to confirming statements and another fourth to clarifying and substantiating them. The latter function is represented by the outward movement of this spiral model. The progress toward decision is represented as the onward movement.

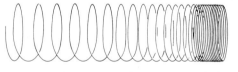

Figure 7.10

[20]Bruce Tuckman, "Developmental Sequence in Small Groups," *Psychological Bulletin*, 63 (1965), 384–99.

[21]B. Aubrey Fisher, *Small Group Decision Making: Communication and the Group Process* (New York: McGraw-Hill, 1974), pp. 140–45.

[22]Thomas M. Scheidel and Laura Crowell, "Idea Development in Small Discussion Groups," *Quarterly Journal of Speech*, 50 (1964), 140–45.

Agendas

If a group discussion is a *systematic and cooperative form of reflective thinking and communication,* then we had better explore reflective thinking in detail to see what kind of system or scheme it suggests for orderly *agendas*—that is, discussion outlines. That orderliness pays off in agreement is shown in a study of seventy-two conferences by Collins and Guetzkow. They report:

> Those meetings in which discussion is orderly in its treatment of topics, and without backward references to previously discussed issues, tended to end in more consensus. . . .When participants discussed but one issue at a time, instead of simultaneously dabbling in two or three, it was more possible for the group to reach consensus.[23]

THE REFLECTIVE THINKING PROCESS.   Reflective thinking was defined by John Dewey as "active, persistent and careful consideration of any belief or supposed form of knowledge in the light of the grounds that support it, and further conclusions to which it tends,"[24] as opposed to nondeliberate, everyday thinking. Dewey thought of reflective thinking as a scientific habit, one that consisted of acquiring the attitude of *suspended judgment* and mastering the various methods of searching for materials. Maintaining an intelligent state of doubt and practicing systematic inquiry are the essentials of reflective thinking.

Dewey's view of general education is also pertinent to group discussion, both as an agenda and as a way of self-conduct. Dewey thought the aim of education was the establishment of a kind of *self-discipline* in students. This self-discipline consisted of *systematic observation, thorough examination,* and, most important to us, agendas, or the *methodical arrangement of thought.* The *Dewey system of reflective thinking* contains five steps:

1. The occurrence or awareness of a *felt difficulty:* you know something is wrong, unexpected, or unidentified.
2. The *definition* of the felt difficulty to see what kind of problem you have and how serious it is: look carefully, don't misdefine; suspend your judgment regarding solutions.
3. The formulation of alternative suggestions, explanations, and hypotheses as *possible solutions:* inference and analysis take place here.
4. The rational working out of the possible solutions by gathering facts, evidence, and inferences: further analysis of the consequences of alternative solutions.
5. Further testing, rejecting, or confirming of the solution chosen in step 4—by observation, measurement, hypothetical case or model building, or actual experiment if applicable: you now have a reasoned solution in your thoughts.[25]

[23]Barry E. Collins and Harold Guetzkow, *A Social Psychology of Group Processes for Decision-Making* (New York: John Wiley, 1964), p. 111.

[24]John Dewey, *How We Think* (Boston: D. C. Heath, 1910), p. 68.

[25]Ibid., pp. 68–78.

Although it is addressed to the individual, the reflective thinking system would make just as much sense to a group of individuals solving a problem or making a decision. More recent research tends to confirm the five stages of Dewey's system.

The best agenda systems found in the literature are derived from research findings coupled with creative insight. Some excellent examples follow:

A visual aid depicting the agenda such as a chart, handout, or program may prove helpful to participants.[26]

EIGHT-STEP AGENDA (Barker, Wahlers, Cegala, and Kibler)

1. Define the problem.
2. Limit the problem.
3. Analyze the problem.
4. Establish criteria.
5. Suggest possible solutions.
6. Check the solutions against the criteria.
7. Implement the solution(s).
8. Evaluate the success of the solution.[27]

FOUR-STEP AGENDA (Goldberg and Larson)

I. Are we all agreed on the nature of the problem?

II. What would be the *ideal solution* from the point of view of all parties involved in the problem?

III. What conditions within the problem could be changed so that the ideal solution might be achieved?

IV. Of the solutions available to us, which one best approximates the ideal solution?[28]

---

[26]John K. Brilhart, "An Experimental Comparison of Three Techniques for Communicating a Problem-Solving Pattern to Members of a Discussion Group," *Speech Monographs*, 33, no. 2 (June 1966), 176.

[27]Larry L. Barker, Kathy J. Wahlers, Donald J. Cegala, and Robert J. Kibler, *Groups in Process* 2nd. ed. (Englewood Cliffs, N.J.: Prentice-Hall, 1983), pp. 138–43.

[28]Alvin A. Goldberg and Carl E. Larson, *Group Communication* (Englewood Cliffs, N.J.: Prentice-Hall, 1975), p. 149; see also C. E. Larson, "Forms of Analysis and Small Group Problem-Solving," *Speech Monographs*, XXXVI, no. 4 (November 1960), 452–55.

TWO-PHASE AGENDA (Gulley)

I. The Analysis Phase
   A. Definitions: What does the question mean?
   B. Limitations, if any: What part of the problem do we intend to concentrate on if we cannot discuss the whole problem now?
   C. What are the important facts about this problem?
      1. What is its history?
      2. What are its causes?
      3. What has happened or is happening?
      4. What has happened elsewhere that illuminates the problem under discussion?

II. The Solution Phase
   A. What are the advantages and disadvantages of each alternative course of action?
   B. By what or whose standards must any decision be evaluated?
   C. What decision should we reach?[29]

ROSS FOUR-PHASE AGENDA

I. Definition Phase
   a. Limit the question
   b. Determine the nature: fact, policy, value

II. Analysis Phase
   a. Puzzles
   b. Probabilities
   c. Values

III. Criteria Phase
   a. Mini-max limits
   b. Order of importance (weighting)

IV. Solution Phase
   a. Test solutions against criteria
   b. Decision and implementation

---

[29]Gulley, *Discussion, Conference and Group Process*, pp. 215–16; see also Gulley and Leathers, *Communication and Group Process*, pp. 120–21.

ELABORATING THE AGENDA SYSTEMS. Using the Ross four-step system as a point of reference, but with the understanding that what is said here applies, for the most part, to all the agenda systems shown, let's look at some of the finer points of an agenda:

I. THE DEFINITION PHASE

In most problem-solving discussions, a suggestion to take stock of the felt difficulty, to ventilate it fully, is pertinent. This phase helps remove emotional heat, if any, from the topic; it allows a quick audit of feelings (for example, there may be more than one felt difficulty in the group). It helps the group formulate the problem and determine goals.

The definition phase consists of the definition and, if pertinent, the limitation of the problem. For example, a group may talk about unemployment and limit the problem to unemployment in Chicago. If a group defines a problem in several different ways and, worse, is not aware of the differences, confusion and irritation are sure to follow.

In some cases (for example, medical diagnosis), a definition of the problem and a knowledge of previous identical situations may make the solution obvious. Most often, however, defining the problem helps to determine its *nature*. Is the problem a question of *fact, policy,* or *value?* The meaning of fact appears obvious to most of us. However, one cantankerous professor claims that he has never heard a good definition of a fact. For the most part, facts are actions, events, or conditions that have been properly observed, described, classified, and reported. Can the phenomenon under discussion be verified by facts, to the satisfaction of group members? Policy is concerned with any plan or course of actions designed to influence and determine future decisions. Our American foreign policy, or a particular company's personnel policy are examples. The nature of this kind of problem usually revolves around desirability. Discussion time is well spent on the definition step. Agree on the nature of the problem and/or goal *before* you proceed. Of course, facts will also be a part of this kind of deliberation. *Value* is concerned chiefly with judgments about attitudes, beliefs, and feelings—very often the things most difficult to measure. More is said about value shortly.

II. THE ANALYSIS PHASE

PUZZLES The *puzzle* dimension refers to questions of *fact*. This dimension is easier to apply than the fact dimension, though it may be less comprehensive. As an illustration, consider a common jigsaw puzzle. No one would deny that a jigsaw puzzle can be difficult or frustrating (or capable of solution by group effort). Yet there is definitely a solution—and only one solution. Indeed, the solution is recognizable when you achieve it. Early detection of and agreement on a problem, as with a puzzle, can save much time and aggravation. If we were to view the jigsaw puzzle as a question of value—perhaps as a threat to our intelligence—then the problem would become more difficult and the solution (putting the pieces together) would probably be delayed.

Some puzzles are complicated. We use computers to solve engineering problems and adding machines and cash registers to solve addition problems in supermarkets. But such problems are still puzzles, and we are well advised not to involve our emotions, morals, or value systems too quickly.

PROBABILITIES The *probability* dimension of a problem refers to common sense reduced to calculation. The suggestion here is that certain problems can be solved according to probability theory or to the laws of chance. Although the word *probability* itself indicates that such problems may never be solved with certainty, the mathematical chance of a solution's being correct may often be treated as an operational fact. Gamblers can predict their odds with relative certainty. They know that they have a 50 percent chance of getting a head in flipping a coin. Even in simple games, however, determining probabilities can quickly become complicated. If your winning number is 5 in a dice game with two dice, you have only four possible combinations: 1–4, 4–1, 3–2, and 2–3. Since theoretical probabilities are multiplied—two six-sided dice give 36 (6 × 6) possible combinations—the odds of your winning are 4/36 or 1/9. The six combinations yielding the number 7 have a probability of 6/36 or 1/6. The number of rolls is, of course, a significant variable. The larger the number of rolls, in general, the greater the likelihood that the theoretical probability becomes an established fact.

Not all probability and prediction problems have odds that are as theoretically absolute as those in a coin flip or a dice game. An insurance company never knows exactly how many accidents, deaths, and fires will occur among its policy holders, but it can make quite accurate predictions on the basis of past experiences. This science of probability prediction is called *statistics*. From statistics we learn not only to ask "What caused the difference?" but also how to test whether the difference is merely a random variation or indicates some known or

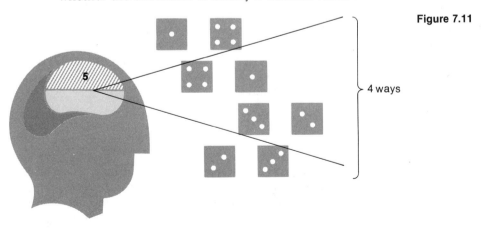

Figure 7.11

4 ways

unknown factor at work. *Significance tests* make it possible to express and interpret the differences mathematically. The resulting numbers may be considered indicators of the "level of confidence" we may justifiably have in the data, or they may reflect our chances of being wrong. Discussants need not be statisticians, but they should be aware of probability problems and of how theory can influence decisions about problems of large masses of data.

VALUES The *value* dimension concerns desirability rather than probability or certainty. Value systems held by group members are commonly considered as deriving from their past experiences. It is in this light that questions of value must, partly, be evaluated.

Your general value system is determined by your past experiences; your understanding and acceptance of the concept of law as natural, universal, and/or pragmatic; and your interpretation of various concepts such as good and bad, pleasure and pain, noble and ignoble, and loyal and disloyal; as well as by a multitude of minor preferences that often defy any search for an underlying principle (preferences for certain foods, colors, architecture, and so on). By knowing the experiences, interpretations, and preferences that make up a person's general value system, it is often possible to make fairly reliable nonnumerical predictions and analyses of questions of value.

To the extent that preferences and attitudes (a form of preference) may be considered as values, it is possible to measure attitudes toward many things, from the size of next year's cars to the latest fashions. Differences in attitudes toward a given subject can, in fact, be measured fairly accurately through the use of the standard statistical techniques.

Although the *value* dimension of analysis is the part most resistant to numerical measurement, this does not mean that we should not try to measure, objectify, and analyze problems. It does mean that we must know our own intelligently derived values and how they may be applied to the group's analysis of a specific problem. It also means that we must make every effort to determine the differences in preferences and values among the people in our group and among the people who may be affected by this group's decision. This kind of analysis should lead to better and more prudent group decisions regarding questions of value.

The Goldberg-Larson agenda system analysis also includes consideration of what an ideal solution would or should look like. It can help you find criteria that your perhaps less-than-ideal solution should at least try to meet.

III. THE CRITERIA PHASE

Whether one thinks of this phase as really a continuation of analysis or as the beginning of the solution phase is of no great importance. It is, however, an important enough agenda item to warrant your close attention. A *criterion* is a standard or yardstick by which we may measure or evaluate something. In the case of

Figure 7.12
Daiwa Corporation, Gardena,
California.

group discussion, a criterion refers to an *agreed-upon standard*. If a group has reasonably clear and agreed-upon criteria in mind, the evaluation or testing of suggested solutions is a lot easier, or at least more systematic. If a group were discussing the problem of a clubhouse for its organization, it would want to clearly establish the criteria of *cost, size, location, new or old,* and so on. The concept of *limits* can help a group at this point. If we are talking about cost in terms of $100,000, what do we really mean? Is that the top limit or the bottom? If the group really meant $75,000 to $110,000, it should state this, at least to itself. The same could be said for size and location. Criteria can also be negative. The group could, for example, name locations that it would not consider under any conditions.

The concept of *weighting* your criteria in terms of importance should also be considered. If size is the single most important criterion, then the group should agree on that point. Say, for example, that the old clubhouse is crowded; unless the next place is X amount larger, however beautiful a bargain, it won't solve the problem. If location is next most important (say the facilities must be close to where the members live), and then cost, parking, architecture, and so on, you have the beginnings of a subagenda for evaluating solutions. Your list of criteria should then appear in some kind of rank in terms of importance. *Weighting* may be used profitably by a group if some of the criteria are close together in importance. Assuming a 100-point weighting scale and the determination that both size and location are very important, the group might assign to size 90 points, to location 80 points, to cost 50 points, to architecture 20 points, and so on, along with specific upper and lower limits for each criterion (see Figure 7.13). Such a scale gives the group considerably more insight into the distances among its ranked criteria. Further, it gives the group a more logical, systematic approach to the solution phase.

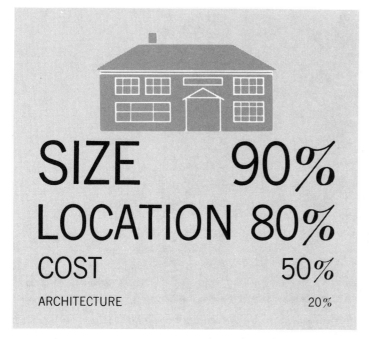

Figure 7.13
Weighting criteria

IV. THE SOLUTION PHASE

To continue the illustration of the clubhouse under the criteria phase, the group may now consider solutions that individuals may offer. If Steve A. offers pictures and real-estate data on a building he's found, but the building fails the criterion of size because it doesn't meet the lower limit (and no plan for enlargement is provided by the contributor), then the group is quickly and systematically ready to go on to the next possible solution. It is possible that a group may come up with several solutions that meet the major criteria; the discussion may then focus on the less heavily weighted criteria. This is progress and the group should be aware of it. Without stated criteria to follow, the group might engage in lengthy argument over minor aspects of a problem while virtually ignoring the major aspects.

A group may wish to discuss and evaluate alternate solutions further, according to the puzzle-probability-value analysis suggested earlier. Or it may wish some additional firsthand observation or action testing. But in any case the group is ready for *decision*.

Remember that discussion may sometimes be called upon to solve inappropriate questions. We do not need a group to solve most questions of fact or even some questions of probability. The library, the computer, the map—these solve some problems without group discussion. Nor does discussion solve the unsolvable. Some questions of value belong here. Once past the educational value, we sometimes may be well advised to adjourn. We should, of course, always look for viable solutions of the moment, if not for all time.

CONFORMITY DYNAMICS

Groupthink

The Orwellian sounding term *groupthink* was coined by Irving Janis, who defines it as ". . . a concurrence-seeking tendency that interferes with critical thinking . . . when members' strivings for unanimity override their motivation to realistically appraise alternative courses of action . . . a deterioration of mental efficiency, reality testing, and moral judgment that results from in-group pressures."[30]

For Janis the Cuban Bay of Pigs invasion was a decision fiasco caused by groupthink. Perhaps our corporate auto executives became complacent in the early seventies and talked only to each other about energy and car size. A failure to consider the full range of alternatives and a failure to work out contingency plans for possible setbacks now seem obvious. Were they too the victims of groupthink? Of course, we had regulated gasoline prices, Ralph Nader, and many government regulations. These outgroups may have caused an even tighter Detroit ingroup which, in Janis's words, ". . . fosters overoptimism, lack of vigilance, and sloganistic thinking . . ."[31]

Figure 7.14

[30]Irving L. Janis, *Victims of Groupthink* (Boston: Houghton Mifflin, 1972), p. 9.
[31]Ibid., p. 13.

Perhaps Parkinson's *law of triviality* is part of groupthink. "The time spent on any item of the agenda will be in inverse proportion to the amount of money involved."[32] The decision to spend millions of dollars for new, big-car production may be approved with relatively quick analysis and discussion while the issue of flying first or second class at company expense might lead to long and acrimonious debate.

Some super conservative or super liberal groups have also been known to develop a group mentality that views anyone not of their persuasion as a "nut" or dangerous character. Members of such groups feed on one another, reinforce one another, and may eventually lose their ability to cope with reality. They obviously may have trouble coping with change.

At its worst groupthink fosters an illusion of invulnerability, a holier-than-thou inherent morality, a stereotyping of opponents as evil, and a heavy pressure to conform to the group mentality.

This is not to deprecate togetherness, dedication, loyalty, team effort, or even group protestation. In fact, we seek these virtues in our work and policy-making groups. These issues are, however, two-sided. To make cohesion work for us we need to constantly take perspective on what we're about. We need feedback from other viewpoints. We should collectively consider as many alternate courses of action as we can. We have to consider contingency plans for things going wrong. We must do everything we can to protect independent, critical thinking whatever the pressures to conform. Organizations don't have to hire obnoxious personalities or "nuts" to keep them honest and defend against groupthink, but perhaps a little eccentricity isn't all bad if it keeps us honest.

Risky Decisions

Risky decisions are those decisions one is willing to take given the possible gains.[33] A ten-to-one longshot bet of $10 will return $100 if the horse wins. An

---

[32]C. Northcote Parkinson, *Parkinson's Law* (Boston: Houghton Mifflin, 1957), p. 24.

[33]This is also referred to as the risky-shift or risky-choice phenomenon. See Dorwin Cartwright, "Risk Taking by Individuals and Groups: An Assessment of Research Employing Choice Dilemmas," *Journal of Personality and Social Psychology*, 20 (1971), 361–78.

eight-to-five bet is more *likely* to pay off (it says here) but you'll only get $16. Of course, how much you're into horse racing and how much the $10 are worth to you in the first place have a lot to do with your decision. Deciding between a high-paying job with little security versus an adequate-salaried job with much security is another example.

Perhaps risky decisions are harder to make when you're alone. Are they? Will a small group, other things being equal, make riskier decisions than the average of the individual decisions made privately?

Consider a car full of teenagers who decide to race all comers at every red light—a risky decision not likely to be made by one person alone in the family car. Such conformity pressure can also lead to heroic as well as foolish decisions. The Canadians who sheltered six Americans in Iran did so at great risk, a risk their *group* had agreed to take. Their risky shift in policy was one unlikely to be made by any single individual, but was easier to make together. Probably not everyone was gung-ho but they went along with the decision, which is what most of the risky-shift research of today would have predicted.[34] Why did they do it? What factors are present in small groups that encourage such risk taking?

Sometimes having a bold, ambassador-type leader has a lot to do with it, but such a leader still needs a cohesive, dedicated group with similar views to exercise such influence.[35] On the other hand, a passive leader might have dampened such spirit.

The *values* one has about risk generally may have a lot to do with one's behavior. Both Canadians and Americans reward and admire bold risk takers. The

[34]See Nathan Kogan and Michael Wallach, *Risk-Taking: A Study in Cognition and Personality* (New York: Holt, Rinehart & Winston, 1964); see also Kenneth Dion, Robert Baron, and Norman Miller, "Why Do Groups Make Riskier Decisions than Individuals?" ed. Leonard Berkowitz, *Advances in Experimental Social Psychology*, vol. 5 (New York: Academic Press, 1970), pp. 306–78.

[35]Michael Wallach, Nathan Kogan, and R. Burt, "Are Risk Takers More Persuasive than Conservatives in Group Discussion?" *Journal of Experimental Social Psychology*, 4 (1968), 76–88.

fact that the Canadians too could have been seized by fanatics gave them special motivation to take some risks. All of these fine people wanted to be judged positively by an outraged free world. This kind of *social comparison* probably also promoted the risky decisions the little group continued to make.[36] Of course, the group comprised experienced diplomats with a strong sense of duty. A practical pooling of critical information and experience undoubtedly bred confidence and a greater willingness to gamble.

SUMMARY

The unique aspect of discussion is that a participant is both a sender and a receiver at the same time. Discussion is dynamic, interactive, and interpersonal. If decision is impossible through discussion, discussion may very well lead to debate. Debate is competitive and two-sided, discussion cooperative and many-sided. A discussion-debate continuum is shown in Figure 7.1.

A small group is dynamic, whereas an audience is most often passive. If we consider small-group discussion in terms of subgroups and feedback loops, we quickly see why "two's company, three's a crowd."

Characteristics pertinent to coacting groups are:

1. They share relevant common interests and engage in frequent interaction.
2. They define themselves as members and find that fact rewarding.
3. They identify with one another and share interlocking roles and goals.
4. They tend to act as a unit.

Research generalizations about coacting small groups include these:

1. Groups can change attitudes and behavior.
2. A group's consensus judgment tends to be better than individual judgment.
3. A small, agreeing group may develop a strong feeling of personal involvement.
4. Cooperative group communication can be taught.

Assuming a real group—persons with a common goal, not just a loose collection of individuals—we can define group discussion as a systematic and cooperative form of reflective thinking and communication.

Group discussion uses a cooperative thinking approach among twenty persons or less. The basic forms of group discussion are dialogue, panel, and symposium. Three techniques that may be used with any of these forms are the buzz

[36]For more on social-comparison theory, see Jerry M. Suls and R. L. Miller, eds., *Social Comparison Processes* (New York: Halsted Press, 1977).

group, role playing, and brainstorming. A forum is simply that part of a discussion in which the audience may speak.

These forms of discussion may be used for information sharing, problem solving, and instruction. Information-solving groups include staff meetings, study groups, and workshops. Problem-solving groups include committees, conferences, and boards or councils. Instructional formats include case conferences, role playing, and to some extent all the forms and techniques of discussion.

Discussion is a dynamic phenomenon that may progress in a more circular than linear course. Modern research suggests that there are phases to problem-solving discussions. There are three in the Bales and Strodtbeck system: Phase 1 employs orientation, information, repetition, and confirmation. Phase 2 uses analysis, evaluation, and the seeking or giving of opinions and feelings. Phase 3 controls possible directions and ways of action. There are four phases in the Tuckman system: (1) forming; (2) storming; (3) norming; and (4) performing. The Fisher system also has four phases: (1) orientation; (2) conflict; (3) emergence; and (4) reinforcement.

Systematic inquiry and an intelligent state of doubt are the essentials of reflective thinking. There are five steps in the Dewey system of reflective thinking: (1) felt difficulty; (2) definition; (3) possible solutions; (4) rational elaboration; and (5) further testing or confirming. Ross' four-step adaptation includes: (1) definition; (2) analysis using puzzle; probability, and value; (3) establishing criteria; and (4) solution.

Four agenda systems that creatively reflect and synthesize the literature are shown.

Two conformity dynamics are explained: (1) groupthink ". . . a concurrence-seeking tendency that interferes with critical thinking . . . when members' strivings for unanimity override their motivation to realistically appraise alternative courses of action . . . a deterioration of mental efficiency, reality testing, and moral judgment that results from in-group pressures";[37] and (2) risky decisions. A small group, other things being equal, will make riskier decisions than the average of the individual decisions made privately. Other risk-encouraging factors are *leadership*, *values*, and *social comparisons*.

A successful group discussion is the product of an interacting reflective group of individuals that is characterized by goals, agenda, leadership, high cohesion, high productivity, and cooperative interpersonal communication.

STUDY PROJECTS

1. After being assigned to a group, pick one of the following problems. Prepare for a ten- to fifteen-minute panel discussion in which you spend the first two to three minutes setting an agenda and the remaining time following it toward a solution.

[37]Janis, *Victims of Groupthink*, p. 9.

a. While shopping in a grocery store, a customer noticed a cashier taking money from the cash register. Startled by the incident, the customer rushed to the manager and reported what he had seen. The manager could not decide how to approach the situation at that particular moment. Finally, he decided that the best approach would be to:

(1) Go to the cashier and tell her she is fired.

(2) Investigate the matter to be certain the customer had reported accurately.

(3) Report the incident to the union.

(4) Have someone watch the cashier in order to guard against a repetition.

(5) Assure the customer and forget it.

b. George Tuffguy is a student in Ms. Smith's tenth-grade class. George is fairly intelligent but doesn't seem to care about school and spends his time getting into trouble. Ms. Smith has investigated his home situation and has found two alcoholic, uncaring parents. She wants to gain George's trust and encourage him to do better.

Today when she was leaving school, George backed Ms. Smith against the wall with a switchblade. School regulations prohibit the carrying of a switchblade in school at any time. Ms. Smith feels George is testing her to see what she will do. What should Ms. Smith do?

(1) Tell George that if he puts the knife away and doesn't bring it back to school she won't report him.

(2) Report George for breaking the school regulation.

(3) Ignore the situation, hoping that her evident lack of interest will persuade George to get rid of the knife.

(4) Threaten to report George if he brings the knife back to school.

(5) Call the police.

2. Observe live or televised groups of people until you find one clear-cut example of groupthink. Describe in a page or less.

3. Think of a time when you were a part of the *risky-shift* group phenomenon. Describe in a page or less; be ready to discuss your experience in class.

8

Leadership
and interpersonal influence

General learning outcomes

- We should learn the sources of leadership.

- We should learn to distinguish among the various types and functions of leadership.

- We should learn various styles of leadership.

- We should learn a contingency theory of leadership.

- We should learn about positive and negative participant-leader roles.

- We should learn to develop our powers as critics of participant and leader communication in small groups.

SOURCES OF LEADERSHIP

In general, leadership should be thought of as any significant action by any discussant that influences group achievement.[1] A group may have an appointed or role leader, whose duties may range from a modest regulation of participation to near domination and control. It is possible to be in a leaderless group (that is, one with no appointed leader) and still have considerable leadership, should this leadership emerge in some way from the group. By the same token, one could be in a group with a poor assigned leader; if no good leader(s) emerged, this group would really have no leadership. The distinction, therefore, between leader and leadership, and leaderless and leadershipless, is a critical one. All group members have a stake and often a part in leadership. Thus, what follows applies to all group discussants, whether they happen to be assigned group leader, chairperson, moderator, or whatever.

Leadership, however temporary, may fall upon a person in a group simply because he or she was appointed the moderator. This role may be given to a person only on certain issues because he or she happens to be the best *informed* on those issues. It may befall a person by reason of his or her *role, position* or *status* in the group (for example, he or she happens to be the boss, or a full professor). Particularly in leaderless groups, leadership may fall to a person who happens to perform communication skills exceptionally well—who one knows, and how well one knows them is also a possible source of power. Let's briefly examine these four sources of leadership.

[1]See especially Dean C. Barnlund and Franklyn S. Haiman, *The Dynamics of Discussion* (Boston: Houghton Mifflin, 1960), Chapter 13; and Halbert Gulley and Dale G. Leathers, *Communication and Group Process*, 3rd ed. (New York: Holt, Rinehart & Winston, 1977), Chapter 11; see also Dennis S. Gouran, "Perspectives on the Study of Leadership: Its Present and Its Future," *Quarterly Journal of Speech*, 60, no. 3 (1974), 376–81.

Figure 8.1   © 1981 by Chicago Tribune-New York News Syndicate, Inc. All rights reserved.

Information

Information can be a strong source of leadership and power. In the highly technical, surgical group shown in Figure 8.2, that person knowing the most about the special task procedures, and possessing the experience and competence, will probably direct the group. Surgery, like war, supports the old adage, "you're only as good as your information."

Role or Position

The captain in Figure 8.3 has "legitimate" power and leadership by reason of her position. How well she "wears" it has a lot to do with how influential her leadership is interpersonally.

We can define a *leader*, then, as someone in a role position who influences and directs others in conformance with their expectations for that role. It usually takes time and effort to earn respect and appropriate role expectations, especially when situations are new or novel.

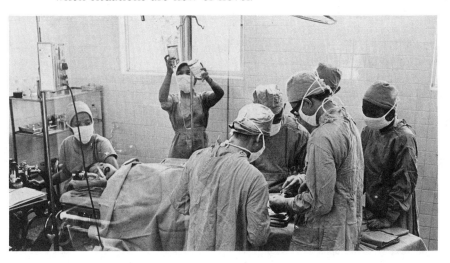

Figure 8.2

Chen, United Nations

Figure 8.3
U.S. Army Photo.

Communication Skills

We learned in previous chapters that general communication elements such as vocabulary, language, choice, and message organization are thought to reflect on the source. Studies show that, other things being equal, people who exhibit a greater linguistic diversity in terms of verb tenses, adjectives, adverbs, and connectives are perceived as more credible. Inarticulate people were rated low in terms of competence, dynamism, and social status.[2] Using nonfluent, inarticulate language generally decreases one's credibility.[3] The same can be said of poor use of voice. As we learned earlier, receivers attribute a person's social status from voice cues alone.[4]

In addition to these general communication skills, there are specific, group-communication skills that often beget leadership. For example, leaders are those group members who happen to be good at performing vital group functions, who know about procedural matters, agendas, reflective thinking, democratic leadership, the communication process, and interpersonal relations.

[2]James J. Bradac, Catherine W. Konsky, and Robert A. Davies, "Two Studies of the Effects of Linguistic Diversity upon the Judgments of Communicator Attributes and Message Effectiveness," *Communication Monographs*, 43 (March 1976), 70–79.

[3]Eldon E. Baker, "The Immediate Effects of Perceived Speaker Disorganization on Speaker Credibility and Audience-Attitude Change in Persuasive Speaking," *Western Speech*, XXIX (1965), 148–61; Gerald R. Miller and Murray A. Hewgill, "The Effect of Variations in Nonfluency on Audience Ratings of Source Credibility," *Quarterly Journal of Speech*, L (1964), 36–44.

[4]James D. Moe, "Listener Judgments of Status Cues in Speech: A Replication and Extension," *Speech Monographs*, 29 (1972), 144–47.

Figure 8.4
©Sony Corporation of America.

Personal Relationships

For Fiedler[5] the *relationship* factor is the most important source of power, whether for a work group or a student group. Do the group members like you? Will they trust your judgment? Can you rely on their support and understanding? Do they perceive you as "a good person speaking well"? Do these judgments and perceptions cross different situations? Test your own perceptions in these matters.

Figure 8.5

[5]Fred Fiedler, *Improving Leadership Effectiveness: The Leader Match Concept* (New York: John Wiley, 1977.) See especially F. Fiedler, "A Contingency Model of Leadership Effectiveness," in Leonard Berkowitz, ed., *Advances in Experimental Social Psychology*, vol. 1 (New York: Academic Press, 1964), pp. 150–90.

Perhaps people are responding to your position power, rather than to your engaging personality. Fair-weather friends can let you down without much warning. Of course, some close friends may love you but not support you in a specific leadership role. It seems obvious that a leader will do much better with healthy interpersonal relationships than with "no love lost" attitudes.

FUNCTIONS OF LEADERSHIP

Leadership, whatever its source (and all group members have responsibility for the source), should in general help a group move toward its goal or help it find its goal. Leadership should also promote a healthy, democratic communication climate within the group.

If your perceived leadership role does not happen to agree with most of your receivers' expectations, you may not exert much influence. In relatively informal, short-lived groups, such as committees or subcommittees, it usually helps all concerned if there is some concordance about role expectations. If your role is strictly procedural and is a random appointment, you may emerge as a George Patton, but not many will be expecting that of you. If, on the other hand, you have been hand picked because of your experience and expertise, you can usually look for different role expectations, but not always! Sometimes your qualifications are not known to the members, and sometimes they don't bother to do their homework. Interpersonal influence may call for role explanation and role assertiveness in such situations. You may risk some embarrassment in so doing, but by not doing so, you may risk charges of entrapping or embarrassing others. "Why didn't you tell me your Dad was a brain surgeon before I criticized high-risk medicine?"

Even when people agree on position descriptions (chairperson, president, supervisor, professor), they may not agree on the respective role expectations. Some people express antipathy toward formal leadership, but even such behavior is predictable if in your search for concordance that role expectation appears. To complicate things further, people change and roles and their expectations change; for example, many years ago professors wore their caps and gowns to class.

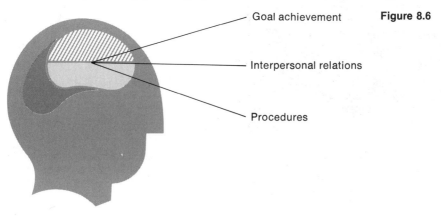

Goal achievement

Figure 8.6

Interpersonal relations

Procedures

The major functions of leadership, then, are in the areas of goal achievement (content or task), procedural functions, and effective interpersonal relations (communication climate).

Goal Achievement

Elements of leadership related primarily to task include such things as contributing and evaluating ideas, locating issues and consensus, synthesizing and cross-relating the ideas of others, and generally seeking specific contributions toward a goal.

Procedural Functions

Leaders, particularly when assigned or designated, must also attend to the more practical functions such as starting the meeting, drafting and/or following the agenda, clarifying statements, summarizing, and ending the meeting. Procedural functions may also include advanced planning and physical arrangements. As a procedural leader, you must review the purposes of the meeting. You should consider the members individually and decide the degree of formality necessary and the specific way you wish to open the discussion. You should consider group goals according to the time available.

As a procedural leader, you are also responsible for participation—that is, for preserving order, for seeing that only one person speaks at a time, and for fairly distributing the right to speak. On occasion you may find it necessary to clarify what has been said as well as to remind the group of the agreed-upon agenda. The agenda should be agreed on by the members unless it has already been designated.

Interpersonal Relations

Qualities of leadership in this area include controlling emotions, setting communication and psychological climates, resolving conflict, regulating the too talkative and the silent, and generally promoting those actions concerned with particularly social and human problems while at the same time keeping the lines of communication open.

Figure 8.7   Reprinted by permission of Tribune Company Syndicate, Inc.

STYLES OF LEADERSHIP

Group Expectations

Style refers in part to method and in part to philosophy. Many times style is determined by the type of organization in which you are operating. For example, a Marine Corps drill instructor (D.I.) understands full well the autocratic style expectations of the Corps, and the recruits put up with this highly directive style because, after all, that was what they expected. If they expected their D.I. to behave differently, they shouldn't have volunteered.

Styles vary with organizational expectations or with situational expectations, as well as with personal and receiver expectations. Styles of leadership are variously described as *laissez-faire, nondirective, permissive, democratic, supervisory, authoritarian,* and *autocratic.* These styles may be ordered on a control continuum as shown in Figure 8.8.

In the preceding example, the Marine Corps was the *leadership* and its attitudes (policies, and so on) were represented by the Corps' role expectations for a D.I. A *leader* attitude is more personal and may or may not reflect the organization of which the leader is a part. Religious leaders usually tend to reflect their churches' or temples' role expectations, but not always. They sometimes reflect the role expectations of their parishioners, which may be different from those of the diocese or larger unit of which they are a part. Then again, a religious leader may elect to go his or her own way apart from either, in which case he or she is usually seeking a new career.

The point being made here is that the role one plays as an influential group leader is dependent, to a large degree, on all of these different expectations.

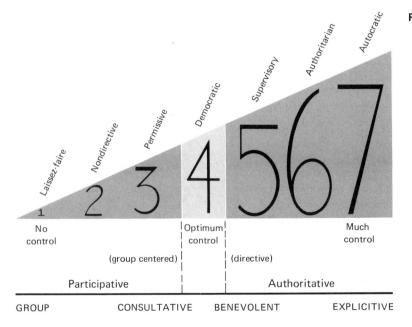

Figure 8.8

Most of us play various roles—leader, friend, teacher, decision maker, and so forth. Which style to use depends in part on the group's expectations, in part on the task, and in large part on the situation of the moment. This often presents a role and style dilemma for leaders.

Contingency Theory

According to Fiedler, life is easier for leaders who have positive regard from their groups, whose tasks are clear, steady, and highly structured, and whose power is based on knowledge, expertise, and/or legitimate authority.[6]

Whether a leader should be group centered or directive is, then, contingent upon all of the matters discussed previously. Interestingly, Fiedler's research suggests that a more directive leader performs best when three influence factors (relations, task structure, and position power) are more favorable but also when they are least favorable. The more permissive, nondirective leader was found to perform best under more status quo conditions—when the bay is calm; when the battle is over.[7] Recall that, for Fiedler, one's interpersonal effectiveness is a critical key to influence and leadership.

The important thing is to be aware that there are a range of leadership styles. Understand that you can be a consistent leader and still have flexibility based on all of the contingencies just discussed.

According to Julia Wood leadership is an adaptive process. She argues that:

> . . . effectiveness in leading is most probable when a leader is sufficiently perceptive to analyze the unique situation and the group members in relation to the goals for discussion and is able to employ appropriate behaviors in light of this analysis. . . . In order to assess "the forces that determine his most appropriate behavior," a leader must analyze group members and the situation. Understanding what members need, want, and expect from their work and their leader has direct bearing on a leader's ability to act effectively.[8]

Professor Wood capsulizes her adaptive approach to leading as follows:

> The focus, then, of the adaptive approach to leading is on (1) analyzing the unique group members and situation requiring leadership so that (2) the leader may adjust his or her personal behaviors or self-presentation to meet the requirements of the circumstances. A primary implication of the

---

[6]Fiedler, *Improving Leadership Effectiveness*; see also Debra J. Stratton, "How to be a Successful Leader: Match Your Leadership Situation to Your Personality, an Interview with Dr. Fred Fiedler," *Leadership*, November 1979, p. 27.

[7]Fiedler, "A Contingency Model," pp. 155–58.

[8]Julia Wood, "The Leader's Brief: Teaching an Adaptive Approach to Leading," *Communication Education*, 26, no. 4 (1977), 355; see also Warren G. Bennis, "New Patterns of Leadership for Adaptive Organizations," in Warren G. Bennis and Phillip E. Slater, eds., *The Temporary Society* (New York: Harper Colophon, 1969), pp. 97–123; and Robert S. Tannenbaum and Warren M. Schmidt, "How to Choose a Leadership Pattern," *Harvard Business Review*, 36 (March–April 1958), 101.

adaptive approach is that the behavioral strategies of an effective leader must *vary* according to the particular situation, task, and members with which he or she must deal.[9]

As with most general adaptation strategies, virtue usually lies near the middle (see Figure 8.8). Experience advises that a *democratic* style is generally superior to an absolute or nonresponsible style. However, in some groups in which *goal achievement* becomes unusually pressing, leadership should go up the scale if such an action can help. On the other hand, to achieve sincerely healthy *interpersonal relations*, particularly when emotions are strained or personalities are in conflict, the best strategy may be to go down the scale.

An interesting study by Simons indicates that the more participation oriented patterns or styles of deliberation, even with relatively large groups (fifteen to twenty persons), were more productive in problem-solving discussion than were the more formal patterns.[10]

In review, contingency theory is an adaptive approach to leadership requiring group analysis, style adjustments in terms of that analysis, and then communication accommodation in terms of the specific situation and the task.

Participant-Leader Roles

Most people play different roles: They change. A "playboy" in one phase of a small-group interaction might play a more serious, evaluator role in another phase. Some personalities are more consistent in their interactive styles and the stereotypes come closer to fitting.

Roles can be related primarily to the task or problem with which a group is faced, as well as to the socioemotional or psychological tensions that occur. There are also negative or disruptive roles that all of us play on occasion, such as flat disagreement with almost every idea a group has. These roles are often compensatory behaviors for personal problems which may or may not be related to the group. Such disagreement can, of course, affect cohesion or togetherness. A true incorrigible can really disrupt a leader and a group's productivity.

The just-discussed role categories have been described and explained by Benne and Sheats.[11] The *group maintenance* (socioemotional) roles help morale and reduce tension. The *task* roles tend to help leadership and advance group goals. The *individual* roles are the negative or disruptive ones. See Tables 8.1, 8.2, and 8.3.[12]

[9]Wood, "The Leader's Brief," p. 355. Wood describes a leader's brief, which should prove useful in training leaders.

[10]Herbert W. Simons, "Representative versus Participative Patterns of Deliberation in Large Groups," *Quarterly Journal of Speech*, 52, no. 2 (April 1966), 164–71.

[11]Kenneth D. Benne and Paul Sheats, "Functional Roles of Group Members," *Journal of Social Issues*, 4, no. 2 (1948), 41–49.

[12]Ibid., pp. 42–46.

Table 8.1 Group Building and Maintenance Roles (Socioemotional)

ROLE	DESCRIPTION
(a) encourager	praises, agrees with, and accepts the contribution of others
(b) harmonizer	mediates the differences between other members, attempts to reconcile disagreements, relieves tension in conflict situations through jesting or pouring oil on the troubled waters, etc.
(c) compromiser	operates from within a conflict in which his ideas or position is involved
(d) gatekeeper-expediter	attempts to keep communication channels open by encouraging or facilitating the participation of others or by proposing regulation of the flow of communication
(e) standard setter	expresses standards for the group to attempt to achieve in its functioning or applies standards in evaluating the quality of group processes
(f) group-observer	keeps records of various aspects of group process and feeds such data with proposed interpretations into the group's evaluation of its own procedures
(g) follower	goes along with the movement of the group, more or less passively accepting the ideas of others, serving as an audience in group discussion and decision

Table 8.2 Group Task Roles

ROLE	DESCRIPTION
(a) initiator-contributor	suggests or proposes to the group new ideas or a changed way of regarding the group problem or goal
(b) information seeker	asks for clarification of suggestions made in terms of their factual adequacy, for authoritative information and facts pertinent to the problem being discussed

(*cont.*)

Table 8.2 Group Task Roles (*cont.*)

ROLE	DESCRIPTION
(c) opinion seeker	asks not primarily for the facts of the case but for a clarification of the values pertinent to what the group is undertaking or of values involved in a suggestion made or in alternative suggestions
(d) information giver	offers facts or generalizations which are authoritative or relates his own experience pertinently to the group problem
(e) opinion giver	states his belief or opinion pertinently to a suggestion made or to alternative suggestions
(f) elaborator	spells out suggestions in terms of examples or developed meanings, offers a rationale for suggestions previously made, and tries to deduce how an idea or suggestion would work out if adopted by the group
(g) coordinator	shows or clarifies the relationships among various ideas and suggestions, tries to pull ideas and suggestions together or tries to coordinate the activities of various members of subgroups
(h) orienter	defines the position of the group with respect to its goals by summarizing what has occurred, points to departures from agreed-upon directions or goals, or raises questions about the direction which the group discussion is taking
(i) evaluator-critic	subjects the accomplishment of the group to some standard or set of standards of group functioning in the context of the group task
(j) energizer	prods the group to action or decision, attempts to stimulate or arouse the group to greater or higher quality activity
(k) procedural technician	expedites group movement by doing things for the group—performing routine tasks, e.g., distributing materials, or manipulating objects for the group, e.g., rearranging the seating or running the recording machine
(l) recorder	writes down suggestions, makes a record of group decisions, or writes down the product of discussion

Table 8.3 Negative and Disruptive Individual Roles

ROLE	DESCRIPTION
(a) aggressor	may work in many ways—deflating the status of others, expressing disapproval of the values, acts or feelings of others, attacking the group or the problem it is working on, joking aggressively, showing envy toward another's contribution by trying to take credit for it, etc.
(b) blocker	tends to be negativistic and stubbornly resistant, disagreeing and opposing without or beyond reason and attempting to maintain or bring back an issue after the group has rejected it
(c) recognition seeker	works in various ways to call attention to himself, whether through boasting, reporting on personal achievements, acting in unusual ways, struggling to prevent his being placed in an "inferior" position, etc.
(d) self-confessor	uses the audience opportunity which the group setting provides to express personal nongroup-oriented "feeling," "insight," "ideology," etc.
(e) playboy	makes a display of his lack of involvement in the group's processes
(f) dominator	tries to assert authority or superiority in manipulating the group or certain members of the group
(g) help-seeker	attempts to call forth "sympathy" response from other group members or from the whole group
(h) special interest pleader	speaks for the "small business man" "the grass roots" community, the "housewife," "labor," etc., usually cloaking his own prejudices or biases in the stereotype which best fits his individual need

PARTICIPANTS AS WELL AS LEADERS HAVE INTERPERSONAL RESPONSIBILITIES WHENEVER THESE SITUATIONS ARISE:	A GOOD PARTICIPANT, LIKE A GOOD LEADER, SHOULD, IN GENERAL:
1. One or two members dominate. 2. Some apparently lack interest. 3. Conflict occurs between members. 4. Some members will not talk. 5. Discussion "techniques" backfire. 6. Discussion drifts to irrelevant matters.	1. Use tact. 2. Be enthusiastic. 3. Exhibit a sense of humor. 4. Be cooperative. 5. Minimize differences. 6. Be friendly. 7. Identify with the group's goals. 8. Interact. 9. Consider the rewards of membership. 10. Work to help group.

OBSERVING AND EVALUATING DISCUSSION

One of the most popular observational schemes for small-group research was developed by Bales. This system, which is called *interaction process analysis,* is a classification of communicative acts; *act* is defined as verbal and nonverbal behavior. An observer is responsible for three areas of observation: positive social-emotional acts, "task" acts, and negative social-emotional acts. A modified outline of the system is presented in Figure 8.9.

Observers' tabulations of acts in various research studies (usually of college students) indicate an average group profile of 25 percent positive reactions (category A in Figure 8.9), 56 percent attempted answers (B), 7 percent questions (C), and 12 percent negative reactions (D).

A group-observation report based on the Bales' subcategories can provide group members with valuable descriptive information. See FORN in Figure 8.10.

A self-explanatory general-discussion rating form for evaluating participants is shown in Figure 8.11.

Observing a discussion can also be done by diagramming the participation. The resulting charts are called *sociograms* and may provide graphic insights into group behavior. Methods of diagramming include simply tabulating the number and length of contributions or classifying the contributions according to categories or types, as Bales does. One can also draw circles representing the discussants, and then lines and arrows to diagram the flow and amount of interpersonal communication. This method often results in graphic evidence of overtalkativeness (see Figure 8.12).

MAJOR CATEGORIES	SUBCATEGORIES	ILLUSTRATIVE STATEMENTS OR BEHAVIOR
Social-Emotional Area	A. Positive (and mixed) reactions	
	1. Seems friendly	Jokes, gives help, rewards others, is friendly
	2. Dramatizes	Laughs, shows satisfaction, is relieved
	3. Agrees	Passively accepts, understands, concurs, complies
Task Area	B. Attempted answers	
	4. Gives suggestion	Directs, suggests, implies autonomy for others
	5. Gives opinion	Evaluates, analyzes, expresses feeling or wish
	6. Gives information	Orients, repeats, clarifies, confirms
	C. Questions	
	7. Asks for information	Requests orientation, repetition, confirmation
	8. Asks for opinion	Requests evaluation, analysis, expression of feeling
	9. Asks for suggestion	Requests direction, possible ways of action
Social-Emotional Area	D. Negative (and mixed) reactions	
	10. Disagrees	Passively rejects, resorts to formality, withholds help
	11. Shows tension	Asks for help, withdraws, daydreams
	12. Seems unfriendly	Deflates other's status, defends or asserts self, acts hostile

Reciprocal or Opposite Pairs: a b c d e f

a. Problems of Communication
b. Problems of Evaluation
c. Problems of Control
d. Problems of Decision
e. Problems of Tension Reduction
f. Problems of Reintegration

Figure 8.9 Categories for interaction process analysis   Based on Robert F. Bales, *Interaction Process Analysis* (Cambridge, Mass.: Addison-Wesley, 1950), p. 9; A. Paul Hare, *Handbook of Small Group Research* (New York: Free Press of Glencoe, 1962), p. 66; and Robert F. Bales, *Personality and Interpersonal Behavior* (New York: Holt, Rinehart & Winston, 1970), pp. 91–97.)

Group Report (FORN)
Insert appropriate letter:

(F) Frequently   (O) Occasionally   (R) Rarely   (N) Never

Descriptive Terms

	1	2	3	4	5	6	7	8
PROJECT CLASS HOUR DATE								
1. SEEMS FRIENDLY								
2. DRAMATIZES								
3. AGREES								
4. GIVES SUGGESTION								
5. GIVES OPINION								
6. GIVES INFORMATION								
7. ASKS FOR INFORMATION								
8. ASKS FOR OPINION								
9. ASKS FOR SUGGESTION								
10. DISAGREES								
11. SHOWS TENSION								
12. SEEMS UNFRIENDLY								

General Comments on the Group:

Figure 8.10   FORN

176

DISCUSSION EVALUATION FORM, WAYNE STATE UNIVERSITY

1-2-3	4-5-6	7-8-9
Weak	Average	Strong

Criteria for evaluating discussion participation include the following:

A. Information about the problem (breadth, accuracy, and use of information).
B. Analysis of the problem (sensing problem's importance; finding the issues; avoiding irrelevant matters).
C. Ability to think cooperatively (open mindedness; alertness; willingness to abandon weak arguments; ability to synthesize the contributions of others).
D. Skill in speaking (adapting voice, action, and language to the occasion; ability to state ideas clearly and briefly).
E. Good manners (listening attentively; quoting others accurately; giving others a chance to speak; general courtesy).
F. Overall effectiveness.

Participants	1	2	3	4	5	6	7	8	9	10	11
Project											
Class Hour											
Date											
A. Information											
B. Analysis											
C. Cooperative Thinking											
D. Speaking Skill											
E. Good Manners											
F. Overall Effect											
Total Scores											
Rank order of Participants											

General comments on the group as a whole (use back sheet as needed):

Figure 8.11

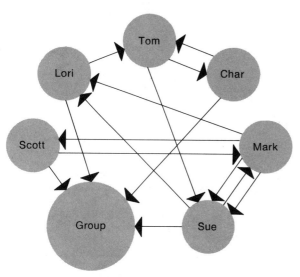

Figure 8.12
A sociogram describing participation

LEADER EVALUATION FORM		
1-2-3 WEAK	4-5-6 AVERAGE	7-8-9 STRONG
Leader's name		
A. GOAL ACHIEVEMENT	Rating	Comment below.
Locates issues and consensus. Synthesizes and relates ideas. Promotes systematic problem solving. Reaches some sensible solutions.		
B. PROCEDURAL FUNCTIONS	Rating	Comment below.
Starts and ends meeting on schedule. Clarifies and summarizes. Supervises physical arrangements. Preserves order.		
C. INTERPERSONAL FUNCTIONS	Rating	Comment below.
Establishes appropriate climate. Controls emotions. Resolves conflict. Regulates participation. Promotes cooperative thinking.		
D. PERSONAL SKILLS	Rating	Comment below.
Communicates clearly and fairly. Listens to others. Understands the issues. Uses an appropriate style.		

Figure 8.13

When a leader is designated, an evaluation form for that person may also be used. Figure 8.13 suggests and describes behaviors thought to enhance leader effectiveness.

SUMMARY

Leadership should be considered as any significant action by any discussant that has significant influence on group achievement. It is possible to have no appointed leader and still have leadership; it is also possible to have an appointed leader and no leadership. The distinction between *leader* and *leadership*, and *leaderless* and *leadershipless*, is a critical one. All group members have a stake and often a role in leadership.

Leadership may fall upon a person through designation or as a result of that person's superior information, role or position, special ability to perform vital group functions, or personal relationships. The major functions of leadership are ensuring goal achievement and effective interpersonal relations. Leadership, particularly when designated, also has procedural functions. These functions may be planning, making physical arrangements, and deciding purposes, degree of formality, goal setting, and the agenda. The procedural leader is also responsible for general control of participation and for preserving order.

Style of leadership may be described as autocratic, authoritarian, supervisory, democratic, permissive, nondirective, and laissez-faire. One's style is dependent upon group expectations, contingencies that arise, and participant behavior. One's interpersonal effectiveness is a critical key to influence and leadership. Contingency theory is an adaptive approach to leadership requiring audience (group) analysis, style adjustments in light of that analysis, and then communication accommodations in terms of the specific situation and task.

Participant-leader roles include group building and maintenance roles, group task roles, and negative and disruptive individual roles.

Interaction process analysis is an observational system that classifies communicative acts (verbal and nonverbal behavior). An observer is responsible for three major areas of observation: positive social-emotional acts, task acts, and negative social-emotional acts. These three areas and twelve subcategories of analysis are shown in Figure 8.9.

STUDY PROJECTS

1. Consider all the groups of which you have been a member. Who was the best leader? Why? Compile a list of roles or behaviors that your ideal leader plays or enacts. How does your group-related behavior differ from that of your ideal leader?

2. Observe a radio or television discussion and attempt to classify the various leadership functions that emerge (goal achievement, interpersonal relations, or pro-

cedural). Be alert for changes in function by the participants. Assess their effectiveness.

3. Write a two- to three-page report of an out-of-class "contemporary form of discussion" you have observed or in which you were involved, and evaluate it according to *interaction process analysis* (Bales's system).

4. Select a class-discussion project on an important social issue suitable for two or three days of research. Describe the issue as a question, prepare a one-hour agenda, select a procedural leader, do your research, and prepare for class discussion(s). You may use combinations of the various forms of discussion. You might choose from these topics of general interest:

Abortion	Fraternities and sororities	Gambling
Narcotics	Changing morals	Population
Welfare	Lotteries	Euthanasia
Sex education	Censorship	Prostitution
Medicare	Crime	Quarter system
Birth control	Capital punishment	Communal living
Gun laws	Busing	Space travel
Pollution	Transportation	Nudism
Advertising	Prisons	Ecumenism
Pornography	Amnesty	Big cities
Sexism	Homosexuality	UFOs
Witchcraft	Gerontology	Inflation

5. After you have completed this lesson, write a three-page personal, introspective report about the attitudes and behaviors you exhibit in group communication. What have you learned about yourself as a participant or leader in cooperative communication?

9

Audience psychology

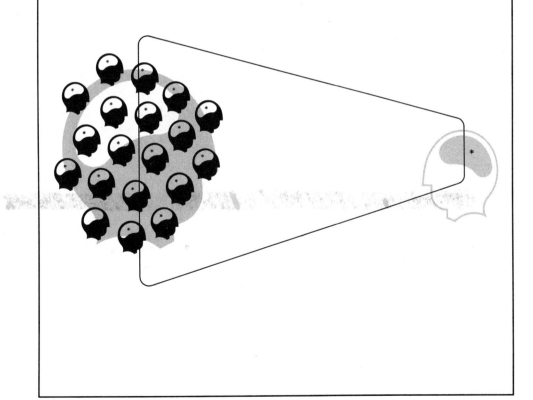

General learning outcomes

- We should learn to match the message we are sending to the requirements of the audience.

- We should be able to distinguish between mobs and audiences, and gain insight into the influence of such groups on speech communication.

- We should become familiar with the importance of audience analysis and audience characteristics affecting speech communication.

- We should be able to explain the differences between dyadic models and audience models of the communication process.

- We should learn to cope with speech fright.

It has been estimated that there are over 3000 speech audiences on any given day in Los Angeles alone, 30,000 in Chicago, and 50,000 in New York. These include Rotary Clubs, universities, women's groups, and conventions. In today's golden age of the lecture business, Henry Kissinger earns $25,000 a speech, and Bob Hope gets $30,000. Ralph Nader earns $800,000 a year speaking.[1]

Public speaking for a fee is obviously big business. Approximately 60,000 conventions or major meetings are held each year in hundreds of cities across America. Many of these gatherings include intelligent, entertaining, or humorous paid presentations. Add to this the number of unpaid speeches made (for example, 960 program participants at the yearly Speech Communication Association convention) and the total grows quickly. Evidently, public speaking is a skill you may need. The key to making this skill effective is knowledge of audiences and how to analyze them.

COLLECTIVE BEHAVIOR

The emphasis in speech communication training is generally on passive audiences. However, the modern speaker also meets active, expressive, and aggressive collections of people. In recent times we have seen demonstrations, panics, riots, and other types of collective behavior that challenge long-standing rhetorical advice. Most research and theorizing assumes relatively passive audiences; we can understand audiences by looking at what happens in more stimulated groups.

Mobs

In 1977 John Davidson was singing before an audience of 3500 spectators at the Beverly Hills Supper Club in Southgate, Kentucky. Fire and panic there resulted in 160 deaths, 130 hospitalizations, and as many as 250 trapped individuals. Asked how so many could become trapped, Kentucky Deputy Fire Mar-

[1]Karen Feld, "Lecturers: Their Talk Isn't Cheap," *Parade*, September 30, 1979, pp. 23–24.

shal Tom Wald said, "Panic. They panicked. That about covers it. They lost their cool, to put it in the vernacular. A lot of them stacked up in doorways. As soon as the smoke started rolling pretty good, they bolted and headed for the exits."[2] The death toll made this the worst nightclub fire in the United States since the Cocoanut Grove tragedy in Boston in 1942, when 492 died.

On December 3, 1979, eleven young Cincinnatians were stampeded to death in a tragic mob insanity while waiting for a rock concert by The Who. Some randomly collected comments by psychologists try to explain:

> A blurring effect occurs.
> The sense of self is lost.
> The mob becomes your identity.
> . . . regressive behavior, kid behavior, impulsive behavior.
> Peer pressure to go along is very strong.
> They lose a sense of physical self.
> People actually forget they are crushing someone.
> This could have happened at any large gathering.[3]

When an audience becomes a mob, as in a panic, we see people at their worst. To account for this kind of superstimulation we need to know about more active psychological mechanisms than those usually associated with more passive audiences. A classification system is shown in Figure 9.1. The general term *crowd* is divided into *mobs,* which are described as *active,* and *audiences,* which are described as passive. Mobs are divided according to their overt behavior.

Figure 9.1 Varieties of crowds   Adapted from Roger Brown, "Mass Phenomena," in The Handbook of Social Psychology, vol. 4, ed. G. Lindzey (Cambridge, Mass.: Addison-Wesley, 1954), p. 510 (material in parenthesis added). Photo credit: Irene Springer.

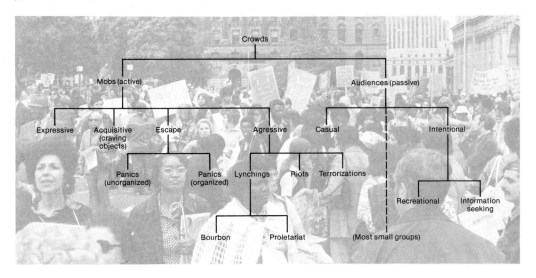

[2]*The Detroit News,* May 30, 1977, p. 1A.
[3]*Detroit Free Press,* December 5, 1979, p. 1.

Gustave Le Bon suggests that when a crowd is focused into a mob, a *psychological law of mental unity* comes into play.[4] The participants become a sort of *collective mind,* and conscious personality is lost. Each person thinks and behaves quite differently from the way he or she would be acting alone. This is the same phenomenon that E. D. Martin describes as *crowd mentality.*[5] Martin classified this collective mind into dreams, delusions, and automatic behavior. It is as if our animal nature, or id, were unleashed. According to Martin the mob becomes "a device for indulging ourselves in a kind of temporary insanity by all going crazy together."[6] For Martin and Le Bon alike, the mob lurks under the skin of us all. In this view mobs may be weapons of revenge. They are always uncompromising in their demands, and in no way do they respect individual dignity. Even their achievements are less a testament to their leadership than a consequence of their unbridled fury.

Figure 9.2
Photo by United Nations/John Isaac

[4]Gustave Le Bon, *The Crowd* (New York: Viking Press, 1960), p. 26.
[5]E. D. Martin, *The Behavior of Crowds* (New York and London: Harper & Brothers, 1920), pp. 4–5.
[6]Ibid., p. 37.

For Le Bon, Martin, and others, the mob is a group in which people's normal reactions become secondary to unconscious desires and motivations. The major mechanisms leading to a state of collective mind or mob mentality appear to be *anonymity, contagion,* and *suggestibility.* One who is lost in the press of the mob loses much of his or her sense of responsibility. This anonymity produces an inflated feeling of power. Contagion is best illustrated by the panic attending the Beverly Hills Supper Club fire, described earlier. It is a kind of high-speed, infectious mayhem. A heightened state of suggestibility leads to hasty, thoughtless, and rash action. Many of our restraining emotions are lost. Fear is often gone in battle, pity in a riot or a lynching.

A complete concept of collective mind includes, of course, the ethical and legal issues of sanity and guilt or innocence. We can argue that stupidity, suggestibility, and irrationality exist in individuals as much as in mobs, and that individuals vary in their degree of participation in mob action.[7] We can also argue, as has Floyd Allport, that mobs simply supply a form of *social facilitation.*[8] Individuals' desires are stimulated merely by the sight and sound of others making similar movements. Contemporary social psychologist Roger Brown argues that "something new is created. To describe this new thing, this 'emergent,' as a 'group mind' does not seem to be seriously misleading. It may be a degree more illuminating to say that what emerges in the crowd is a payoff matrix that does not exist for the members when they do not compose a crowd."[9]

Audiences

In a typical audience there is far less emotionality and irrationality than in a mob; the "group mind" is nowhere near as evident. Mobs may regress to adolescence or violence—audiences, rarely. Nevertheless, motivational forces are present even in very casually organized audiences. More formal audiences—such as classes of students, church groups or temples, and lecture gatherings, which are intentionally and purposefully organized—are motivated by more readily identifiable forces.

Audiences, like mobs, can vary considerably in size; here we are more concerned with relatively formal, intentional audiences of roughly twenty or more persons. We are concerned mainly with audiences that are present physically. When you are dealing with vast, unseen audiences, as in the mass media, you are, for the most part, beyond interpersonal influence and must utilize a more sociological and political analysis. Nevertheless, much of what follows also applies to the mass media audience.

In general, the audience we are talking about is a fairly formal collection of individuals who assemble for a specific purpose. Patterns of interaction are rea-

[7]Ralph H. Turner and Lewis M. Killian, *Collective Behavior* (Englewood Cliffs, N.J.: Prentice-Hall, 1972).

[8]Floyd N. Allport, *Social Psychology* (Cambridge, Mass.: Riverside Press, 1924).

[9]Roger Brown, *Social Psychology* (New York: Free Press, 1965), p. 760.

sonably predictable in such groups, given enough information. Three of these patterns are polarization, interstimulation, and feedback-response.

Polarization describes unusually homogeneous audience attitudes. When two relatively homogeneous but opposing factions are present in an audience, the audience is referred to as *bipolar*. Debates often attract bipolar audiences. *Interstimulation* refers to some of the volatile behavior characteristic of mobs and, more specifically, to Allport's concept of social facilitation. It includes ritual, suggestion, and the reinforcement we receive from similar behavior occurring at the same time. When all of those around us are angry, we are apt to be angry; when all are happy, we are apt to be happy. *Feedback-response* is a *positive* response to the efforts of the speaker; a *negative* response is quite another matter. If the speaker is strongly reinforced by positive feedback, he or she may become closely identified with some ideal. With strong interstimulation, this identification may lead to exceptional, if only temporary, polarization among the speaker's listeners—an enviable situation as long as the persuader can control it and live with the results over a period of time. An aroused audience, let us remember, is only a few steps removed from a mob.

AUDIENCE CHARACTERISTICS

Classifications

The classic categorization of audiences was made by H. L. Hollingworth, who suggested five types: (1) pedestrian; (2) discussion group or passive; (3) selected; (4) concerted; and (5) organized. Hollingworth's categories make sense not only for dyadic and small-group situations but also for more formal settings. Hollingworth used the term *orientation*, by which he meant "the establishment of a pattern of attention, when the group is considered, or a set and direction of interest, when we consider the individuals comprising the group."[10]

The *pedestrian audience* is a temporary audience, such as a group of pedestrians on a busy street corner. No common ties or lines of communication bind the members of the audience to the speaker. The first step, that of *catching attention*, is crucial with this type of audience. How far the process goes beyond that varies with the purpose of the speaker.

The *discussion group* or *passive audience* is one whose attention is already secured or guaranteed by rules of order. The persuader's initial problem is more likely to be the second step, that of *holding attention* or interest. Again, how long the persuader can do so depends upon the occasion or the success of the persuader.

The *selected audience* is one whose members are assembled for some common purpose, but not all of whom are sympathetic to one another or the speaker's

[10]H. L. Hollingworth, *The Psychology of the Audience* (New York: American Book, 1935, 1977), p. 21.

point of view. Impression, persuasion, and direction characterize the speaker's undertaking here.

The *concerted audience* is one whose members assemble with a common, active purpose in mind, with sympathetic interest in a mutual enterprise, but with no clear division of labor or rigid organization of authority. A sense of conviction and delegation of authority are the speaker's chief responsibilities.

The *organized audience* is a group with a rigid division of labor and authority supported by specific common purposes and interests. The tasks of the members are well learned, having already been assigned by the leader. The persuader has only to issue instructions, since the audience is already persuaded.

Before appearing in front of the audience, according to Hollingworth, the speaker ought to secure as full a knowledge as possible of the mode and degree of the audience's orientation. The speaker must be prepared to shift tactics if the first reactions of the audience show that the initial judgment was wrong.

According to Hollingworth, the five fundamental tasks of a persuader are *attention, interest, impression, conviction,* and *direction.* From these we can gain a better picture of what distinctions Hollingworth saw among the five types of audiences. In Figure 9.3 we have listed these five tasks under the types of audiences to which they are most relevant. For instance, the principal tasks of a person speaking before a concerted audience are to instill conviction and to delegate authority.

According to Hollingworth, the craving for an audience is one of humanity's fundamental needs. One of the most significant characteristics of individuals is the type of audience that most readily motivates their thought and conduct. Hollingworth observed that there is often a striking conflict between one's craving for an audience and one's fear of it. Individuals probably seek a certain amount of confrontation or encounter and at the same time resist it.

Speaker-Audience Model

Let's now try to adapt the Ross communication model (Figure 1–10), a dyadic model, to audiences (Figure 9–3).

Most of what was said in Chapter 1 about the Ross dyadic model applies here. The audience model obviously has a larger potential for collective stimulation and its consequences, and the problems of physical setting, climate, and feedback are more important. The analysis of audiences by types becomes an averaging process, and we must realize that such generalizing inevitably fits some members of the audience poorly and others perhaps not at all. Accordingly, the model in Figure 9.3 places some of the members outside of the general audience concept.

The audience has frequently been considered as a statistical concept—a means of assembling a large amount of information about individuals into manageable form (average age, income, nationality, education, and so forth).[11] Audi-

[11]Theodore Clevenger, *Audience Analysis* (Indianapolis and New York: Bobbs-Merrill, 1966), pp. 13–22.

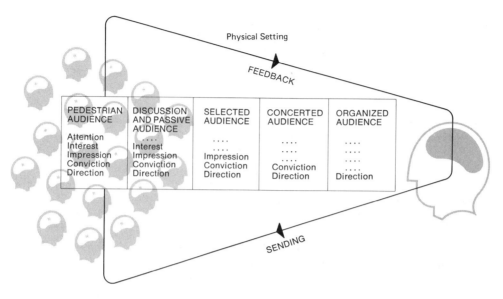

Figure 9.3

ences have also been classified into many general types, such as organized-unorganized, unified, heterogeneous, apathetic, hostile, polarized, and bipolar. More is said about types of audiences shortly.

AUDIENCE ANALYSIS

Audience-Message Relationships

Audience psychology encompasses rhetorical sensitivity, which involves an effective matching of the message the speaker is sending to the requirements of the receivers. Recall that rhetorical sensitivity was defined earlier as " . . . a particular attitude toward encoding spoken messages. It represents a way of thinking about what should be said and then a way of deciding how to say it."[12]

Applying this concept to audience analysis, to be a rhetorically sensitive speaker, you must:

1. *Attempt to accept role taking as part of the human condition.* To make this kind of adjustment you should decide what is an appropriate role to play at a given time. You cannot *not* play a role; the choice is among the roles available.

[12]Roderick P. Hart, Robert E. Carlson, and William F. Eadie, "Attitudes toward Communication and the Assessment of Rhetorical Sensitivity," *Communication Monographs*, 47, no. 1 (March 1980), 2.

2. *Attempt to adjust verbal behavior.* You need not be all things to each and every complex audience, but you must try to adapt your language so that an audience is not so turned-off that it misses your message or viewpoint.

3. *Be willing to undergo the strain of strategy adaptation.* Audiences differ in knowledge, mood, situation, and attitude. These differences call for organizational and rhetorical adaptations that often mean extra effort and extra patience.

4. *Discern which information is acceptable for a given audience.* You must plan your speeches rather than speak off-the-cuff. You cannot say everything about anything, but you can easily say something stupid or offensive if you are not alert. Recall that a rhetorically sensitive person knows (or plans) when to "shut up" as well as when to "speak up."

5. *Discern which form and style are appropriate for communicating ideas.* There is more than one way to present information. You should calculate responses to different ways, approaches, or styles of speaking when you are analyzing the audience and preparing the message.[13]

Unless you are on a deserted island, it seems obvious that you, the speaker, have great need of audience analysis and rhetorical sensitivity. That some audiences are less rhetorically sensitive toward speakers is also a given.

Figure 9.4

Several useful questions relating to audience-message analysis have been suggested by Jon Eisenson and his associates:

1. *What is the significance of the subject for the audience?* Is its interest in the subject only casual, or is it motivated by real needs and wants? How far has its thinking about the problem progressed?

[13]These five characteristics are adapted from Roderick P. Hart and Don M. Burks, "Rhetorical Sensitivity and Social Interaction," *Speech Monographs*, 39, no. 2 (June 1972), 75.

2. *What does the audience know about the subject?* Does it have essential factual information, or only opinions and sentiments? Are its sources of information sound ones, unbiased and complete?

3. *What beliefs or prejudices does the audience have about the subject?* In either case, what are the probable sources or influences in the formation of these existing notions?

4. *What is the attitude of the audience toward the subject?* Is it possible to estimate the percentage who are favorable, neutral, or unfavorable toward the problem?[14]

Descriptive Measures

Some general descriptive measures worth considering in audience analysis are:

Age. Obviously an audience of ten-year-olds will call for different preparation by the speaker than will a group of forty-year-olds—even if the subject is Little League baseball! A few children in an otherwise all-adult audience sometimes present a problem. Even if you choose (or are advised) to ignore them, you can be certain that the members of the audience will not: They usually establish norms of appropriateness and understanding based on the youngsters. Often an off-color story is even less well received than usual when a child is present.

Education. A person's education is the sum of that person's learning. Do not confuse schooling with education, for attending school does not guarantee an education. There are many uneducated college graduates! Nevertheless, formal schooling is in most cases a more efficient way of acquiring knowledge than other ways. You should take your audience's educational level and previous schooling into account when you select your language and vocabulary. An audience with a highly technical education requires a different approach than one with a liberal arts background. The problem again is a difference in educational background. Time invested in this kind of audience analysis is usually well spent.

Gender. In modern America, male-female descriptions are often less meaningful than determining the attributions *people* (men or women) make about gender roles. An assessment of masculinity, femininity, and androgyny (people high on both measures) may provide a better measure of the sex-role adaptability of your audience.[15]

[14]Jon Eisenson, J. Jeffrey Auer, and John V. Irwin, *The Psychology of Communication* (New York: Appleton-Century-Crofts, 1963), p. 279.

[15]Sandra L. Bem, "Sex Role Adaptability: One Consequence of Psychological Androgyny," *Journal of Personality and Social Psychology*, 31 (1975), 634–43; see also Charles L. Montgomery and Michael Burgoon, "The Effects of Androgyny and Message Expectations on Resistance to Persuasive Communication," *Communication Monographs*, 47 (1980), 56–57.

Occupation. Stereotyping a person by his or her occupation is as dangerous as classifying a person according to schooling. Nevertheless, knowing people's occupations is often useful. For instance, the average income level of your audience can often be predicted by knowing the occupations of most of its members. Furthermore, you can predict that teachers will have college degrees, top management executives will have similar opinions about some kinds of legislation, and so on. Knowing such information can help you appropriately address an audience.

Primary-Group Memberships. Most of us belong to many groups. Predicting what groups are represented in an audience is shaky at best. For example, an audience at a political convention may be all Republican or all Democratic. However, it may also represent many religious, ethnic, and occupational groups, not to mention attitudes. The more you can learn about the groups to which an audience does or does not belong, the better you can prepare your speech.

Special Interests. Whatever their differences, audience members are often of one mind about some special interest they have in common. A small community with a winning high-school basketball team may ignore a guest speaker who is unaware of this special interest. Sometimes these interests are temporary. Seek out and become familiar with any special interests about which the audience *expects* you to know.

Audience-Subject Relationships. This part of your analysis concerns an audience's *knowledge* about your speech topic. What *experience* and *interest* does the audience have in your subject? What is its *attitude* toward your specific purpose? It is often valuable to know to what extent the audience is uniform in its beliefs and knowledge.

Some audiences are very firm in their beliefs, whatever their levels of knowledge or experience. Specific strategies for persuading them are covered in Chapter 12. In general, an audience is either interested or uninterested in your speech *subject,* but the audience's attitudes are directed toward your *purpose.* A useful scale for determining the general audience attitude toward the purpose of your speech is shown in Figure 9.5. Your preparation of a speech and your arrangement of its material depend heavily on how accurately you analyze your audience.

Figure 9.5

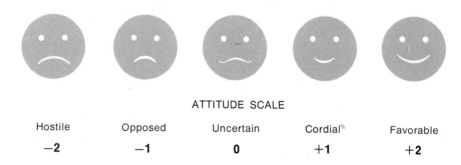

ATTITUDE SCALE

Hostile	Opposed	Uncertain	Cordial	Favorable
−2	−1	0	+1	+2

FEAR OF AUDIENCES

A sample of 2543 adults rank ordered a list of fears ranging from escalators and flying to death and darkness.[16] Heading the list (40.6 percent) was "speaking before a group."

Beginning speech-communication students also consider this a problem. Surveys indicate that 60 percent to 75 percent of a class may admit that they are bothered by "nervousness in speaking," an expectation that they have more to lose than to gain from speaking.[17] Twenty-five percent may be concerned enough to ask for help in the form of instructor conferences, reading assignments, or desensitization (exercises that help ease speech fright). Most of this is typical, if not always normal. Much of it is temporary and based upon expectations of anxiety in speaking situations.[18] Most of you will find that the more formal the audience or the situation, the more speech fright (or what has been called stage fright) you will experience.

Psychologists and speech communication scholars stress the difference between a general proneness to anxiety and a kind of particular anxiety of the moment.[19] We are most interested in the latter type in public speaking and in small-group communication. The level of anxiety and the kinds of experience that cause it may vary in conversation, small groups, and public-speaking situations. A

[16]"What Are Americans Afraid Of?" *The Bruskin Report* (New Brunswick, N.J.: R. H. Bruskin Associates, July 1973), p. 1.

[17]James C. McCroskey, "Validity of the PRCA as an Index of Oral Communication Apprehension," *Communication Monographs*, 45, no. 3 (August 1978), 192–203; Gerald M. Phillips, "Rhetoritherapy versus the Medical Model," *Communication Education*, 26, no. 1 (January 1979), 34–43; see also William T. Page, "Rhetoritherapy versus Behavior Therapy: Issues and Evidence," *Communication Education*, 29, no. 2 (May 1980), 95–111.

[18]William T. Page, "The Development of a Test to Measure Anticipated Communicative Anxiety," in *Bibliographic Annual Speech Communication*, ed. Ned A. Shearer (New York: Speech Communication Association, 1971), p. 99.

[19]Douglas H. Lamb designates the first type of anxiety as "A-Trait" and the second as "A-State" in "Speech Anxiety: Towards a Theoretical Conceptualization and Preliminary Scale Development," *Speech Monographs*, 39, no. 1 (March 1972), 62–67; see also Ralph R. Behnke, Larry W. Carlile, and Douglas H. Lamb, "A Psychophysiological Study of State and Trait Anxiety in Public Speaking," *Central States Speech Journal*, 25, no. 4 (1974), 249–53.

pattern of fear that extends across all or nearly all interpersonal relationships involving oral communication may be called *reticence.* According to research at the Pennsylvania State University, reticence may affect as much as 5 percent of a class.[20] McCroskey calls this phenonemon "communication apprehension."[21]

If it is true that misery loves company or that there is safety in numbers, then you may be reassured to know that you are not alone in experiencing stage fright. Even professional performers report intense emotional reactions before some public performances. Consider these reports:

> *It's really not fun, acting. Always that tremendous fear . . . Do you know that before a performance sometimes Laurence Olivier goes back to the foyer and, to release his tension, swears at the audience? Some actors even stick pins in themselves.*

Jane Fonda

> *Acting scares me senseless. I hate everything I do. Even if it's a crummy radio show with a script, I throw up, I tell ya—it's the equivalent of going voluntarily to hell.*

Judy Holliday

Figure 9.6 THE WIZARD OF ID by permission of Johnny Hart and Field Enterprises, Inc.

That audiences generally do not view your fright as seriously as you do indicates that you do not appear and sound as bad as you feel; this should be reassuring. But whether your fear is visible or not, the result may be the same. As

[20]Gerald M. Phillips, "Reticence: Pathology of the Normal Speaker," *Speech Monographs,* 25, no. 1 (March 1968), 44; see also Gerald M. Phillips, symposium editor, "The Practical Teachers' Symposium on Shyness, Communication Apprehension, Reticence, and a Variety of Other Common Problems," *Communication Education,* 29, no. 3 (July 1980), 213–14.

[21]James C. McCroskey, "Oral Communication: A Summary of Recent Theory and Research," *Human Communication Research,* 4, no. 1 (Fall 1977), 78; see also Lynne Kelly, "A Rose By Any Other Name Is Still A Rose: A Comparative Analysis of Reticence, Communication Apprehension, Unwillingness to Communicate, and Shyness," *Human Communication Research,* no. 2 (Winter 1982), 99–113.

in other fright-producing situations, you may feel a dryness in the mouth, a rapid heartbeat, a sinking feeling in the stomach, even difficulty with abdominal control. Mulac and Sherman suggest that the following symptoms are found in frightened people:[22]

ANXIETY BEHAVIORS

Voice	1. Quivering or tense voice
	2. Too fast
	3. Too slow
	4. Monotonous: lack of emphasis
Verbal Fluency	5. Nonfluencies: stammering; halting speech
	6. Vocalized pauses
	7. Hunts for words: speech blocks
Mouth and Throat	8. Swallows
	9. Clears throat
	10. Breathes heavily
Facial Expression	11. Lack of eye contact; extraneous eye movements
	12. Tense face muscles; grimaces; twitches
	13. Deadpan facial expression
Arms and Hands	14. Rigid or tense
	15. Fidgeting; extraneous movement
	16. Motionless; lack of appropriate gestures
Gross Bodily Movement	17. Sways; paces; shuffles feet

Speech courses do help with this all-too-common problem. Mulac and Sherman found that after eight weeks and four speeches, observable anxiety was significantly reduced. Actual speaking experience appears to help students gain confidence.

In most studies of specific techniques for helping students with anxiety problems, all forms of counseling, group therapy, group desensitization, and cognitive restructuring have been found helpful.[23] A general state of anxiety (such as

[22]Anthony Mulac and Robert A. Sherman, "Behavioral Assessment of Speech Anxiety," *Quarterly Journal of Speech*, 60, no. 2 (April 1974), 134–43.

[23]Donald H. Meichenbaum, J. Barnard Gilmore, and Al Fedoravious, "Group Insight versus Group Desensitization in Treating Speech Anxiety," *Journal of Consulting and Clinical Psychology*, 36, no. 3 (June 1971), 410–12; James C. McCroskey, David C. Ralph, and J. E. Barrick, "The Effect of Systematic Desensitization on Speech Anxiety," *Speech Teacher*, 19, no. 1 (January 1970), 32–36; see also William J. Fremouw and Michael D. Scott, "Cognitive Restructuring: An Alternative Method for the Treatment of Communication Apprehension," *Communication Education*, 28, no. 2 (May 1979), 129–33.

reticence) that extends beyond the normal speech communication contexts discussed here (but including these) seems most treatable by a form of insight counseling and group therapy. Some interpersonal instruction has also had positive effects.[24]

An important question you may ask is, "Even if I overcome speech fright in this class, using whatever help I can get (perhaps just reading the rest of this chapter), will my speech communication training carry over and help me in another situation?" Several researchers have explored this question, and their findings are reassuring. This question concerns the psychological and learning problem referred to as *transfer.* In a study by S. F. Paulson, speakers were taken from their regular classes and were made to speak before strange class audiences. The results of an adjustment inventory test indicated no decrease in confidence scores; it was concluded that transfer of training did take place.[25] It is also encouraging to note that even three-fourths of a group of students at Penn State defined as reticent indicated noticeable improvement in their out-of-class behavior after ten weeks of speech training.[26]

To a great extent, we humans are afraid of what we do not understand. Young children may be paralyzed with fear during severe electrical storms until their mothers or fathers explain what causes the thunder and lightning. Afterwards, children may still experience fear, but not of a paralyzing nature. Loud noises make all of us jump, but knowledge and understanding of what causes the loud noises make it possible for us to stop jumping between noises. Because we are dealing with the symptoms and causes of emotional reactions, we are better able to control emotions if we know in some detail what emotions are and how they operate.

The Nature of Emotion

In 1884 the famous psychologist William James presented a simple and useful theory of emotion:

> Our natural way of thinking about . . . emotions is that the mental perception of some fact excites the mental affection called the emotion [for example, fear] and that this later state of mind gives rise to the bodily expression. My thesis on the contrary is that the bodily changes follow directly the perception of the exciting fact [stimulus] and that our feeling [awareness] of the same changes as they occur is *the emotion.*[27]

[24]Richard E. Barnes, "Interpersonal Communication Approaches to Reducing Speech Anxiety" (paper delivered at the Central States Speech Convention, Chicago, Ill., 1976).

[25]Stanley F. Paulson, "Changes in Confidence during a Period of Speech Training: Transfer of Training and Comparison of Improved and Nonimproved Groups on the Bell Adjustment Inventory," *Speech Monographs,* 18, no. 4 (November 1951), 260–65.

[26]Phillips, "Reticence," p. 49.

[27]William James and Carl Lange, *The Emotions,* vol. 1 (Baltimore: Williams & Wilkins, 1922), p. 12 (emphasis added).

The point is that it is our awareness of our *reactions* to a frightening situation that is the *real* emotion. James' favorite illustration of this theory was that of a man coming upon a bear in the woods. In a nonscientific way, we might say the bear triggers the emotion of fear in us. Not so, for according to James, our bodies react most automatically to the bear. Our natural survival devices take over to prepare us for an emergency. Our muscles tense for better agility, our heartbeats and breathing quicken to provide larger supplies of fuel, our glands secrete fluids to sharpen our senses and give us emergency energy. All of this happens in an instant. Then we become aware of our bodily reactions. We sense our heavy breathing, our muscles tensing to the point of trembling, perhaps adrenalin surging into our systems. It is this *awareness* of our reactions that frightens us; in other words, the awareness is the emotion. Of course, the bear still has a lot to do with our condition! It would be ridiculous to tell you that if you understand clearly all the physiological reactions just described, you've eliminated the bear. However, this knowledge and understanding *will* help you better control what action you take and thereby improve your chance for survival. This is what we mean by emotional or speech-fright control, and this is why we use the term *control* rather than *eliminate* when speaking of fear.

Our fear of the bear is caused not by the bear itself but by our *awareness* of our bodily reactions to the bear. In speech fright it is our *awareness* of our internal and external reactions that provides us with the emotion and that may therefore cause a large part of our trouble. Giving a speech, though obviously less dangerous than facing a bear, poses a more difficult problem. Our natural survival reactions typically prepare us for "flight or fight," so we either flee from the bear or attack it. The speech situation rules out survival tactics, for you can neither attack the audience nor run for the woods. In your favor, however, is the fact that there are no recorded instances of an audience eating a speaker! The problem is to drain some of your excess energy while holding your ground.

The purpose of the bear story is to help you better understand the nature of emotion, for understanding and knowledge almost always reduce fear. The story contains a second lesson that may be of even more use to you. This is the principle of *objectification*. That is, if you have a clear explanation of what's happening to you, the edge is taken off the emotions. Imagine a great lover who, when kissing his beloved, decides to analyze exactly what he is doing. A former student, reporting on one of his own experiments, reported, "You know, prof, it takes all the kick out of it!" By the same reasoning, detailed explanation of speech-fright experiences should help take some of the "kick" out of them.

Have you ever asked yourself, "Why do my arms and hands tremble? Why do I have that sinking feeling in my stomach?" The issue is not *whether* you experience these things, but rather *why*. If you do ask *why* and answer, "Because I'm scared to death," you probably only add to the emotion. This is the time to apply both the theory of emotion and the principle of *objectification*. Remember that the emotion is primarily the result of your *awareness* of your own bodily reactions and that an objective explanation of these reactions will take the edge off them.

Let's take the case of the trembling arms and hands. Skeletal muscles are usually arranged in *antagonistic* groups—that is, one group opposes the other. The muscles located on the inside (anterior) surface of the arm and forearm are called *flexors*; those on the back or outside (posterior) surface are called *extensors*. The flexors bend or draw up your arm, the extensors extend or straighten the arm. When either set of muscles contracts, the opposing set relaxes—but not completely, for skeletal muscles have *tone*, which gives them a certain firmness and maintains a slight, steady pull upon their attachments. Suppose you "tell" your forearm to rise, as in Figure 9.7: try it. Your flexor muscles contract and the extensor muscles on the other side of your arm are forced to relax. If you tell your arm to straighten itself, the antagonistic muscles simply reverse functions. Now try something more interesting. Position your arm as shown in Figure 9.7, tell it to stay there, and at the same time tell both sets of muscles to contract simultaneously. If you are really working at it, you will notice a tremble in your arm. If you extend your fingers, the tremble is usually quite evident in your hands. You have just produced a state very similar to the trembling that takes place in speech fright.[28] Fright increases the natural tension of your antagonistic muscles and causes the same kind of trembling. Understanding this explanation, you will still experience some trembling, you will still be aware of it, but—theoretically, at least—not in exactly the same way as before. Having increased your knowledge of why your arms and hands tremble, you are better equipped to adjust to this event when it occurs. Some of the "kick" has been taken out of it. Although the lightning still startles you, you're somewhat better off because science has explained *what* it is.

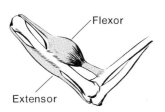

Figure 9.7
Antagonistic muscles of the arm and forearm

Flexor

Extensor

[28]Ralph R. Behnke, Michael J. Beatty, and James T. Kitchens, "Cognitively-Experienced Speech Anxiety as a Predictor of Trembling," *Western Journal of Speech Communication*, 42, no. 4 (Fall 1978), 270–75.

A detailed and vivid description of the bodily reaction to threatening situations is provided by W. B. Cannon. These were his conclusions, based on experiments with animals:

> The adrenalin in the blood is increased . . . which causes strong, rapid heartbeat, suspended activity of the stomach and intestines, wide opening of the air passages in the lungs, release of sugar from the liver, delay of muscle fatigue, free perspiration, dilation of the pupils of the eyes, more red corpuscles to carry oxygen, faster blood coagulation, and increased blood pressure.[29]

The sinking feeling that we experience in the stomach under stress can be explained in great detail. When faced with fear, the body calls upon its glandular secretions, mainly adrenalin, for emergency energy. These secretions chemically interfere with and halt the digestive system. This process tends to make the stomach contract and produces a sinking feeling. At the same time, we also become aware of many lesser reactions, such as rapidly beating heart (for added circulation) and heavier breathing (for extra oxygen), that help prepare the body for survival. These explanations should help you maintain your composure.

Most individuals cannot experience two different emotional reactions at the same time. For example, when you are boiling mad, you are probably not afraid. This is not to suggest that you freely substitute anger for your fright, but you may already have observed that when you are really involved in a subject, you tend to be less frightened.

This helps explain, in part, our almost instinctive actions to ward off fright situations. It explains why, for example, we whistle while walking through a dark alley. We are acting "as if" we are unafraid—perhaps happy, indignant, or angry. Acting "as if" has helped all of us through emotionally charged situations. It is healthy to whistle in the dark; it often makes the difference between poise and panic. Your choice of a speech topic may therefore be important to you emotionally as well as rhetorically. If you are excited or can become excited about your subject, you are making this theory work for you—you are exhibiting a kind of natural and intelligent whistling in the dark.

Controlling Emotion

Let's talk about some specific actions you can take to make further use of the theory of emotion.

KNOW ABOUT EMOTION. Remember that emotion is primarily the result of your awareness of your own bodily reactions. Analyzing these reactions should help you control fright. Emotion loses its intensity under examination and objec-

---

[29]W. B. Cannon, *Bodily Changes in Pain, Hunger, Fear, and Rage* (Boston: Charles T. Branford, 1953), p. 368; see also Ralph R. Behnke and Larry W. Carlile, "Heart Rate as an Index of Speech Anxiety," *Speech Monographs*, 38, no. 1 (March 1971), 65–69.

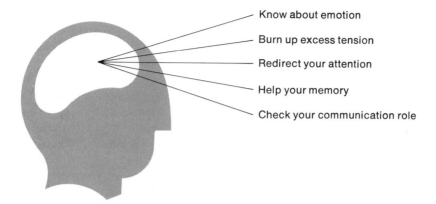

Know about emotion

Burn up excess tension

Redirect your attention

Help your memory

Check your communication role

Figure 9.8

tification. Face up to your problems and get the facts straight. It is healthy to talk objectively about your fright. Instructors are good listeners. Let yours help you talk out your fright. In these ways you will meet your fright on a conscious level, where you have the most control. If your mouth feels dry, find out why. If your knees shake, find out why. If you feel faint, find out why. The *why* is usually rather unexciting, but it is extremely logical and objective. Should unusual speech fright persist, you may find it useful to review this entire chapter at a later date.

BURN UP EXCESS TENSION.   It should be clear from the previous discussion, particularly the bear story, that we direct our actions most usefully once we break the wall of tension with the first step. Physical motion—either away from the bear at full speed or toward him—bursts the dam of tension. In your speech situation you are in no real danger. Your primary problem is to release some of the extra energy that your body dutifully provides. Once again, the *first* step is very important. Bodily activity will help you utilize your extra energy or tension.

In a speaking situation you might be concerned about how your activity looks and what it communicates to the audience. The strategy here is very simple: Plan and direct some of your bodily movement in advance, complete with options. For example, at the close of your introduction or perhaps at a transition between points, you might plan on moving a step to the side or raising a book or card for

Figure 9.9   © PEANUTS 1963 United Feature Syndicate, Inc.

emphasis. You have the option of selecting the precise time and action, depending on how natural it seems and how tense you are. Another very natural kind of activity is that associated with visual aids. The communication values of visual aids are almost self-evident, but their value as emotion-controlling devices may not be as obvious. If you comment on a picture, demonstrate an object, or write on a blackboard, you have to make perfectly natural movements in the process. This is an excellent way to utilize excess energy, and it is why you will probably be asked to give a demonstration or visual-aid speech early on in a speech communication course. The lesson is obvious: Use planned activity freely as a means of burning up excess tension.

Physical activity before you speak can help you reduce your tension and relax. A brisk walk has helped many an athlete unwind. Even moderate exercises are in order. Although you cannot do pushups in the classroom, deep breathing is possible. Lifting or pressing your chair has helped. Isometric exercises should help. A yawn is a natural outlet as long as you do not look *too* relaxed! Another useful prespeech exercise is repetition of those activities that produce anxiety. If the journey from your chair to the speaker's platform is a real torture, rehearse this activity in an empty classroom or in measured distances at home. Keep rehearsing it until you sense a monotony in the repetition. College debaters repeat certain strategies and argument patterns so often in practice that they risk becoming stale when presenting the same ideas in debate. Football teams have had similar experiences. The point is that monotonous repetition can help drain keyed-up feelings.

Good health and a reasonable amount of rest are necessary for sound emotional adjustment. Speech and communication demand both because so much energy is involved.

REDIRECT YOUR ATTENTION.   Let your emotions work for you when you can. In moments of strain, redirect your attention to more happy things. Try to become so involved in something that you are less aware of your anxiety. If you can become excited about your subject or develop a positive desire to communicate it, you will often find your fright lessening. If you can find humor in your task or in your reactions to it, you may have found a very healthy distraction.

You can redirect your attention by concentrating on the smiling and pleasant faces in the audience for moral support. Most of your audiences are on your side. One professor reported that he started to overcome his speech fright when he began concentrating on the sleeping faces. He didn't say whether he was substituting anger or whether he decided his fear was a little ridiculous if he was talking only to himself.

HELP YOUR MEMORY.   Our memories, like our perceptions, may become less dependable under severe emotional strain. Beginning speakers are often frightened by just the thought of forgetting their speeches. Apparently, speech fright becomes a cause of forgetting and the thought of forgetting causes speech fright— a vicious circle.

As in redirecting attention, the topic you select can help your memory. The more you know about a subject and the more enthusiastic you are about it, the less likely you are to forget your material.

In preparing your speech, the key word for memory protection is *system*. We remember better, we learn better, we speak better if the material we're dealing with is arranged systematically. Your organization of your material can affect your ability to remember it. More is said about rhetorical organization in later chapters. The point here is simply that it is easier to remember a list of twenty automobile names grouped according to some system (that is, according to manufacturer, size, horsepower, or whatever) than one in a random order. Have you ever noticed how rapidly you can learn the names of baseball players? Obviously, it is because of the system of positions they play. If you do not know the positions, you will be slower at learning the names. Find a way that is natural and meaningful to you of ordering your speech materials and you will find it much easier to remember what comes next. Your audience, incidentally, will probably find your material easier to follow as a result.

One of the most effective memory aids is a visual aid. If you are explaining how an internal combustion engine works, it is obviously easier to remember functions and parts if you have the engine before you to point to. If your speech deals with numbers and statistics, a large card with the numbers listed eases the pressure on your memory. Tucked in your pocket as a precaution, a note containing testimony, statistics, or other details is also helpful. Just the knowledge that you have such a backstop is often worth more than the material on the cards. Some of the best speeches are delivered from a visual outline. All the major points and supporting statements are put on large cardboard visual aids in much the same way that one might put notes on file cards. These aids serve much the same function, except that now you are credited with using visual aids instead of criticized for depending too much on your notes.

Despite all the protection you can give your memory, all speakers occasionally "blank out," or momentarily forget. A good question is, "What do I do now?" If you have ever watched youngsters delivering memorized poems at elementary school convocations, you have probably heard them forget their materials. They almost always keep repeating the last line they *do* remember in a frantic effort to rerail their memory. This effort may help, but often the prompter also has a busy day. Word-for-word memorization is really not a very intelligent "system," because the memory cannot relate so many small, unrelated parts. But the principle of repeating the last thing you *do* remember is useful. The practical application is to *review* the material you have just covered. If your memory fails toward the end of your speech, you can *summarize* the key points you have made. Practical experience indicates that such a technique does help you reawaken your memory. One student who found this suggestion useful formulated her own rule: "When in doubt, summarize."

CHECK YOUR COMMUNICATION ROLE. We talked earlier of a professor who felt less speech fright when he discovered that most of his class was asleep.

With all due respect to student audiences, you may find that they are not eagerly awaiting the wisdom you are about to deliver. Audiences may on occasion be lively, but more often than not this is due to the efforts of the speaker. Experienced speakers live for such moments. Be objective about your audience. An analysis of speech-rating charts, particularly the write-in comments, indicates that the audience sympathizes with the speaker. This means that if your audience is listening at all, it is rooting for you.

However important your speech message, it will probably not be recorded for the future. If every speaker in a class of twenty-five gives ten speeches, any particular speech is only one out of 250. If it helps to be part of the crowd, then relax. Be realistic about your speech goals and their effect upon your audience. Instead of worrying about the damage your ego may suffer, worry about *not* being able to motivate an audience to listen.

SUMMARY

The first key to making public speeches effective is a knowledge of audiences and how to analyze them. Audience behavior also includes behavior observed in mobs and small groups. When a crowd turns into a mob, suggests Le Bon, a psychological law of mental unity, or "collective mind," makes the mob think and behave quite differently from the way its members would act individually. The major mechanisms that alter mob behavior appear to be anonymity, contagion, and suggestibility. Mobs stimulate and aid in the expression of individuals' repressed desires.

In an audience, as contrasted with a mob, the "group mind" is nowhere near as evident, regressive acts are less gross, and emotionality and irrationality are generally less widespread. More formal audiences, such as classes of students, church or temple groups, and lecture gatherings, which are intentionally and purposefully organized, are groups whose motivating forces are more identifiable than those of casual groups. Three reasonably predictable patterns of interaction are polarization, interstimulation, and feedback-response.

H. L. Hollingworth enumerates five types of audiences: (1) pedestrian; (2) discussion group or passive; (3) selected; (4) concerted; and (5) organized. In his view, persuaders undertake five fundamental tasks—attention, interest, impression, conviction, and direction—all of which are necessary when speaking to non-polarized pedestrian audiences and only one of which—direction—is necessary when speaking to highly polarized, organized audiences.

Audience psychology encompasses rhetorical sensitivity, which involves an effective matching of the message you are sending to the requirements of the receivers. Rhetorical sensitivity denotes an attitude toward encoding spoken messages.

An ideal speaker: (1) attempts to accept role playing as part of the human condition; (2) attempts to adjust verbal behavior; (3) is willing to undergo the strain of strategy adaptation; (4) discerns which information is acceptable; and (5) discerns which form and style are appropriate for communicating ideas.

Audiences may be considered as a statistical concept—a means of assembling a large amount of information about individuals into manageable form (average age, income, nationality, education, and so forth). Audiences have also been classified into many general types, such as organized-unorganized, unified, heterogeneous, apathetic, hostile, polarized, and bipolar.

Most beginning speech students admit that they are bothered by nervousness. Professional performers report similar feelings of tension. Significantly, though, reports indicate that speakers do not appear and sound as bad as they feel. Research also indicates that frightened people do not differ from the confident minority in very basic ways, such as intelligence and the important aspects of personality. Research reveals, further, that most students do gain confidence during a course in speech and are able to transfer this learning to other situations.

Understanding the nature of emotion is useful because it helps us objectify our feelings and reactions. The James-Lange theory of emotion suggests that awareness of our reactions to frightening situations is the real emotion. Emotion is a good and necessary phenomenon. The problem is one of control.

An understanding of our bodily reactions to frightening situations helps us control our emotions. The objectification of emotional reactions tends to take the edge off emotion, making it easier to control. An increase in intellectual activity helps reduce emotional intensity. We are afraid of what we do not understand.

Most individuals cannot experience two different types of emotional reaction at the same time. If you are excited or can become excited about your subject, you are making theory work for you—a kind of natural and intelligent whistling in the dark.

Here are some specific suggestions for controlling emotion:

1. Understand emotion.
2. Utilize excess tension.
3. Redirect your attention.
4. Help your memory through logical systems of organization.
5. Evaluate your communication role.

STUDY PROJECTS

1. Observe live or televised groups of people until you find clear-cut examples of (1) a mob and (2) an audience. Describe each in a page or less.
2. Describe in one page an audience situation that approached the "crowd [mob] mentality" description of E. D. Martin.
3. Remain near the center of an active group (for instance, a demonstration, revival meeting, athletic event, fight, or political rally) until you feel a sense of interstimulation (anonymity, contagion, suggestibility) or collective mind. Write the most detailed account possible of how you felt, what impulses came over you, what seemed to cause these impulses, and how you might have avoided them.

4. Attend the meeting of a relatively ritualized group (for example, a religious service, an award ceremony, a graduation, or a funeral service), and write a short audience analysis. Include "descriptive measures" and "audience-message" relationships.

5. Assess your speech-anxiety level according to the following inventory. If you check twelve or more items and feel nervous, it would probably be a good idea to confer with your instructor. You're probably not the only one.
Check only those statements that you feel apply to you to an abnormal or extraordinary degree.

☐ 1 Audiences seem bored when I speak.
☐ 2 I feel dazed when speaking.
☐ 3 I am continually afraid of making some embarrassing or silly slip of the tongue.
☐ 4 My face feels frozen while I am speaking.
☐ 5 I have a deep sense of personal worthlessness while facing an audience.
☐ 6 Owing to fear, I cannot think clearly on my feet.
☐ 7 While preparing my speech I am in a constant state of anxiety.
☐ 8 I feel exhausted after addressing a group.
☐ 9 My hands tremble when I try to handle objects on the platform.
☐ 10 I am almost overwhelmed by a desire to escape.
☐ 11 I am in constant fear of forgetting my speech.
☐ 12 I dislike using my body and voice expressively.
☐ 13 I feel disgusted with myself after trying to address a group of people.
☐ 14 I feel tense and stiff while speaking.
☐ 15 I am so frightened I scarcely know what I'm saying.
☐ 16 I hurry while speaking in order to finish and get out of sight.
☐ 17 I prefer to have notes on the platform in case I forget what I'm saying.
☐ 18 My mind becomes blank before an audience and I am scarcely able to continue.
☐ 19 I particularly dread speaking before a group that opposes my point of view.
☐ 20 It is difficult for me to search my mind calmly for the right word to express my thoughts.
☐ 21 My voice sounds strange to me when I address a group.
☐ 22 My thoughts become confused and jumbled when I speak before an audience.
☐ 23 I am completely demoralized when suddenly called upon to speak.
☐ 24 I find it extremely difficult to look at my audience while speaking.
☐ 25 I am terrified at the thought of speaking before a group of people.
☐ 26 I become so confused at times that I lose the thread of my thinking.
☐ 27 My posture feels strained and unnatural.
☐ 28 Fear of forgetting causes me to jumble my speech at times.
☐ 29 I am fearful and tense throughout the time I am speaking before a group of people.
☐ 30 I feel awkward.

- ☐ 31 I am afraid the audience will discover my self-consciousness.
- ☐ 32 I am afraid my thoughts will leave me.
- ☐ 33 I feel confused while speaking.
- ☐ 34 I never feel I have anything worth saying to an audience.
- ☐ 35 I feel that I am not making a favorable impression when I speak.
- ☐ 36 I feel depressed after addressing a group.
- ☐ 37 I always avoid speaking in public if possible.
- ☐ 38 I become flustered when something unexpected occurs.
- ☐ 39 Although I talk fluently with friends, I am at a loss for words on the platform.
- ☐ 40 My voice sounds as though it belongs to someone else.
- ☐ 41 At the conclusion of the speech I feel that I have failed.[30]

[30]Adapted from the research of Howard Gilkenson by Raymond S. Ross and Wilbur J. Osborne, Wayne State University.

10

Preparing and organizing

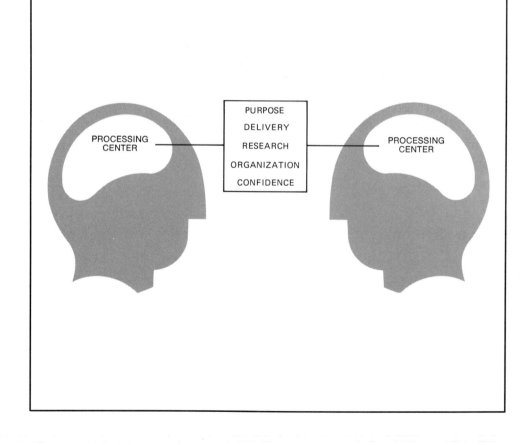

PROCESSING CENTER

PURPOSE
DELIVERY
RESEARCH
ORGANIZATION
CONFIDENCE

PROCESSING CENTER

General learning outcomes

- We should learn the general purposes and goals of speaking.
- We should learn the four principal types of delivery and when to use them.
- We should learn how and where to locate materials.
- We should learn ways of organizing ideas.
- We should learn systems for arranging the parts of a message.
- We should learn the basic principles of outlining.

Preparing and organizing a message are to the speaker what planning and drawing are to the architect. Purpose and goal are very important to both. As a speaker you need a specific and understandable purpose. If you don't know where you're going, how will you know when you're there? If you don't know what your purpose is, how will you know if you've achieved it? More to the point, how will you go about preparing, organizing, and presenting your message? You'll need to know how to locate materials, take notes, arrange materials, and prepare outlines.

A well-organized message and outline help give you confidence: You know you've done your homework and you have a system. You should find it easier to remember your material and the audience should find it easier to understand and retain your message.

THE GENERAL PURPOSES OF SPEAKING

The insurance agents who come to your door are interested primarily in selling you a policy. Though they may present an armload of practical information, their purpose is to persuade. A speech billed as an "Informative Talk on the Arts" may really turn out to be persuasion for abstract painting, even if most of the material is informative. There is probably no such thing as a purely informative, purely persuasive, or even purely entertaining speech. Even the most flowery oratory probably presents some information. Entertainment ranging from court jesters to comedy players has for ages been a means of gentle persuasion. Some very effective persuasive speeches have sounded like informative talks. Some, in fact, have contained almost wholly information.

By itself the sheer volume of informative, entertaining, or persuasive elements in a speech does not determine the kind of speech or the speaker's purpose. The arrangement of the material, the audience, the speaker's style and voice, and many more factors must also be considered.

If your instructor asks you to prepare an informative speech for the next class and you state your purpose as being "to inform the class why they should join the Republican party," you had better be prepared for criticism. The instruc-

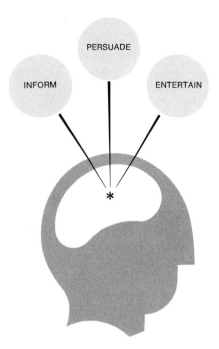

Figure 10.1
General purposes of speaking.

tor will probably suggest that you save the subject for the persuasive speech assignment and state your purpose more accurately as being "to persuade the class to join the Republican party." You might choose as your purpose "to inform the class about the history of the Republican party." The speech could then be either informative or persuasive, depending on your treatment and emphasis.

Your real purpose can be determined by the primary reaction you want from your audience. The general purposes and goals of speaking are:

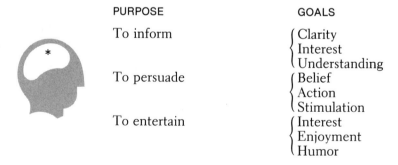

PURPOSE	GOALS
To inform	Clarity, Interest, Understanding
To persuade	Belief, Action, Stimulation
To entertain	Interest, Enjoyment, Humor

To Inform

One of the most common purposes of speaking is to inform people of something about which the speaker has knowledge. This is the purpose of a typing teacher who is showing students how to use the keyboard. The speaker who would inform has an obligation to make the information or instruction clear, interesting, and easy for the audience to learn, remember, and apply. To achieve these goals, a speaker should know something of how humans learn (this is discussed in detail in Chapter 11). Briefly, we learn through our previous knowledge and experience. We learn more easily when the material follows some sequence. We remember better because of reinforcement (repetition), verbal emphasis, organization, effective use of voice, and other techniques. The primary goal in informative speaking is *audience understanding*. The key means to this goal are *clarity, interest,* and *organization of material.*

To Persuade

The goals of a persuasive speech are to convince people to believe or do something, or to stimulate them to a higher level of conviction.

These divisions (belief, action, and stimulation) often overlap. When no immediate action is being called for, the speaker may be attempting to convince or to bring about *belief.* Such persuasive topics as "Foreign Policy," "The Threat of Fascism," or "Uphold the United Nations" might have this purpose. No specific and immediate action is asked. The listeners are only asked to agree with the speaker, to believe and be convinced. This, of course, assumes that the audience does not have the power to act. If the audience were the United States Congress, these belief purposes could become action purposes.

When the audience is asked to do something specific following the speech, the purpose is action—for example, a speech asking for donations to the Red Cross that is ended by passing a container for contributions. Election speeches asking people to vote or to sign petitions are also examples. Most sales talks, even TV commercials, are action speeches—even though the speaker or TV announcer does not really expect you to run out and buy the particular product advertised at 11:30 P.M. The desired action is specific and available.

When a speaker is seeking a higher degree of audience enthusiasm or devotion, the purpose is *inspiration* or *stimulation.* An example might be a speech for party unity at a political convention after the nominee has been selected. In short, speeches of stimulation are found in those situations in which the speaker is (1) not trying to change any basic attitudes, but rather to strengthen them; (2) not trying to prove anything, but rather to remind the listeners; or (3) not calling for any unusual action, but rather trying to inspire the listeners.

To Entertain

When you sincerely want people to enjoy themselves, your general purpose is to entertain. The "fun," after-dinner, or radio-television speeches that involve jokes, stories, and a variety of humor are examples. Their success depends on the experience, skill, and personality of the speaker and mood of the audience. In a speech designed solely to entertain, the members of the audience should understand that purpose and genuinely relax and enjoy themselves.

A word of warning to both beginning and experienced speakers: The speech to entertain is the most difficult of the three. Feedback is rapid and blunt. You know without doubt when a funny story or joke does not succeed. Practice is critical!

TYPES OF DELIVERY

The four principal methods of delivering a speech are: (1) by reading from a manuscript; (2) by memorization; (3) by impromptu delivery; and (4) by speaking extemporaneously. The subject and the occasion are the primary factors in determining which method or which combination should be used at a given time.

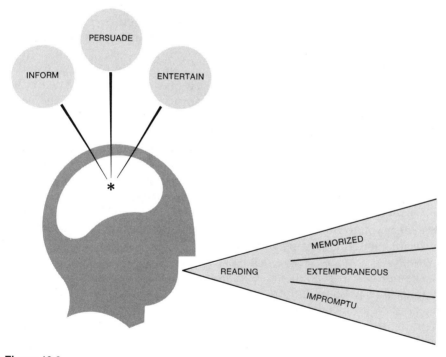

Figure 10.2

Reading from a Manuscript

In this delivery the speaker presents a manuscript by reading it word for word. It is the most difficult type of delivery. Fortunately, the subjects and occasions that demand this method are few, although they are increasing in number. An important policy speech by the United States Secretary of State, for example, may be analyzed word by word by foreign governments; therefore, maximum accuracy in wording is needed to avoid ambiguity. The demands of today's mass media also encourage word-for-word delivery. Very often, the media receive a copy of the manuscript before the speech is given. They can then set type or make a tape quoting the speech before it has been delivered. If the speaker then deviates from the manuscript, trouble and confusion ensue. Complicated and technical subjects demanding absolute accuracy also may call for manuscript reading. So too may the very rigid time limits in live radio and television.

The problems with this type of delivery are clear. The preparation must be painfully accurate; worse, there is little chance for instant adaptation of the material. Unless the reader is exceptionally good, the actual delivery is hamstrung by a lack of eye contact and directness. The speaker's eyes are typically glued to the manuscript. If the speaker steals a glance into outer space, he or she is apt to lose his or her place. This ensuing embarrassment may cause the speaker to lose emphasis and vocal variety. A lively sense of communication is almost impossible to maintain in this situation—for some, the word to describe the results is *dull*.

The beginner, in an effort to avoid the audience, may hide behind the manuscript. And because this usually results in poor audience reaction, it only delays the speaker's development.

When preparing a manuscript to be read to an audience, we have to change our style. A writer, for example, might use the terms *person, people, the reader;* a speaker talks of *I, you, they.* The other differences are not as obvious. Although we speak in short, simple sentences, we tend to write in longer, more complex ones. It's easy to see why. When we are writing material to be read silently, the reader can reread and review! The listener, however, cannot stop the speaker to go back over the material or to consult a dictionary. Therefore, in a speech, we use shorter, less complex sentences, more repetition, and frequent restatement. The spoken words must be instantly clear to the listener. And so we use more illustrations, examples, analogies, and vivid words. The secret is to write "out loud."

The delivery of a manuscript speech is also different. Normal eye contact and vocal patterns are often disrupted. The manuscript may be hard to see if the lighting is bad. The noise of a fan has been known to drown out a speaker's words. Even deciding how to hold the manuscript creates problems. If you hold the manuscript in your hand at about waist level, you inhibit your hand gestures. If you put it on a lectern, you hide most of your body. Either way, you have an added problem of letting your eyes drop to the paper while keeping your head erect.

Most good manuscript reading involves memorizing some blocks of language that are held together for you by meaning. You can then look at the audience while you recite. When your memory fails, you can refer back to the manuscript for the next memorized language group. The problem is trying to find your place! Marginal notes, underlinings, and color markings can help, but the secret lies in a thorough understanding of your message and practice, practice, practice. To be successful you must learn to spend more time looking at your audience than at your manuscript.

Figure 10.3
"For some it's easier"

Memorization

Unless you're an actor, who must sound spontaneous, there is little reason to completely memorize a speech. The effort required for a word-for-word memorization is enormous. The delivery is often stiff, overly rhythmical, and impersonal. Nor does memorization offer any easy way to adapt the material to the audience. All the same, many frightened beginners will undertake the enormous task of memorization. Unfortunately this method can result in panic if their memories fail. There is neither a place to go nor a specific thing to do. Grade schoolers repeating a memorized poem are far better off. They have a prompter. And it is only a poem, not a personal message, that is in danger.

This is not to say that you should not memorize *parts* of your speech. A dramatic introduction, a conclusion that involves poetry, a piece of testimony—all are likely passages for memorization.

Impromptu Delivery

An impromptu speech is one delivered on the spur of the moment. Typically, you will not be asked to make even an impromptu speech unless you have some special experience that makes you vulnerable to unexpected requests for a "few words." Then you had better carry at least a mental outline with you at all times. In this way you reduce the risks of being caught completely off guard. A student from Kenya once observed that he was routinely asked to tell about Kenya and give his reaction to America. He found himself in a true speaking situation as more and more people gathered around and as he did more and more of the talking. To improve these presentations, he prepared several brief outlines. He committed the outlines to memory, then tried to anticipate each situation and group in which he was apt to find himself. He explained that he has become so expert at this that he is now disappointed when he *isn't* asked to say a few words. People are amazed at his fluent and well-organized "impromptu" remarks!

Here are some general rules that may help you:

1. Anticipate the situation. Try to avoid a true impromptu speech. Figure the odds of your being called upon, and try to determine what topic you would be asked to discuss.
2. Relate the topic to your experience. You will speak more easily about something with which you have had specific experience.
3. When in doubt, summarize. There may be moments when you lose the thread of what you were saying or where you were going. At this moment, a quick review or summary often sets your mind back on the right track.
4. Be brief! The shorter your impromptu speech, the less chance for you to lose track of what you are saying.
5. Quit when you are ahead! All too often we make a good impromptu speech, then, instead of stopping, ramble on.
6. If you really have nothing to say, don't speak! Better to be thought a fool than to open your mouth and remove all doubt.

Extemporaneous Delivery

For an extemporaneous delivery, the speaker prepares a thorough but flexible outline, catalogs usable material, and uses a general outline (either memorized or written out). The language and wording of the speech are adaptable, as are the material and details to be included.

In this method you must know your subject and know your audience. You should collect a lot more material than you think you will use. Then, if one illustration or piece of evidence does not satisfy your audience, you can select another. If your audience finds one approach unclear, you can switch to your alternative approaches.

The chief advantage of extemporaneous delivery is that it gives you flexibility and adaptability. You can respond to problems as they develop. You are thinking on your feet in the best sense of that term.

In general, an extemporaneous speech is best given from a brief outline, carried either in your head or your hand. This is the type of preparation and delivery expected of you most often.

CHARACTERISTICS OF DELIVERY

Extemporaneous delivery gives you flexibility of thought, adaptability of material, and sensitivity (or *empathy*) toward your listeners. These are the qualities of good conversation and interpersonal communication. These same qualities should be present in all good speeches as well. The speaker who seeks to inspire need not sound artificial. A speaker can be eloquent without sounding pompous. On the other hand, adapting conversational qualities to public speaking does not mean employing a monotonous voice, poor preparation, or careless language.

A famous speech teacher, James A. Winans, once noted, "It is not true that a public speech to be conversational need sound like conversation. Conventional differences may make it sound very different.[1]" We are seeking the best qualities and moods of conversation.

Characteristics of a good delivery include:

1. Clear organization.
2. Clear concepts, language, and wording.
3. A clear, pleasant voice and articulation.
4. A sense of communication indicated by some direct eye contact.
5. An alertness of body and mind that indicates enthusiasm.
6. Controlled yet flexible bodily activity that helps meaning.

Characteristics of an annoying delivery include:

1. Clear lack of preparation and knowledge.
2. A dangling conclusion. The speaker seems unable or unwilling to close and simply repeats the message.
3. A mumbling of words.
4. A general vagueness.
5. Monotonous, stiff delivery from a manuscript.
6. Excesses of "ah," "er," and "uh."
7. Mispronunciations and grammatical mistakes.

Figure 10.4
"We loved your talk! You didn't take our minds off our knitting the way a lot of other speakers do." THE GIRLS, by Franklin Folger

[1]James A. Winans, *Speech Making* (New York: Appleton-Century-Crofts, 1938), p. 17.

Other aspects of delivery that lead to poor speaking include:

1. Stiff body action.
2. A refusal to look at the audience.
3. A weak, unclear, or monotonous voice.
4. Excessive nervousness or fidgeting.
5. A clear lack of enthusiasm.

LOCATING MATERIALS

We have discussed the *general* purposes of speaking: to inform, to persuade, and to entertain. Now we turn to the *specific* purpose of speaking, the specific audience, and methods of locating, organizing, and outlining materials.

Specific Purpose and Audience

The specific purpose is the *objective* or *response* your speech is designed to achieve. Let's look at teaching for an example. A teacher works from lesson plans (outlines). Every lesson a geometry teacher plans has the *general* purpose of informing the class about geometry. A particular lesson might have the *specific* purpose of teaching the class to apply principles of geometry to map reading.

If you choose the subject flying for a speech, you might start with the general purpose of informing the class about flying. But obviously, flying is far too

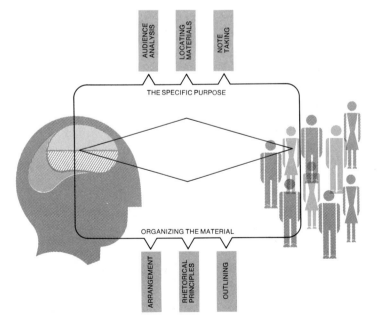

Figure 10.5

big a subject for a short speech. You'll want to restrict your subject. You might state your specific purpose as follows: to inform the class about the principle that allows a wing to "lift." Or you might talk about weapon and propeller synchronization in World War I Jennys. The more precisely you can state what it is you are trying to say or do, the easier your preparation will be. When your purpose is to persuade, you may not wish to tell the audience your intentions. But when preparing and outlining your speech, always start with a precise statement of your specific purpose.

Close on the heels of your specific purpose should come a careful consideration of your audience. In fact, if possible, consider your specific purpose and audience at the same time. Most often, we know the general type of audience we will meet (for example, business people, teachers, homemakers). In your classroom speeches you will know the specific audience.

Suppose your specific purpose were "to explain the five managerial functions of planning, organizing, controlling, coordinating, and communicating to an audience of management personnel." Your preparation and organization would be different if in checking your specific audience you discovered that they were executives rather than first-line supervisors. Preparation and organization are essential in either case, but the specific material and organization might vary widely. To continue the example, you might revise your specific purpose as follows: "To explain the five managerial functions of planning, organizing, controlling, coordinating, and communicating to an audience of *executive-level* personnel."

Factors to consider before you collect speech materials are the occasion, the environment, and the general descriptive measures of an audience (size, age, education, and so on), as discussed in the previous chapter.

The speech subject, the language you use, the clothes you wear—these and many other matters are often directly related to the purpose of the gathering. Consider: Why have you been chosen to speak? If there are other speakers, when, in what order, and for how long does each person speak? You must answer all these questions as you prepare.

If possible, know the special rules, habits, rituals, and practices you are likely to meet. Organizations such as the Kiwanis, Rotary, and Lions have standard meeting formats. Many organizations have certain "fun" rituals, which, though great sport if you are warned, can be a nightmare if you are unaware. A speaker was once fined a dollar before saying his first word because he was wearing a red necktie! Know your occasion so that you can predict these things and take them into account in your preparation.

Part of the speech occasion is the introduction. The chairperson almost always asks the speaker for help with what to say. The novice speaker almost always answers, "Oh, it doesn't really matter." But it *does* matter, so *do* help. The introducer will appreciate it, and you will reduce your risks at the same time.

Closely related to the occasion is the environment. This is the location and arrangement of the room or building in which the speech will be made. The same speech delivered in a church or temple, a restaurant, or a fraternity house

Figure 10.6 THE WIZARD of ID. By permission of Johnny Hart and Field Enterprises, Inc.

changes with the location. People expect different things in different types of buildings.

If you'll be using a PA system, it may strongly affect the way in which you use your visual aids. The effects of most microphones fade if you move more than two feet away from them. It's a good idea to check the system *before* you speak.

Visual and audio aids should be closely related to these environmental factors. A chart big enough for a group of twenty-five may be too small for a group of 300. Slides may be useless if the room will not darken, and a tape recording may not be heard in a room filled with echoes.

The message, of course, is most critical. The audience-message analysis is very important. Some practical questions that the speaker should answer are:

1. What is the importance of the subject for the audience?
2. What does the audience know about the subject?
3. What beliefs or prejudices does the audience have about the subject?

Sources

Once you have considered your specific purpose and have related it to your audience and occasion, you are ready to start locating and collecting materials. The question now is, "Where do I find these materials?" Your own knowledge and experience can give you a head start. Conversations with experts can also be very valuable sources. However, any serious interviewing should usually follow some reading and observing. If you start your research early you will better understand which questions are important. If, for example, you were to interview a professor of electrical engineering on information theory, you would be well advised to first browse through one or two books or articles in the field. The same would be true if you were going to interview a speech professor on semantics, psycholinguistics, or congruency.

Your next question, is, "Where do I find references to browse through?"

THE LIBRARY. The simplest source is your *library card catalog*. This is a vast treasure house of information; take advantage of it. Almost every library has the *Reader's Guide to Periodical Literature*. This lists magazine articles by author, title, and subject. The *Reader's Guide* is typically bound into volumes by year and is located in the reference section of the library. You use it much as you would the library card catalog. You might also look through *Books in Print*, the *Cumulative Book Index*, and its predecessor, *The United States Catalog*; these sources do for books about what the *Reader's Guide* does for magazines. The *Cumulative Book Index* is arranged according to author, title, and subject. While you're in the library, see if it has *The New York Times Index*. This is the only complete newspaper index in the United States; it can be a real time-saver. Some libraries also have the *Index to the Times* of London, England.

Many libraries also have a good selection of general encyclopedias, such as *Britannica, Americana,* and *New International,* and special ones, such as the *International Encyclopedia of the Social Sciences, New Catholic Encyclopedia,* the *Jewish Encyclopedia,* and the *Encyclopedia of Religion and Ethics.* Very often, these sources present the best short statement on a given subject to be found anywhere. These encyclopedias are typically kept current by annual supplements called yearbooks.

Do not overlook your dictionary. Good dictionaries contain much more than a good vocabulary.

For descriptions of cultural and political events, see *The Official Associated Press Almanac*; for geographical topics, see *The Information Please Almanac.* The *Reader's Digest Almanac* offers facts and household hints and advice. When you need statistics and short statements of factual data, see the *Statesman's Yearbook,* the *World Almanac and Book of Facts,* and the *Statistical Abstract of the United States* from the U.S. Bureau of the Census. This last source covers social, political, and economic facts of a wide range. Smaller general encyclopedias, such as *Columbia* or *Everyman's,* also contain compact statements and facts. Finally, an atlas can provide political facts as well as detailed maps. Try *The Hammond Citation World Atlas* or the *National Geographic Atlas of the World.* Check the date of publication on all of these sources before you use them; the world has changed dramatically in the last few years.

To learn more about famous individuals, you can consult some of the better-known directories and biographical dictionaries, such as *Who's Who in America. Who's Who in American Education, Who's Who in Engineering, American Men of Science,* and the *Directory of American Scholars.* For information on prominent Americans of the past, see *Who Was Who in America,* the *Dictionary of American Biography, Lippincott's Biographical Dictionary,* and *The National Cyclopedia of American Biography.*

Most professional or trade associations publish journals of their own—for example, the American Bar Association, the American Bankers' Association, the American Medical Association, the Speech Communication Association, the American Psychological Association, and the AFL-CIO. Many of the articles in the journals published by these organizations are indexed by special publications that are often available in your library (*Biological and Agricultural Index, Art Index, Index to Legal Periodicals, Index Medicus, Psychological Abstracts,* and many more).

In addition to the *Statistical Abstract of the United States,* mentioned earlier, other government publications can be excellent sources of speech materials. The *Commerce Yearbook* and the *Monthly Labor Review* provide much valuable information. The *Congressional Record* is an especially fruitful source for speech students. It includes a daily report of the House and Senate debates—indexed according to subject, name of bill, and representative or senator—and an appendix that lists related articles and speeches from outside of Congress.

Other sources of speech materials are the thousands of organizations that issue pamphlets and reports, often at no cost. You can write directly to these organizations for information and in some cases (for example, Planned Parenthood League, the World Peace Foundation, the American Institute of Banking, and the AFL-CIO) you will receive a speech outline or manuscript in return. If you would like to know the addresses of these or other organizations, refer to the *World Almanac* under the heading, "Associations and Societies in the United States."

If you cannot find enough information in all of these sources, or if you would like to *start out* with a printed bibliography on your subject, you may obtain in some libraries a bibliography on bibliographies—an index of bibliographies called the *Bibliographic Index.* Many college and community libraries have a computerized information service where a search is done for the reader by library personnel. Other libraries are installing coin-operated computers. Check with your librarian for these sources.

CONVERSATION AND INTERVIEW. Another way to gather materials is to talk with people about your topic, to "try it out" on somebody. If the somebody has

Figure 10.7
"It is not strange that remembered ideas should often take advantage of the crowd of thoughts and smuggle themselves in as original.—Honest thinkers are always stealing unconsciously from each other.—Our minds are full of waifs and estrays which we think our own.—Innocent plagiarism turns up everywhere."—*O.W. Holmes* From *Communication Education,* 29, no. 3 (July 1980), 272.

firsthand or secondhand experience with your topic, you may be in luck. If experts are available you may be able to interview them. Before interviewing anyone, always do some basic research so you can ask clear and brief questions. Explain early in the conversation why you want this person's opinion or information. Avoid loaded or biased questions (even if you have a bias), and try to be objective throughout. Note any sources the person mentions. Listen carefully, letting your subject do most of the talking. Remember to give credit to your sources later.

NOTE TAKING. Now you must consider how to select, sort, evaluate, and, finally, record the material. You'll find that a good system for taking notes will save you time and strain.

A good way to begin is to give your material a quick sorting, dividing it into two stacks: useful and not useful. Now you're ready to record details that might support your specific purpose. Before you write anything down, decide if you want to revise your specific purpose as a result of your findings. This decision can affect the materials you will use or the issues you will discuss. In other words, set up temporary categories of speech materials, issues to be discussed, and so forth. Then add, omit, or subdivide later as your search becomes more specific This will also give you a head start on the organizing and outlining of the speech itself.

Now you're ready to start making *systematic* notes. Note the emphasis on the word *systematic*. Use file cards. You should write only one subject, source, classification, and note on each card. The big advantage of file cards over a notebook is that you can rearrange the file cards and thus easily organize your material.

The next problem is what to write on the card. If you have found a general source about which you are undecided, make a short summary in your own words.

Figure 10.8   Sample file card to note quotation

```
(Subject) Prehistoric man        (Classification)
                                       Dinosaurs

"... you will often see cartoons showing cave men being
chased by dinosaurs.  But this could never have happen-
ed.  The physical anthropologists tell us which bones
are the bones of the prehistoric men who lived in
caves.  The paleontologists tell us which bones are
the bones of giant reptiles.  The geologists tell us
that the human bones come from layers of earth that
are 50,000 years old, and the dinosaur bones come
from rocks 150,000,000 years old.

SOURCE:  Donald Barr, Primitive Man (New York:
         Wonder Books, 1961), p. 10.
```

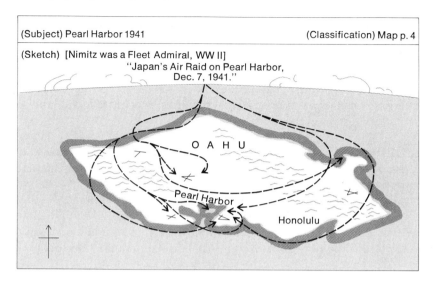

(Subject) Pearl Harbor 1941   (Classification) Map p. 4

(Sketch) [Nimitz was a Fleet Admiral, WW II]
"Japan's Air Raid on Pearl Harbor,
Dec. 7, 1941."

O A H U

Pearl Harbor

Honolulu

Figure 10.9   Sample file card for visual aid

You can then decide later whether to reread the source. If you find a statement by an authority that you may decide to use, take it down word for word and put quotation marks around it. Be sure to record the name and qualifications of the authority. In taking down testimony or statistics, make sure you record the date. Things change! If you add explanations or interpretations of your own, bracket these words so that later on you will not confuse your words with those of your sources.

Some sample note-taking systems are illustrated in Figures 10.8 and 10.9.

ARRANGING IDEAS

Let's look first at some useful methods for arranging the raw materials.

Methods of Organizing

CHRONOLOGICAL METHOD.   Materials are arranged according to the order in which events took place. In speaking on "Life on Earth," we would probably discuss the geologic periods chronologically. Most historical subjects lend themselves readily to this method; so do processes of a sequential, 1–2–3 order, such as developing film. Remember, however, that these subjects do not have to be handled in this way. History, for example, is often more interesting and meaningful if discussed topically.

TOPICAL METHOD.   Material is ordered according to general topics or classifications of knowledge. To continue the example of history, we might concentrate on the history of religion, war, government, education, or science. The importance of the topic may be such that you'll ignore historical time. The topical method can help in breaking down very broad topics. One can, for example, look at integration of the races in several topical ways: educationally, socially, militarily, economically, and so forth. A city may be described topically in terms of its industry, employment opportunities, recreational facilities, schools, climate, and so on.

LOGICAL METHOD. This method is useful for subjects with generally accepted or obvious cause-and-effect relationships such as the fall of the Japanese empire or the building of a house or a boat. When the order is naturally present in the subject, this may be a convenient way to organize speech materials. This method differs from the topical method in that subpoints almost always illustrate or explain whatever they are subordinate to. You must analyze your audience thoroughly before using this method. What seems logical to you may not seem logical to them.

DIFFICULTY METHOD. For some subjects, particularly technical ones, it may help to organize your materials in their order of difficulty—that is, proceeding from the easiest aspect to the most difficult one. In discussing general principles of electricity, we might arrange a series of ideas as shown in Figure 10.10.

Figure 10.10 Organization by order of difficulty

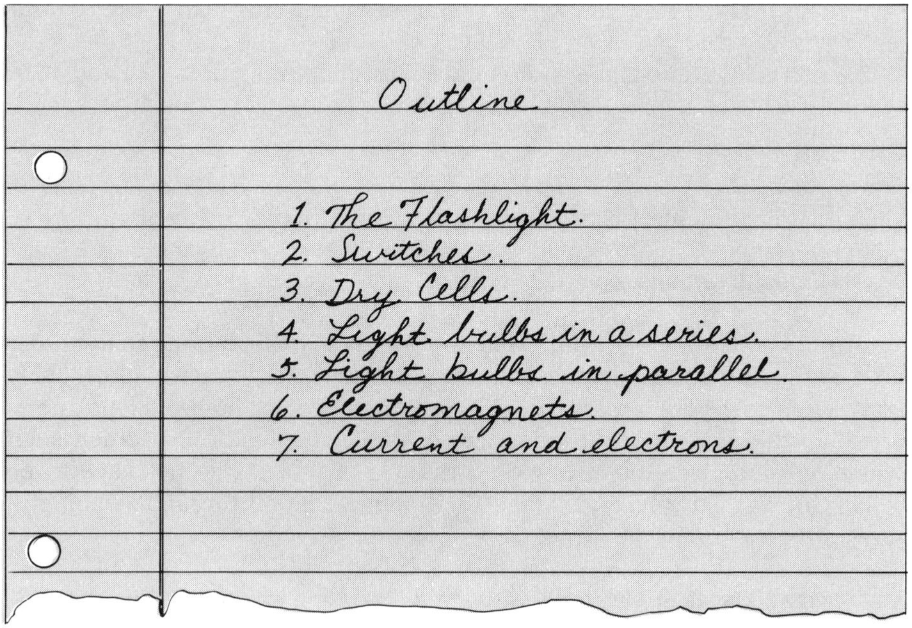

Outline

1. The Flashlight.
2. Switches.
3. Dry Cells.
4. Light bulbs in a series.
5. Light bulbs in parallel.
6. Electromagnets.
7. Current and electrons.

SPATIAL METHOD. In a speech about the United Nations we might first describe each building, then discuss the offices in each building one floor at a time. These ideas are organized spatially. The ideas could also be organized topically if the audience were familiar with the political structure of the United Nations. In discussing "Nationalism in Africa," we might organize geographically and simply divide the ideas from north to south and east to west. This subject might also be organized historically.

NEED-PLAN METHOD. Materials can also be organized according to problems (needs) and solutions (plans). An affirmative debate team arguing about government health programs could divide its material into needs and plans. The first speaker could concentrate on the needs. The second speaker could discuss the various plans and indicate why one is better than the others. The needs can be subdivided into economic needs, health needs, and social needs.

Rhetorical Principles

The *major* parts of a speech are: *beginning, middle,* and *end,* or *introduction, body,* and *conclusion.* Other parts are the speech details and ideas. Before analyzing each part, let's look at three rhetorical principles that are important in the arranging of the parts. These are *unity, coherence,* and *emphasis.*

UNITY. Aristotle once said that a play must be constructed so that the omission of any part damages the whole. He also noted that each part of the plot must contribute to the purpose or end of the play. He said a play must have a total unity in the same manner as a living thing. We still use the term *organic unity.* In speech, organic unity means that the material should be so unified that it can be summarized in a single statement of purpose. In some speeches this statement takes the form of a proposition that is openly announced. In others it is left unstated for strategic purposes. But the speaker must always understand his or her specific purpose if the speech is to have unity. This specific purpose helps the speaker evaluate materials and ideas during preparation. The arrangement of the parts of a speech should be so unified that the purpose is clear to both the audience and speaker. Unity, of course, presumes some substance.

Figure 10.11   THE WIZARD of ID.   By permission of Johnny Hart and Field Enterprises, Inc.

COHERENCE. Coherence refers to the connections among the parts of the speech. It involves the methods of ordering ideas and speech details. To *cohere* is to be connected. The connecting of the parts and ideas of a speech is done with words or phrases. To achieve coherence, we must carefully consider our connecting words. Unlike the reader, the listener cannot go back and recheck the text to locate a lost thread of meaning. Thus, we must connect our thoughts carefully, often repeating the connectives. Coherence must involve the audience. In going from one point to another, we may lose our audience if we assume that it will see the relationship of ideas just because we do.

EMPHASIS. Emphasis involves the location, space, and form you give your ideas. Should you present your most important idea first, last, or as a climax? Does the amount of space you give the idea affect emphasis? Your main point should not be buried under some subpoint. Since a number of really important ideas may compete for attention, which idea should you emphasize most strongly? These questions can be answered best in terms of your subject, knowledge, audience, and the occasion. Location, space, form, and order do make a difference. They do affect emphasis. Successful emphasis involves the use of these devices.

Figure 10.12 THE WIZARD of ID. By permission of Johnny Hart and Field Enterprises, Inc.

Systems of Arrangement

Aristotle thought that good arrangement was related to normal thinking habits. So do modern rhetoricians. Aristotle suggested four steps: *introduction* (he called it proem), *statement* (of the purpose), *argument*, and *conclusion* (he called it epilogue). Hollingworth listed the parts of a speech as *attention, interest, impression, conviction,* and *direction*. The speaker may eliminate some parts as he or she adapts to the audience.

Monroe suggested that the basic parts are *attention, need, satisfaction, visualization,* and *action*. He believed that the emphasis given each element would depend on the audience's mood and knowledge as well as on the purpose of the speech. A speech to inform might use only three elements. A speech to persuade might call for all five.

These systems of arrangement are useful. They show the complicated interaction of subject, audience, speaker, and arrangement.

Table 10.1   Some General Systems of Arrangement

INTRODUCTION →	Attention	Attention	Attention	Attention
BODY →	Statement	Interest Impression	Need Satisfaction	Overview
	Argument	Conviction	Visualization	Information
CONCLUSION →	Conclusion	Direction	Action	Review

Other divisions of your speech are possible. The *general* purpose of your speech (to persuade, to inform, or to entertain) will dictate how complex a system you will need. Let's view these parts in terms of the more common divisions of *introduction, body,* and *conclusion.*

Let's look now at the requirements of a good introduction, body, and conclusion.

INTRODUCTION. Table 10.1 shows that arousing attention is always an important first step. The number of attention-getting devices to use depends on how attentive the audience already is. If listeners are on the edge of their seats and are ready to hear what you have to say, a lengthy introduction to arouse their attention is unnecessary.

Arousing attention is only one requirement of an introduction. Your introduction should also attempt to establish or strengthen good will between you and the audience. In those rare cases where good will is hard to come by (as when you're facing a hostile audience), establishing a mood for a fair hearing is perhaps the most you can hope for. For example, Adlai Stevenson once used humor to establish rapport with a tough Labor Day audience: "When I was a boy I never had much sympathy for a holiday speaker. He was just a kind of interruption between hot dogs, a fly in the lemonade." Mark Twain once told a story of his early lecturing days. Arriving in a town where he was to speak in the early afternoon and seeing that the evening lecture was poorly billed, he stopped in at the general store and, addressing the owner, said, "Good afternoon, friend. Any entertainment here tonight to help a stranger while away his evening?" The storekeeper straightened up, wiped his hands on his apron, and said, "I expect there is going to be a lecture—I have been selling eggs all day."

In some situations, a purpose of the introduction is *orientation.* That is, the speaker must supply certain background explanations to help the audience better understand the rest of the speech. Not defining new words, for example, will cause confusion in the audience. A brief historical sketch often helps orient the audience. A good example is John F. Kennedy's opening address to a conference on African culture held in New York City on June 28, 1959:

Some 2,500 years ago the Greek historian Herodotus described Africa south of the Sahara as a land of "horned asses, of dog-faced creatures, the creatures without heads, whom the Libyans declared to have eyes in their breasts, and many other far less fabulous beasts." Apparently when Herodotus found himself short on facts, he didn't hesitate to use imagination—which may be why he is called the first historian.

But we must not be too critical of Herodotus. Until very recently, for most Americans, Africa was Trader Horn, Tarzan, and tom-tom drums. We are only now beginning to discover that Africa, unlike our comic strip stereotypes, is a land of rich variety—of noble and ancient cultures, some primitive, some highly sophisticated; of vital and gifted people, who are only now crossing the threshold into the modern world.

Your introduction should seek to make your purpose clear. It is often a preview of what is to follow. Again, remember that an *audience*, unlike a *reader*, cannot go back to a previous page. Therefore, more repetition is called for.

To summarize, the purposes of an introduction are: (1) to secure *attention*; (2) to establish *good will*; (3) to assure a *fair hearing*; (4) to *orient* your audience to the subject; and (5) to make your *purpose* clear.

You can achieve good introductions in many different ways. However, any introduction should relate to both the subject and the situation. An unusual story describing your troubles in getting to the meeting is acceptable. So are humorous anecdotes. Most experts agree that if you are going to use jokes or humorous stories, they should relate in some way to the subject or situation. Appreciation, personal reference, quotations, and related stories or experiences are also useful. When the purpose of the speech is obvious and both speaker and subject are well known, a related story or incident with built-in attention often gives the audience a fresh orientation. Booker T. Washington's introduction to his address at the Atlanta Exposition is a good example:

> **[Attention]**
> Mr. President and Gentlemen of the Board of Directors and Citizens: One-third of the population of the South is of the Negro race. No enterprise seeking the material, civil, or moral welfare of this section can disregard this element of our population and reach the highest success.
>
> **[Good Will]**
> I but convey to you, Mr. President and Directors, the sentiment of the masses of my race when I say that in no way have the value and manhood of the American Negro been more fittingly and generously recognized than by the managers of this magnificent Exposition at every stage of its progress. It is a recognition that will do more to cement the friendship of the two races than any occurrence since the dawn of our freedom.
>
> **[Fair Hearing]**
> Not only this, but the opportunity here afforded will awaken among us a new era of industrial progress. Ignorant and inexperienced, it is not strange that in the first years of our new life we began at the top instead of at the bottom; that a seat in Congress or the state legislature was more sought than real estate or industrial skill; that the political convention or stump speaking had more attractions than starting a dairy farm or truck garden.

[Orientation]

A ship lost at sea for many days suddenly sighted a friendly vessel. From the mast of the unfortunate vessel was seen a signal, "Water, water; we die of thirst!" The answer from the friendly vessel at once came back, "Cast down your bucket where you are." And a third and fourth signal for water was answered, "Cast down your bucket where you are." The captain of the distressed vessel, at last heeding the injunction, cast down his bucket, and it came up full of fresh, sparkling water from the mouth of the Amazon River.

[Purpose]

To those of my race who depend on bettering their condition in a foreign land or who underestimate the importance of cultivating friendly relations with the Southern white man, who is their next door neighbor, I would say: "Cast down your bucket where you are"—cast it down in making friends in every manly way of the people of all races by whom we are surrounded.[2]

During World War II, President Roosevelt used a story in an introduction to one of the many appeals he made for the purchase of war bonds.

Once upon a time, a few years ago, there was a city in our Middle West which was threatened by a destructive flood in a great river. The waters had risen to the top of the banks. Every man, woman, and child in that city was called upon to fill sandbags in order to defend their homes against the rising waters. For many days and nights destruction and death stared them in the face. As a result of the grim, determined community effort, that city still stands. Those people kept the levees above the peak of the flood. All of them joined together in the desperate job that had to be done—businessmen, workers, farmers, and doctors, and preachers—people of all races.

To me that town is a living symbol of what community cooperation can accomplish.[3]

BODY. This is where the bulk of the information or argument is located. All the previous discussions of organization, rhetorical principles, and arrangement come into focus here. Forms of the *body* are explained and illustrated in the next section, *Outlining*.

CONCLUSION. Concluding words from Table 10.1 on p. 225 are *direction*, *action*, and *review*. We could add *visualization, restatement*, and *summary*. These devices are all intended to regain attention and to assist the memory. Aristotle suggested that the major purpose of the conclusion is to help the memory.

The conclusion is generally shorter than either the introduction or the body. It may and generally should include a short summary that reinforces the message and makes it easier to understand. It may call for clearly stated directions if certain actions are part of the speaker's purpose. When your purpose has been

[2]Quoted in A. Craig Baird, *American Public Addresses: 1740–1952* (New York: McGraw Hill 1956), p. 189.

[3]*Vital Speeches of the Day*, 9, no. 23 (September 15, 1943), 703.

inspiration, you may need a more impressive conclusion. Some of the devices suggested in the discussion on introductions (an impressive quotation, incident, or experience) apply here. Martin Luther King, Jr., gave an inspirational conclusion in his famous speech in support of civil-rights legislation before an estimated 200,000 people:

> So let freedom ring—from the prodigious hilltops of New Hampshire, let freedom ring; from the mighty mountains of New York, let freedom ring—from the heightening Alleghenies of Pennsylvania!
> Let freedom ring from the snowcapped Rockies of Colorado!
> Let freedom ring from the curvaceous slopes of California!
> But not only that; let freedom ring from Stone Mountain of Georgia!
> Let freedom ring from Lookout Mountain of Tennessee!
> Let freedom ring from every hill and mole hill of Mississippi.
> From every mountainside, let freedom ring, . . .
> When we allow freedom to ring, when we let it ring from every village and every hamlet, from every state and every city, we will be able to speed up that day when all of God's children, black men and white men, Jews and Gentiles, Protestants and Catholics, will be able to join hands and sing in the words of the old Negro spiritual, "Free at last! thank God almighty, we are free at last!"[4]

Most important, make it evident when you are finished; consider your exit lines carefully. Speakers who do not know when they are going to finish appear awkward and confuse the audience. The never-ending conclusion, caused either by the ham in all of us or by poor preparation, is all too familiar. The remedy is obvious: Prepare your conclusion as carefully as the rest of your speech. Doing so serves as a good check on unity. And quit while you're ahead. Don't let an audience hypnotize you so much that you ruin a good speech with an overly long conclusion.

Figure 10.13   THE WIZARD of ID.   By permission of Johnny Hart and Field Enterprises, Inc.

[4] Quoted in Robert T. Oliver and Eugene E. White, *Selected Speeches from American History* (Boston: Allyn & Bacon, 1966), pp. 289–94.

Outlining

WHERE TO START. The outline is to a speech what a blueprint is to a house. A good, clear outline can help you discover mistakes, weaknesses, and unnecessary information *before* you speak. Imitate the builder or architect who saves costly mistakes by taking a hard look at the plans before starting to build the house.

Begin by reviewing your specific purpose. This serves to narrow and unify the subject matter further and should result in a precise statement of purpose. Your statement of purpose attempts to capture the point of the entire speech in a single sentence. It should not be confused with a title or a general subject area, although both may be closely related to your purpose.

Start your serious outlining with the body of the speech. The introduction and conclusion, important as they are, only enrich the content-loaded main body. State your main points or ideas in terms of your purpose. Locate your supporting material under the main points. After roughing out the body of your speech, outline the introduction and conclusion.

Your rough outline should eventually become a *complete-sentence outline* (one in which all the major and minor points are written out as complete sentences). This will force you to *think* your way through the material and help you avoid embarrassment on the platform. The sentence outline will also make it easier for your instructor to evaluate and help you with your speech planning. After making a thorough outline, you may want to simplify the outline in topical or key-word form for use on the platform. Such an outline is an aid to clear, orderly thinking. It is a blueprint of the speech.

PRINCIPLES OF OUTLINING. Here are six principles that apply to all outlines:

1. *Simplicity.* Each numbered or lettered statement should contain only one idea.
2. *Coordination.* A subordinate list of topics must have a common relationship.
3. *Subordination.* Related lesser points supporting a general statement should be grouped separately from the statement, usually by means of indentation. Items of equal importance should be given equal billing.
4. *Discreteness.* Each item in an outline should be a distinct point and should not overlap other items.
5. *Progression.* Related items should be arranged in some natural sequence, such as time or space. Keep the items in sequence and don't switch patterns in midspeech.
6. *Symbolization.* Similar symbols (I, II, and III; A, B, and C; and so on) should represent items or points of equal importance. The symbol and its indentation should indicate the relative importance of the item that follows.

Usually, main points are roman numerals, major subpoints are capital letters, minor subpoints are arabic numerals, and so on.

Logical outlining involves (1) divisions of ideas and (2) headings that make these divisions clear. If a topic is divided, it should have two or more subordinate parts. In other words, if you're going to have a *1*, you should also have a *2*; if you're going to have an *A*, you should also have a *B*. If your *2* or *B* is not important to your speech, the first point should be incorporated into its superior heading. For example,

    A. Wagon trains.
       1. Role in development of West.

becomes

    A. Wagon trains as factor in development of West.

The numbers and letters you use as labels must be consistent. Let your symbols show clearly that the main ideas are equal in importance, and that the subpoints are secondary to the main points.

The standard system of symbols and indentations is shown in Figure 10.14.

Figure 10.14   Standard outline indentation

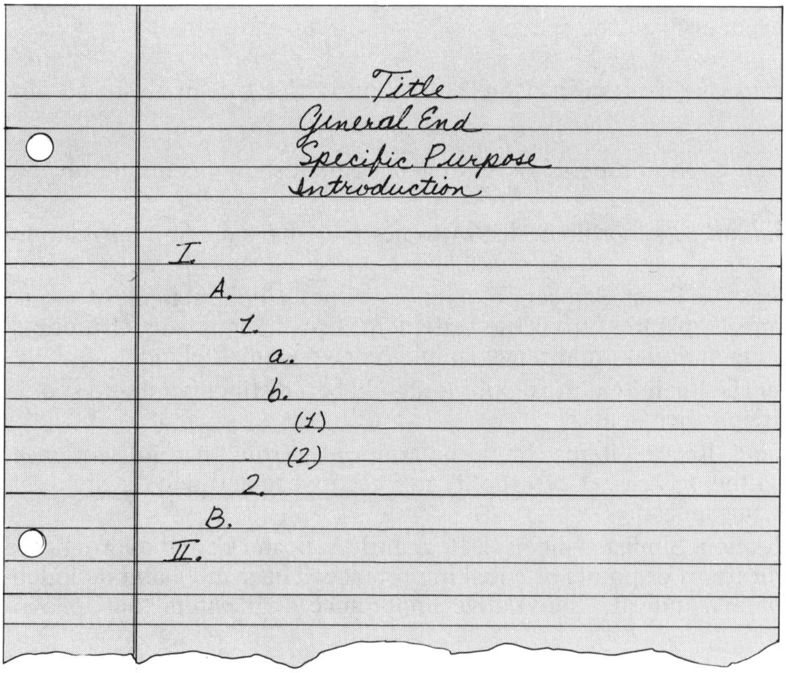

How many main points should you have in a speech? If you include more than four or five, your listeners will have difficulty remembering the points and relating them to one another. Your main points should be of equal importance. Each main point should be worded carefully and completely and should contribute to the central purpose of the speech. You should present your main points in an order that will aid the logical development of your speech and strengthen audience understanding.

How you arrange your outline may vary with your purpose and your instructor's preference. You may use the system of *introduction, body,* and *conclusion* or some of the other systems. You should probably capitalize, but not number, such words as *introduction, body,* and *conclusion,* and perhaps put words such as *attention, overview, need,* and *reinforcement* in the margins.

TYPES OF OUTLINES. The complete-sentence outline is the most detailed of all the forms. All main and minor points are written out as complete sentences. Your first try at outlining a speech will probably be in a topical, skeleton form. The disadvantage of the topical outline is that your memory may fail you and the thoughts may suddenly be difficult to visualize as complete sentences. Its advantages are fewer notes and more extemporaneous speaking. A key-word outline is an abbreviated topical outline. In terms of indentation and symbols it looks the same as the complete-sentence outline. The key-word outline is usually easier to remember. It makes the reordering of ideas much easier when the situation calls for such adaptation.

You may want to use a combination of forms when you are speaking on a subject with which you are very familiar. The main points might be written as complete sentences, the subpoints as phrases, and the subsubpoints as key words.

The sample outline in Figure 10.15 shows how symbols and indentations are used. The words in parentheses indicate another system of arrangement. Another example is shown in the Appendix C outline of "The Dietary Laws of the Jewish People."

SUMMARY

The general purposes of speaking are to inform, to persuade, and to entertain. Many speeches combine these purposes and are difficult to classify. By itself, the degree of information, entertainment, or persuasion in a speech does not indicate the speaker's purpose; we must also consider the arrangement of the material, the knowledge possessed by the audience, and the speaker's style and voice. Your real purpose can be determined from the principal reaction you desire from your audience.

The goals of informative speaking are clarity, interest, and understanding. In a speech to persuade, the speaker tries to make people believe something, urges them to do something, or attempts to stimulate them to a higher level of enthu-

```
THE LEFT WING

General End:          To inform and entertain.

Specific Purpose:     To inform the audience about left-handed people, their
                      problems, theories as to why some people are left-handed,
                      and what is being done to help them.

                      INTRODUCTION

                  I.  Are you one of those people who have been described
                      as temperamental, unstable, unintelligent, pugnacious,
                      or, in a word, left-handed?

                 II.  Even if you are not, you should know some facts about
                      this persecuted group.
(Attention)
(Overview)            A.  Their number.
                      B.  Their difficulties.
                      C.  Assistance given.
                      D.  Theories as to why they are left-handed.

                      BODY

                  I.  Who are the southpaws?

                      A.  Number.
                          1.  ¼ North Americans originally left-handed.
(Information)             2.  Schools report an 8% increase.
                      B.  Some are famous.
                          1.  Present-day lefties.
                          2.  Historic lefties.

                 II.  Southpaw advantages and disadvantages.

                      A.  Advantages.
                          1.  Mirror writing.
                          2.  Sports.
                      B.  Disadvantages.
                          1.  Eating.
                          2.  Musical instruments.
                          3.  Knitting.
                          4.  Office machines.

                III.  Help for left-handers.

                      A.  The Association for the Protection of Rights of
                          Left-Handers.
                          1.  Oaths.
                          2.  Saluting.
                          3.  Fellowship.
(Visualization)       B.  Manufactured goods for lefties.
                          1.  Golf clubs.
                          2.  Musical instruments.
                          3.  Reversed turnstiles.
                      C.  Theories concerning southpaws.
                          1.  Cerebral dominance.
                          2.  Inherited.
                          3.  Present opinion.
                              a.  Surveys.
                              b.  Tests.

                      CONCLUSION

                  I.  If you are left-handed, be comforted in that:

                      A.  Though your numbers are small, you are not inferior.
                      B.  Your disadvantages are being reduced.
                      C.  The theories make you more interesting.
                      D.  Society is trying to help.

                 II.  You righties should now have a right attitude about the
                      left wing.
```

Figure 10.15 A topical and key-word form of outline. From a student speech by Robert Willard,
Wayne State University.

siasm. The goals of a speech to entertain are to help people escape from reality and to enjoy themselves without the threat of some hidden meaning.

The four principal ways of delivering a speech are reading from a manuscript, memorization, impromptu speaking, and extemporaneous speaking. In manuscript delivery the speaker presents the subject to the audience by reading word for word a completely written speech. In memorization the speaker commits every word of the manuscript to memory. An impromptu speech is one that is delivered on the spur of the moment, without advance notice or time for detailed preparation. In the extemporaneous method a thorough but flexible outline is prepared, a wealth of potentially useable material is catalogued, and a general outline is either memorized or carried by the speaker. The language and wording of such a speech may be specific, but they are always adaptable to circumstances, as is the use of speech materials and details.

The characteristics of good delivery include a conversational quality; precise concepts, wording, and pronunciation; a clear, pleasant voice and articulation; direct eye contact, enthusiasm, and controlled yet flexible body action.

The characteristics of bad delivery include evident lack of preparation, dangling conclusions, mumbling, vagueness of meaning, monotonous reading, unnecessary verbalizations, mispronunciation, loss of temper, rigid body action, lack of eye contact, weak voice, fidgeting, and an evident lack of enthusiasm.

One of the most important aspects of preparing, organizing, and outlining a speech is to achieve a clear understanding and statement of your specific purpose—the outcome, objective, or response that your speech is supposed to accomplish. Of almost equal importance is careful consideration of the audience and the situation. The relationships between audience and subject as well as between audience and speaker are other critical factors in the preparation of a speech.

When you have considered your specific purpose thoroughly and have related it to an analysis of your audience and the occasion of your speech, you are ready to start finding and collecting the materials that will make up the speech itself. This chapter provides a list of sources and procedures for making the task much easier than it may appear at first. Taking notes from your readings and sources should be done systematically; that way, you will have to do only a minimum of rereading and returning to the library. The use of file cards rather than a notebook will ease the eventual organizing and arranging of the various parts of the speech.

The principal ways of arranging ideas for speech purposes are the chronological, topical, logical, difficulty, spatial, and need-plan methods. The arrangement of the parts of a speech (beginning, middle, end; introduction, body, conclusion; and other variations) is related to your general end as well as to your specific purpose. Most systems of arrangement consist of a simple introduction-body-conclusion sequence. The rhetorical principles of unity, coherence, and emphasis also have a strong bearing on the arrangement of the parts.

The general functions of a good introduction are: (1) to secure attention; (2) to establish good will; (3) to assure a fair hearing; (4) to orient your audience to the subject; and (5) to make your purpose clear.

The conclusion is generally shorter than either the introduction or the body. It may, and generally should, include a short summary that reinforces the message and makes it easier to understand. It may provide clearly stated directions if certain actions are part of the speaker's purpose. It is important to make it clear when you are through; consider your exit lines carefully. Speakers who do not know when to finish appear awkward and frustrate the audience. Prepare your conclusion as carefully as the rest of your speech; doing so is a good check on organic unity. Remember to quit when you're ahead. Never ruin a good speech by an overly long or overly dramatic conclusion.

An outline is an aid to clear, orderly thinking. It is a blueprint of the speech. Useful principles that apply to all outlines are simplicity, coordination, subordination, discreteness, progression, and symbolization.

Start your serious outlining with the body of the speech. State your main points or ideas in terms of your purpose, and place your supporting material under the appropriate main points. After sketching the body of your speech, outline the introduction and conclusion. Your rough outline should eventually become a complete-sentence outline. After completing a thorough outline, you may then redo it in a topical or key-word form for use on the platform.

The numbers and letters you use as labels in your outline must be consistent. Let your symbols show clearly that the main ideas are relatively equal in importance, and that the subpoints are secondary to the main points. If a topic is to be divided, it should be divided into at least two parts. The number of main points in a speech should seldom go beyond four or five. Your main points should be of approximately equal importance. Each main point should be worded carefully and should contribute to the central purpose of the speech. The order in which you present your main points should aid the logical development of your speech and strengthen audience motivation, remembering, and understanding.

STUDY PROJECTS

1. Write out, word for word, a two- to three-minute message in your best oral style. Then rehearse it and prepare to read it from a manuscript.

2. Observe a speaker (live, on radio, or on TV) for at least fifteen to thirty minutes. On two separate sheets of paper note the characteristics of good and bad delivery that you observed.

3. From newspapers and magazines select and clip items that are clearly (a) informative; (b) persuasive; (c) entertaining; or (d) a combination of these, and identify the specific purposes of each item.

4. Your instructor will assign you two numbers at random from 1 to 48. These refer to the numbered impromptu topics below. Review the suggestions for making good impromptu speeches, choose one of the two topics, take thirty seconds to prepare, and speak impromptu for one minute before the class.

1	Animals I Have Known	25	Something I Do Well
2	The Most Valuable Modern Invention	26	"Pride Goeth before a Fall"
3	A Mystery I Never Solved	27	The Best Purchase I Ever Made
4	Things I Want to Learn	28	The Music I Like Best
5	Learning to Dance	29	My Last Vacation
6	Learning to Swim	30	Why I Like (Do Not Like) to Live in This State
7	My First "Public Appearance"	31	A Buying Experience
8	"It Pays to Advertise"	32	" 'Tis More Blessed to Give . . . "
9	Learning to Play Golf	33	The Time That It Paid to Disobey
10	My Hobby	34	A Selling Experience
11	What to Do on a Rainy Day	35	My Green Thumb
12	The Radio or Television Program I Like Best (or Least)	36	A Camping Experience
13	My Favorite Character in Fiction	37	The First Money I Ever Earned
14	Improvements I Would Suggest for This School	38	An Embarrassing Moment
15	How I Taught Someone to Drive	39	Propaganda
16	How I Got Out of a Difficult Situation	40	Spiritual Aspects of Nature
17	The Most Important Story in This Week's News	41	Beauty Justifies Itself
18	Charisma	42	Censorship in American Life
19	Improvements I Would Suggest for This City	43	When There Is a Will There's Always a Way
20	A Joke That Didn't Come Off	44	The Time I Won
21	My Favorite Relative	45	An Obnoxious Character
22	My Pet Superstition	46	An Unforgettable Moment
23	Styles Have Changed	47	The Love of My Life
24	Books Worth Buying	48	Honesty Is the Best Policy

5. Prepare a detailed outline (see Appendix C) for a two- to four-minute, one- or two-point speech. After your instructor has evaluated the outline, reduce it to a keyword form for use in delivering the speech to the class. In general, choose topics that are mainly explanatory or informative rather than persuasive or entertaining.

6. Make simple one-page, main-point outlines of your classmates' speeches. Then give them to your instructor, who will feed them back to the speakers as a means of giving them insight into their organizational effectiveness.

7. Prepare only the introduction to a five- to ten-minute speech that you might use later. Make your general and specific purposes clear, and try to achieve all of the functions of a good introduction: attention, good will, fair hearing, orientation, purpose. (See the model outlines in Appendix C.)

11

Presenting information

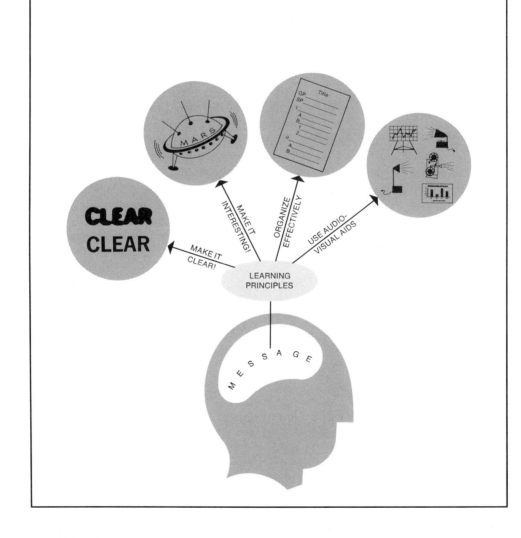

General learning outcomes

- We should learn four ways of increasing message clarity and support in an outline.
- We should learn seven ways to achieve interest in a speech.
- We should learn a four-step system of arrangement for speeches to inform.
- We should learn how to relate the choice and use of audiovisual aids to the cone of experience.
- We should learn to deal with questions and interruptions in audience-participation situations.

ACHIEVING CLARITY

Clarity is a primary objective in speech communication. Here are five verbal means of achieving clarity:

Illustration or Example

In a class speech a student teacher had as her specific purpose "to inform the class of the basic principles of solving discipline problems in the fourth grade." She could have proceeded to discuss "projections of insecurity and overt cognitive intellectualization assistance from an interacting teacher." The class was lucky. Instead she used specific examples from her own experience which made clear the complex problems of discipline and which were much more interesting. She opened her speech by describing an experience involving George Z. and his quirk of putting gum in little girls' hair. She followed this with the story of Bernard B., who, though a gifted child, took a special delight in swearing. Next she explained the psychological reasons for such behavior, then explained the proper means of discipline to apply. In a sense the whole speech was an extended example and it helped make her point clear. The more detail that's included, and the more vivid the incident, the more interesting it generally is. Very often, verbal illustration can be aided considerably by showing pictures or actual objects (perhaps a recording of Bernard B.'s language).

Richard Ryan made the confusing and often dull subject of taxes more understandable through the following illustration:

> Figured on a daily basis, the Tax Foundation estimates that it takes the average taxpayer 2 hours and 35 minutes out of each working day to satisfy the tax collector.
>
> It takes 1 hour and 38 minutes to meet the federal government's tax demands and 57 minutes to pay state and local taxes.
>
> The "tax bite" out of a taxpayer's working day is much greater than any other single expenditure.

The Tax Foundation estimates that it takes the average working man 1 hour and 28 minutes to meet his housing needs and 1 hour and 3 minutes of work each day to pay for food and beverages.

Other expenditures and daily time required to meet them, according to the foundation estimates, are:

Clothing, 30 minutes.

Transportation, 40 minutes.

Medical care, 24 minutes.

Recreation, 20 minutes.

All other needs, 1 hour.

The daily tax requirement is down this year because of the tax cut.

But before you start to applaud the cut, consider this:

In 1930, the worker satisfied his tax needs in 57 minutes. In 1940, it was 1 hour and 28 minutes. Ten years later, it was 2 hours and 1 minute. In 1960, it was 2 hours and 22 minutes.[1]

If you have had no firsthand experience with a particular topic, you can often draw your examples from people who have had such experience. An excellent speech on aerial acrobatics was delivered by a student who had never been in an airplane: He gave examples from the experiences of three veteran stunt pilots. Or you can use a hypothetical example, a made-up story, to illustrate a point. You might start, "Suppose you were flying at 10,000 feet..." or, "Imagine yourself in this predicament..." The hypothetical example does not carry the solid proof of a real one, but it does clarify. The major problem is an ethical one: Make sure the hypothetical is never taken for the factual, and make sure it is in keeping with known facts.

Illustrations and examples are powerful ways of clarifying and supporting a point. In choosing yours make sure that they truly relate to the point being made. A totally offbeat example only hurts clarity in the long run.

Analogy or Comparison

Analogy can make a point vivid and clear. Analogies point out similarities between things already known or understood and things not known. In trying to explain the gigantic size of our galaxy, the following analogies should help:

At 186,000 miles per second light travels 6,000,000,000,000 miles a year, a distance equal to 240,000,000 trips around the earth. At this rate we could reach the sun in 8 1/2 minutes, the next nearest star in 4 1/2 years. If we started at age 20 and moved at the speed of light, we would be 80 before we reached the star Aldebaran. The really distant stars in our galaxy would take us thousands of years to reach!

How big and how heavy are the nuclei and electrons of an atom? Consider Figure 11.1.

[1] *The Detroit News*, May 6, 1975, p. 22.

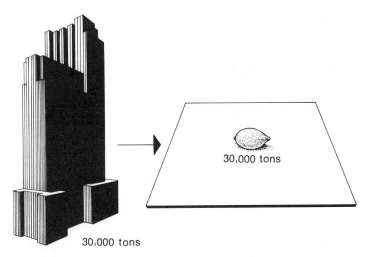

30,000 tons

30,000 tons

Figure 11.1 If all the nuclei and electrons that make up a skyscraper were squeezed together, they would be no longer than a cherry stone. But the cherry stone would weigh 30,000 tons, the same weight as the skyscraper. From Margaret Bevans, ed., *The Golden Treasury of Knowledge* (New York: Golden Press, Inc., 1961), p. 1145.

Statistics

Using numbers to help make a point clear is not simple. Statistics are powerful evidence only if they are (1) meaningful to the audience and (2) related to the point. Statistics may cloud rather than clarify an issue. If you were trying to explain that the Ford Motor Company lost $1 billion trying to sell cars and trucks in North America last year while making $1.4 billion overseas, and that Ford plans to spend $20 billion on new plants and equipment between now and 1985, the following might clarify the billion statistic:

HOW MUCH IS A BILLION?

If you take a crisp $10,000 bill and put it on the ground and then put another $10,000 bill on top and then keep stacking up $10,000 bills until you have $1 million, the stack will be eight inches high. If you keep going until you reach $1 billion, the stack of $10,000 bills would be as tall as the Washington Monument.

With the typical suburban house selling for $72,000 a billion would buy 13,888 new houses. That's enough to provide shelter for all the citizens of Bloomfield Township, about 40,000 people.

A billion could build three Renaissance Centers, with enough change left over to construct a chair lift to Canada.

Taking a figure of $28,000 to cover the full salary and benefit costs of a single auto worker, a billion could employ 35,700 workers for a full year.[2]

[2]*Monthly Detroit*, April 1980, p. 50.

Figure 11.2   WIZARD OF ID. By permission of Johnny Hart and Field Enterprises, Inc.

Make statistics concrete by relating them to things your audience knows. If you say that South America has serious economic problems because the average family income is $650 per year, it is clear. If you compare this figure to the $19, 684 of the United States and show that $650 comes to only $1.78 a day, it is clearer! We live more and more by statistics that predict things: vote predictions, insurance rates, measurements of cancer-causing things in a carton of cigarettes, average number of cavities in a group of children. We have learned to combine statistics with analogies to make sense out of outer-space distances. We express speed as Mach 1, 2, or 3 instead of miles per hour and we speak of distance in terms of light years.

Statistics can give a speech a sense of clarity if the speaker remembers to relate the statistics to known things and to make them meaningful to the audience.

Testimony

Testimony has great value in speeches to persuade but it also helps clarity. In a speech to inform, it may add *interest* to straight explanation.

In describing D-Day, for example, one can express the story more vividly by using testimony from a dozen GIs who hit the beaches:

> **0400, Pvt. Johnson:**   "There were ships and little boats and men all tangled up in one maze of confusion."
>
> **0430, Pvt. Sandrin:**   "The men coming down the cargo nets to the LCIs (Landing Craft Infantry) seemed to be 20 feet from the deck one minute and a step away the next."
>
> **0500, Pvt. Brown:**   "The LCI to our left just seemed to evaporate."
>
> **0600, Sgt. Glover:**   "Where the hell is the air cover?"
>
> **2300, Lt. Rucks:**   "This has been the longest day of my life."

An explanation of events is often clearer and more interesting with testimony.

Restatement

Restatement is not simply repetition. Rather it is saying the same thing in a different way. This is most useful with difficult material.

In Chapter 1 you found many different definitions of communication. All were trying to say the same thing. One definition was a long paragraph; another, a short paragraph. Still another reduced the definition to encoding and decoding. This was restatement to ensure clarity. If the meaning was not clear to you in one definition because of sentence structure or in another because of vocabulary, you were given still more opportunities to understand. If you understood all the definitions at first glance, fine. Assuming that it is not overdone, this kind of repetition can help ensure clarity. Remember the value of restatement. When your subject or vocabulary is difficult or new to the audience, try saying the same thing in different ways.

DEVELOPING INTEREST

Another primary objective in presenting information is developing interest. What things tend to interest all of us? How can they be used to motivate the audience to pay attention? Much of an audience *interest* is, of course, dependent upon the speaker's delivery. But we are now concerned with speech content. The seven factors listed next can promote interest.

Specificity

When a speaker says, "Let me show you what I mean by dog-tired," you probably pay closer attention than if he or she simply stated that some people were tired. For example:

> The men of Hurricane Camille's Red Cross rescue group thought after two days of forced march through wreckage-strewn coastal areas that they were dog-tired. Then they saw the remote victims of the storm, who seemed to be moving on sheer instinct and determination alone. They staggered through their broken homes with drooping shoulders, so physically drained that it seemed to take every last ounce of strength to put one foot in front of the other.

Specificity and reality are more interesting than vague explanations. Instead of saying, "A boy was run over," be specific: Call the boy by name; indicate his age; identify the car. "Mark Scott, age six, ran into the street to greet his mother, who was approaching from the other side, and was dashed to the pavement by a 1984 Thunderbird traveling at the thirty-mile speed limit."

Conflict

TV westerns and police stories always seem to pit "bad guys" against "good guys." This conflict and fighting pay off in viewer interest. Can you imagine *Hill Street Blues, Dallas,* or the soaps without conflict? Sports contests, even those whose outcomes are virtually assured, interest most people. Disagreement and conflict have elected and have destroyed many a politician, but almost always in an interesting way! If in your examples, illustrations, and explanations you can use conflict, your speech should interest the audience.

Novelty

Novel means different, unusual, contrasting, or strange. Novelty adds interest. Of course, if a subject is so unusual that listeners cannot relate it to their experience, interest may be lost rather than gained.

Novelty is not limited to the strange or odd. Average things become novel if the world about them is in contrast. At one time a bikini would have been a novelty because of its contrast with most other swimsuits. Now a woman would probably create more interest wearing an old-fashioned neck-to-ankle suit of the early 1900s. New Yorkers find nothing unusual or novel about their skyscrapers, but visitors themselves might become novelties to the natives by staring up into low clouds that hide the top of the World Trade Towers.

The unusual, the contrasting, the strange, the rare, and the generally different things in life are more interesting than the run of the mill. Let your examples, analogies, and explanations be novel for added interest.

Curiosity

Young children seem to ask an endless series of questions. Grown children (men and women) are not really much different. They may only become a little more specific about the subjects about which they want to know and the questions they ask. Humans seem to have to find out what lies around the corner or beyond the stars. Each new discovery in space leads to added suspense about what the universe is really like and to the big question, "Is there life out there?"

Unanswered questions, uncertainty, suspense—use these to arouse interest.

Immediacy

Issues of the moment or of the occasion can be used to arouse attention and interest. One training director has the rare ability to memorize names and remember facts about a person after just one meeting. He once startled a group of forty on the second day of a course by calling each by name throughout a two-hour period: "Mr. William Sandy, what do you think of . . . ?" Needless to say, interest was high. Class members never knew when he would call their names, state their home towns, and ask their opinions.

A reference to a previous speaker or to a recent incident that is known to the audience can also heighten interest. In a speech in Grand Rapids, Michigan, a speaker noticed several members of his audience staring out the window at the fast-falling snow. They were probably concerned about the snow rather than uninterested in the speaker. In any event, the speaker too looked toward the window, paused, and commented, "Misery loves company. We have eighteen inches of snow in Detroit and you have forty-two inches. The weather forecaster is predicting clearing skies in the next few hours." The audience seemed more attentive after that. Not only had a distraction been acknowledged, but the audience felt more closely attuned to the speaker.

Time spent learning about the speech occasion, the audience, last-minute headlines, and all other matters of the moment is time well spent. It helps make your speech interesting.

Humor

If you do not tell a joke well or if you find it difficult to be humorous, perhaps you need not be too concerned. Research on humor seems to indicate that in *persuasive* speeches humor has little effect on the outcome. Audiences listening to humorous and nonhumorous speeches on socialized medicine were equally persuaded by both speeches. One study of humorous and nonhumorous *information* lectures did show better student *retention* of the humorous lectures. In any event, funny stories, if told well, have probably helped many an otherwise dull speaker.

There is, however, no feeling quite as desperate as the one that results from viewing a poker-faced audience after you have told your best joke. If you do include a humorous story, make sure it is related to either the subject or the occasion. Make sure you can tell it fluently. Make sure you remember the punch line.

Make sure that it won't offend your audience. The best advice of all is to try it out on a small group of your friends. In other words, *practice.*

Vital Factors

If you have the FM radio playing and you hear, "Alert! Alert! Please turn to the Conelrad triangles on your dial," you would probably do as told. The reason is obvious. Staying alive, protecting your loved ones, defending your home—these are all vital concerns to you. You are interested because you have to be!

Using vital factors will gain your audience's attention. Self-preservation, reputation, jobs, property, and freedoms are truly vital. More is said about the role of these factors in Chapter 12.

ORGANIZING INFORMATION

Arrangement Systems

One method of organizing was voiced by the gifted speaker Chauncey Depew: Tell them what you're going to tell them; tell them; and then tell them you've told them.

Let's revise this and add a fourth step in Figure 11.3. Here's what we end up with: *attention, overview, information,* and *review.*

1. Get their attention.

2. Overview what you're going to say.

3. Give 'em the information.

4. Review and reinforce what you've said.   **Figure 11.3**

The interest factors are excellent means of gaining attention. In a speech "to inform the class about the problems facing India," one speaker opened with the following (*attention* and *interest*): "Did you know that half of the world's population is illiterate and that one-third of this half lives in India? Did you know that over 300 languages are spoken in India? That 14,000 babies a day are born in India?" He then discussed each of these three points. He gave us the detailed *information.* At the close of the speech, he repeated the three points. He also summarized some of the details from the *information* step. In other words, he "told them what he told them."

The value of this four-part development is clear. You may add an occasional internal summary, review, or preview in the *information* step. One study clearly shows that audiences listening to well-organized speeches remember more than those hearing poorly organized speeches. Organization may be aided by following the four-part scheme: *attention, overview, information,* and *review.* A model outline follows.

Model Outline

INTRODUCTION TO MUSIC

General End: To inform.

Specific Purpose: To state and explain the fundamental concepts of music theory.

Attention

  I.   Play a few bars of music on the violin. (deomstration)

  II. Poke fun at the music majors in the class.

Overview

  I.   The kinds of notes.

  II. The musical staff.

  III. Methods of counting the notes.

  IV. Relation of these three points to an instrument.

A brackets the above (Introduction)

Information

  I.   The kinds of notes.

     A. Neutral notes: A, B, C, D, E, F, G.
     B. Sharp notes: a halftone up.   **Visual aid D (below)**
     C. Flat notes: a halftone down. **to be used here.**

  II. Explanation of the musical staff.

     A. The treble clef and melody.
        1. Contains 5 lines: E, G, B, D, F.
        2. Contains 4 spaces: F, A, C, E.
     B. The bass clef and rhythm.
        1. Contains 5 lines: G, B, D, F, A.
        2. Contains 4 spaces: A, C, E, G.

  III. Methods of counting the notes.

     A. Whole note gets 4 beats.
     B. Half note gets 2 beats.
     C. Quarter note gets 1 beat.
     D. Eighth note gets half a beat.

  IV. Relation of these points to a musical keyboard.

     A. The notes (whether neutral, sharp, or flat) correspond to the lines and spaces in the staff.
     B. The position of the notes on the staff determines what note or key is to be played on the musical instrument.
     C. The number of beats the note receives tells how long the note is to be played on the instrument.

B brackets the above (Body)

Review

  I.   I have tried to make clear the following four factors of musical theory:

     A. The kinds of notes.
     B. The musical staff.
     C. Methods of counting the notes.
     D. Relating the theory to an instrument.

  II. Now you can start writing your own music or at least sneer at the music majors.

C brackets the above (Conclusion)

D = Visual aid (musical staff)

A = INTRODUCTION   B = BODY   C = CONCLUSION   D = VISUAL AID

Figure 11.4 Model Outline   Adapted from a student speech by Gary Carotta, Wayne State University.

VISUAL AIDS

Types of Aids

Visual aids help make a subject clear and build interest. Valuable as they are to the speaker, they are not without some problems: What kind of aid do I use in what situation? Can I use a *demonstration* as an aid? Teachers almost always ask for a demonstration speech, in part because it helps you to work off tension. Along with discussing familiar visual aids, this section relates the use of visual aids to demonstrations.

THE CONE OF EXPERIENCE. An expert on the use of teaching aids has given us a model for aids in terms of telling, showing, and doing. Those aids that allow the audience to "do" something are more direct than those aids that simply "show" something. "Telling" aids are the least direct. Direct experience is the most interesting.

Specific visual aids are listed in Figure 11.5. The top of the cone (the "telling" area) contains visuals that aid the audience: graphs, charts, cartoons, diagrams, flat pictures, blackboard sketches, and so on. Graphs that a speaker might use include pictograms, bar graphs, area diagrams, and line graphs. Charts include organization charts, stream or tree charts, and tabular charts.

The aids in the middle of the cone (the "showing" area) are self-explanatory. These items bring the audience closer to reality than mere telling, but still not to the involvement found in doing.

The bottom of the cone (the "doing" part) contains aids such as artificial experiences and dramatic participation. These would include LINK trainers for pilots, weightlessness chambers for astronauts, and other simulators, as well as role playing situations. Perhaps in grade school you played a Pilgrim landing at Plymouth Rock or Paul Revere. In job-training programs adults once again play roles: as irate supervisors, shop stewards, unhappy managers. Why? Because it is thought that playing roles involves the individuals and approaches real experience. Figures 11.6 through 11.8 show some visual aids.

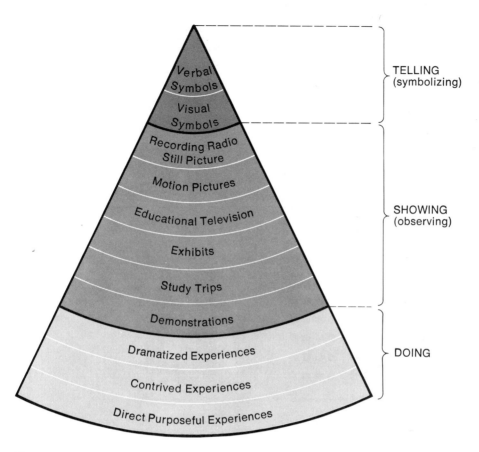

Figure 11.5 The cone of experience   From Edgar Dale, *Audio Visual Methods in Teaching*, 3rd ed., Copyrights 1946, 1954, 1969 by Holt, Rinehart & Winston. Reprinted by permission of Holt, Rinehart & Winston.

Year		Millions
2000		340
1985		258
1975		220
1965		195

100 million
more Americans

Figure 11.6
Pictogram

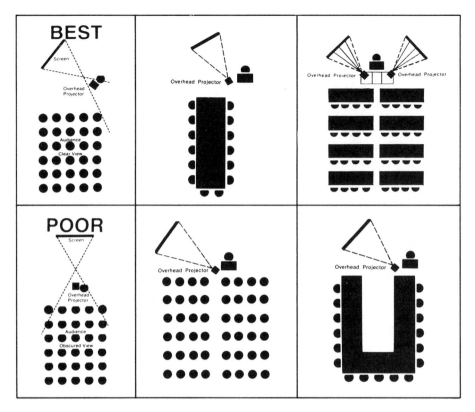

Figure 11.7 Area diagram showing use of overhead projectors From *Leaders Digest*, published by Audio Visual Division/3M.

Figure 11.8 Tree chart explaining the roots of modern languages

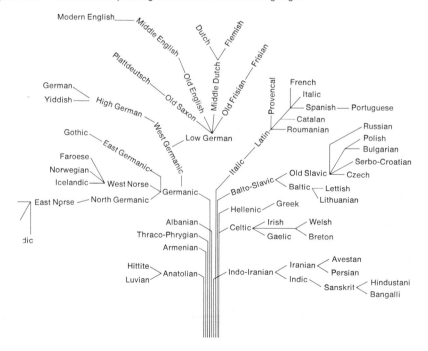

Demonstrations

A demonstration speech is a type of informative speech. A demonstration speech reduces anxiety and clarifies information. The purpose of a demonstration is to show how a skill, a procedure, a process, or a device is used. A demonstration combines showing with telling. "Show-and-tell" sessions in primary-school grades are excellent early speech-training exercises.

The value of demonstration is that the audience can learn by seeing. Demonstration also helps speakers remember their material; it appeals to several senses of the listeners; it saves time; and finally, it has dramatic appeal.

Demonstrations don't always work as planned. A few years ago commercials were not taped, as they are now. In a Westinghouse commercial Betty Furness, while swishing between refrigerator doors, had a door close on part of her lovely, full-skirted dress. Ms. Furness finished the commercial without the bottom half of her dress! The point is that she finished the speech. We can draw a lesson from this. In another fiasco, an announcer tied a Timex watch to the propeller of an outboard motor, lowered the propeller into a can of water, and started the engine. When the propeller was withdrawn, there, before millions of viewers, was a ruined watch badly in need of reassembly. What would you have done?

Sometimes, demonstrations can be dangerous. In another TV commercial a man added water to a bottle of pills and then shook the bottle to liven up the demonstration. The bottle blew up only moments after it was out of his hand!

Figure 11.9   Reprinted by permission of the Chrysler Corporation.

Classroom demonstrations are just as much fun as TV demonstrations, and can often be just as hazardous. A student once demonstrated a tear-gas pencil in an overheated, poorly ventilated classroom with the temperature outside about zero. Talk about audience involvement! Another student demonstrating the toughness of unbreakable, bulletproof glass, dropped the piece of glass on the concrete floor. It did not break—it exploded! This produced one badly shaken speaker. (A glass company spokesperson informed us later that the chances of the angle of impact, the temperature, the force, and other factors being perfectly coordinated—which caused the shattering—were about 1 in 10,000.)

What can you do to reduce the risk? If something does go wrong, what do you do at that moment of truth?

The answer to the first question is plan. Plan exactly *how* you will perform the demonstration. Make sure you have *all* your equipment and have it in the right order. Be sure the demonstration *works*. Emphasize safety precautions. Check for conditions that may vary from the practice session (for example, electric current). Finally, be sure *you* can do the demonstration. A flight instructor was teaching cadets the principles of airfoil and how an airplane wing develops lift. To demonstrate, he put a piece of paper between his lower lip and his chin. He then blew over the paper creating a partial vacuum on top of the paper, which caused it to lift. A new instructor who had observed this demonstration tried it in his next class without practice. Confident that he could do it, he proceeded to blow—with no movement from the paper and with an audience of cadets trying not to explode with laughter. Sometimes defeat is very evident.

The answer to the second question, "What do you do if it happens anyway?" is again plan. Calculate the extent and kind of risk and then plan emergency procedures for every foul-up you can think of. This is a must. You have no time to protect yourself when something does go wrong, and the shock and confusion may cause you to panic.

Pilots of high-performance aircraft have long talked of calculated risk and alternate procedures. There are preplanned procedures to meet emergencies. If two engines go out, what do you do? Talk it over? NO. You go to alternate plan two on a prearranged signal, thereby cutting confusion and perhaps saving your life. There is simply no time to respond in any other way.

The student with the "unbreakable" glass had a calculated risk of 1 in 10,000. One can hardly blame him for not having alternate procedures. These are better odds than a pedestrian has on the Los Angeles freeway. Nevertheless, this student could have had two pieces of glass, just as you should always have two bulbs for your slide or movie projector. However, having extra equipment or spare parts available is only part of the answer. The real problem is what you will say if something goes wrong with your demonstration. Plan this very carefully. *When and if the glass breaks I will say, "The odds on that happening were 1 in 10,000. Let me prove it by beating the next piece of glass with this hammer."* If the next piece breaks, you may have to resort to an alternate plan involving prayer. You can't win them all!

Some Practical Rules

USING AIDS

1. Never obstruct the vision of your audience. Make sure the lectern or stand is out of the way. Try not to stand in front of your materials.
2. Use your aids to help, not to distract. Introduce them when they fit the message.
3. Talk to the audience; "talk" to your visual aid only when you wish the audience to look at it.
4. Make sure you understand how and when you intend to use your visual aid. Orient your audience to the aid (for example, "This is a top view.").

PREPARING AIDS

1. Relate your choice of aids to the cone of experience, the audience, your subject, and your specific purpose.
2. Make a visual aid really visible. Is it big enough? Are the lines heavy and dark enough (one-eighth to one-half inch thick)?
3. Make each visual aid clear. Do not put too much detail or too many ideas on one aid. Label all parts clearly. Keep the aid simple enough so that you will be able to explain it easily and quickly.
4. Organize the aid logically. This will make it easier for you to remember your speech when using the aid.

AUDIENCE PARTICIPATION

Generating Participation

Some audiences just seem to spring into action. Others, even with very skilled speakers, must be given a push. Here are several techniques to start things off:

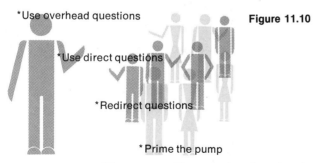

*Use overhead questions

*Use direct questions

*Redirect questions

*Prime the pump

Figure 11.10

[3]For some specific suggestions for using electronic aids (projectors), see Raymond S. Ross, *Speech Communication: Fundamentals and Practice,* 6th ed. (Englewood Cliffs, N.J.: Prentice-Hall, 1983), p. 228.

THE OVERHEAD QUESTION.   This is a direct question to the entire audience. You might try this technique if no questions arise from the audience (or even if they do): "Let me ask this question in order to get a reaction from an intelligent Midwestern audience." The immediate problem is to choose a question that will cause a reaction, for if there is still silence you may be worse off than before. Sometimes you can react to your own question in such a way as to promote participation. Before giving your speech carefully plan a few general overhead questions as a method of encouraging participation.

THE DIRECT QUESTION.   Ask a specific person a direct question. This technique is often very effective if the individual is known to the audience or is in some special way qualified to answer. The size of your audience may present a problem, in that the audience may have difficulty seeing who has been singled out. Classroom-size audiences respond well to this technique. You probably know many teachers who use the direct-question technique. Social and civic groups such as the Lions, Elks, Kiwanis, Knights of Columbus, and Rotary, whose members know one another, often make good use of direct questions.

Try not to call on the same person all the time, but do pick those who are most apt to get participation started. Try to tailor the question directly to the individual chosen. The question should be relatively short and clear and should demand more than a simple *yes* or *no* answer.

THE REDIRECTED QUESTION.   (Also called the reverse method or the relay method.) Redirect a question to the person who asked it: "That's a very good question—how would you answer it?" Or, in the relay method, redirect the question to some other person: "A good question; let's see how Mrs. Wright would answer it." A third approach is to aim the question at the audience in general.

As a rule, do not redirect a question unless you yourself know at least a partial answer to it. An exception to this rule is a simple question of fact upon which you can freely admit ignorance. A beginning teacher redirected a tough question (to which he did not have the answer) to each individual of the class, only to find that it came right back to embarrass him. Do not redirect so freely that you lose control of the situation.

PRIMING THE PUMP.   This is the technique of building questions into your speech. Your questions or implied questions should develop your point, stimulate audience thinking, and encourage participation.

Questions and Interruptions

In this section we discuss methods of dealing with questions and interruptions and we consider the problems of audience participation. Every speech offers a chance for audience participation. Questions, comments, and objections from the audience may come at any time. You should always calculate the risk of

Figure 11.11   BLOOM COUNTY by Berke Breathed © 1982, The Washington Post Company. Reprinted with permission.

being interrupted or even heckled. Some speakers seem to ask for trouble by plead-
ing with the audience to interrupt for any reason whatsoever. Questions from a
very large audience of perhaps hundreds can be a real nightmare if there is no
system of handling questions. The Economic Club of Detroit has the audience of
800 to 1000 people turn in written questions, which are screened while the speaker
is still on the platform. When answering oral questions from the floor, be sure that
everyone in the audience has heard and understood the question. Listening to
answers without having heard the question is highly frustrating.

In some situations the speaker does want immediate audience participation. On the other hand, formal speakers, although they should be democratic,
must also cover their subjects and stay within their allotted times. Unreasonable
numbers of questions and interruptions have ruined many an otherwise good
speech and have shaken many an experienced speaker. The solution to the problem lies in the word *control*. Speakers must retain control. They must control audience participation in such a way as to do justice to the *audience*, the *material* to
be covered, and the *time* restrictions placed upon their speeches.

Most business training programs encourage audience participation. This
is as it should be, since people learn faster and better when they participate and
feel involved. The audience, particularly in training programs, is often invited to
interrupt. But if the speaker chases after every question, relevant or not, he or she
will soon be in serious trouble.

A well-known businessperson came to a training program as a guest instructor. He pleaded sincerely for interruptions and he *got* them—some good, some
bad, some ridiculous. He tried to react, answer, or comment on each equally. The
result was that he was unfair to his audience. He covered only one-fourth of his
material, and even this part was confused because of the free-for-all participation.
The audience's evaluation of him was unfavorable.

Another situation in which you may find yourself is the open forum after
a speech. Although the problems just described also apply here, they are less likely,
because you have much better control of your time. You have probably covered
the main points before opening the forum to questions. You can control whatever

time is left by simply cutting off the questions. Life can be miserable, however, when you are given three hours and have only one hour's material. The situation is just as bad when you have no time for a promised question period.

The third audience situation is the symposium forum. Any discussion situation obviously requires one to participate with the *other* members of the panel. However, a symposium forum usually allows one third of the total time for questions from the audience. Many convention programs are run this way. Once again, the rules and problems are similar to those discussed previously, except that a decision must often be made as to which panel members should respond.

General Principles and Rules

The *first* principle obviously ought to be,

> *"Know your subject and audience."*

If you know your subject and audience, you are in a position to apply the *second* principle,

> *"Second-guess the situation."*

Try to guess what areas of your subject are most questionable and try to predict what questions this particular audience will ask. *Third,*

> *"Try sincerely to answer or at least react to all questions."*

Consider and react courteously to even the irrelevant questions, and attempt, if necessary, to clarify or postpone such questions. The *fourth* principle, and one that is very easy to overlook in your eagerness to meet the question asked, is,

> *"Consider carefully the rest of the audience."*

You must try to satisfy not only the person asking the question, but the total audience as well. Otherwise, you might satisfy the statistician, for example, while thoroughly confusing everybody else. *Fifth,*

> *"Do not feel or act as if you know everything or have to win every argument."*

Finally,

> *"Attempt to encourage good questions and audience participation."*

It is very easy to discourage questions with even a slightly overbearing attitude. However, it is possible to be so overbearing that the audience decides to give you a bad time.

Leaders have to be on guard not to put down others simply because of their positions. The colonel who follows the manual's advice and asks the cadets, "Are there any dumb questions?" is not apt to get many. But he knows *that*. That is why he says it. When such an attitude is *not* intended, however, it is most unfortunate.

RULES FOR ANSWERING QUESTIONS.   At Purdue University an audience of about 400 students was listening to a famous philosopher. At the close of the speech the chairperson asked for questions from the audience. Most of the raised hands were in the first row, where the philosophy club had gathered. The speaker pointed to a hand in the first row, a mouth opened, and to those near the middle of the audience the question sounded like this: "I should zzum ug ask hrump zud Hegel?" The speaker moved to the lectern, stroked his chin, and said, "A very good question." He then proceeded to give what was probably a very good answer. The problem was that most of the audience did not understand the answer because they had not *heard* the question. The speaker handled three or four more questions in the same way. The audience became frustrated, then restless, and finally rude as it started to leave.

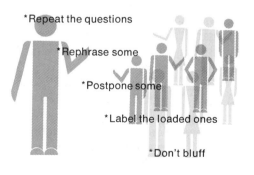

*Repeat the questions

*Rephrase some

*Postpone some

*Label the loaded ones

*Don't bluff

Figure 11.12

Repeat the question. This is the first rule. People who do not hear the question will attempt to figure out what the question must have been in terms of the answer. You can see the invitation this gives to confusion. Counterquestions based on bad guesses can really raise confusion to a high level. It is a good idea to repeat the question even with smaller audiences, for though everyone can hear, not everyone may be listening.

A question might be asked in a loud, clear voice, but with awkward or unclear wording. A famous army general was giving a speech at Ohio State University during a Middle East crisis. In the large audience were foreign students from all of the countries involved. One of these students took the general to task in clear English, but the question was long and complicated. The general said, "I know what you're getting at," and proceeded to answer for about ten minutes. As the general completed his answer, the foreign student leaped to his feet and gave another short speech, which said, "But that's not what I asked." The general tried again, for five minutes this time, but still with no success. After one more attempt, a desperate general finally held up his hand and said, "Let's see if we can agree on what the question is."

Sometimes it is necessary not only to repeat but also to *rephrase the question.* After rephrasing, you should always gain the approval of the questioner. Some ways of checking your restatement of the question are to ask the questioner if your phrasing is fair. See if the person's head is shaking *yes* or *no.* Pause a moment and see if the person objects verbally. You do not always have to rephrase questions. Do so only when it is necessary for clarity, and then always seek approval.

Some long, complicated questions deserve careful attention if they are on the issue and if you can answer in the time available. However, when you receive questions that, long or short, are off the topic, highly technical, or would consume the entire question period, you have a different kind of problem. Answering such questions can ruin an otherwise good speech. Though you do not want to avoid questions, you also owe it to the rest of your audience to stay on the subject and to give more than one person a chance to ask a question. Let us therefore formulate our third rule: *Postpone the off-topic, overly technical, or time-consuming questions.* Postpone these questions until after the official open-forum period or until the end of the period if you have time remaining. In interruption situations this rule becomes more complex, for a person may ask a question that you had intended to cover later in the speech. In this situation you should most often delay the answer until you arrive at that point. (You might say, for example, "Could I hold the answer to that for a few minutes? I will cover the issue a little later.") The problem is trying to remember the questions you may have postponed. One solution is to suggest that the person ask you again, but after you've covered the point at hand.

The loaded question is dangerous. Although sometimes people deliberately ask the *"Are you still beating your wife?"* kind of question, other times questions are posed that are unintentionally loaded. These are difficult to detect because they are frequently asked by people who are not troublemakers by reputation.

"Why is it that textbook writers have such inflated egos?" an author was once asked. If you are a writer, try to answer that without looking bad. Thus, rule four is: *Label a loaded question.* There are several ways to do this if you are lucky enough to detect such a question in time. The most effective way is to pause long enough for the audience to label it for you. An audience is often quick to chuckle if it sees that the speaker is faced with a "heads I win, tails you lose" situation. Or the speaker could say frankly, "That's a loaded question." A more tactful way might be, "It looks like I'm in trouble no matter how I answer this." Another method is to ask the questioner to please repeat the question. The audience will listen more closely and may label the loaded question for you, or the questioner may "unload" it. After you have successfully labeled or unloaded the question as courteously as possible, you should then attempt to answer. With the proper labels applied, the audience is not apt to be prejudiced by the question.

One sure way to get in trouble is to try to bluff your way through a question. Once an audience senses that you are bluffing, you can expect it to ask more questions specifically on this bluff point. The solution is to know your subject thoroughly—but if you do not have an answer, say so right away and save yourself the embarrassment of being trapped later on. No speaker is expected to have all the answers to all the questions in the world. This rule, then, might simply be called the "*I don't know*" rule.

A graduate student once learned the preceding advice the hard way. The occasion was her final oral examination. After twenty minutes of torture, the candidate finally blurted, "I guess I just don't know the answer." The rejoinder from the chairperson is worthy of a piece of marble: "We didn't expect you to answer the question, but we expected you to *know when you didn't know*. It is a wise person who knows when and what she doesn't know."

However, you cannot escape the hard facts of life by simply saying, "I don't know." In some question-answer situations you may wish to say, "I don't know, but I have an opinion," or "I don't know, but I can answer in terms of my specialty." The point is that you answer any question you are capable of answering and yet be honest enough to admit when you cannot.

SUMMARY

The primary principles in informative speaking are clarity, interest, and organization. Methods of achieving clarity include illustration or example, analogy or comparison, statistics, testimony, and restatement. The factors that create or add interest are specificity, conflict, novelty, curiosity, immediacy, humor, and vital concerns of the audience. Psychologically sound organization requires (1) gaining *attention*; (2) preparing the audience through a preview or *overview*; (3) presenting the detailed *information*; and (4) *reviewing* the significant points for added reinforcement.

Teaching aids are a vital part of public speaking, particularly when the goal is clarity. Edgar Dale's cone of experience is a good model for classifying these aids in terms of telling, showing, and doing, and on the basis of audience involvement. The model helps us make decisions about our selection and use of audiovisual aids by grading them according to abstractness. Some typical forms of visual aids that a speaker might use are pictograms, area diagrams, and tree charts.

The practical rules for reducing the hazards of demonstrations all include planning in advance: (1) calculate the risks; (2) devise alternate procedures, including what you will say if something goes wrong; and (3) make practice runs to ensure that you can perform the demonstration.

The general rules for using all teaching aids are: (1) make sure your audience can see your aids; (2) use them to reinforce, not distract; (3) talk to the audience, not to the visual aid; (4) relate your choice of an aid to the cone of experience; and (5) do not put too many ideas or details on any one aid.

To help generate audience participation, you may use the overhead technique—a question from the speaker to the total audience. You may ask a direct question of a specific member of the audience. You may use the redirect technique, which is to reverse or relay the question. In reversing, you redirect the question to the person who asked it; in relaying, you direct it to some other person. You are also counseled to prime the pump: to build questions into the formal part of your speech.

In the participation part of your speech, try not to call on the same person all the time; try to tailor your questions directly to the audience or to the individual you choose; keep your overhead or direct questions short, clear, and free of yes/no answers. In the main, your questions or implied questions should develop your point, stimulate audience thinking, and obtain attention and interest.

Typical audience-participation situations include open forums, symposium forums, instructing situations, and group discussion before an audience. Some general principles of speaking in an audience-participation situation are:

1.   Know your subject and audience.
2.   Second guess the situation.
3.   Try to answer or at least react to all questions.
4.   Consider the total audience.
5.   Do not grant opposing arguments reluctantly.
6.   Generally encourage questions.

Specific rules for answering questions are:

1.   Repeat the question.
2.   When necessary, rephrase the question.
3.   Postpone irrelevant or overly complicated questions.
4.   Label loaded questions.
5.   Don't bluff. Instead, say "I don't know."

STUDY PROJECTS

1.   Prepare a detailed two- to three-page outline for a four- to six-minute speech to inform that meets the message preparation tests of Chapters 9 through 11. (See Appendix C.)
2.   Prepare visual aids to accompany a four- to six-minute speech to inform that are designed to increase clarity and interest.
3.   Prepare a three- to four-minute speech to teach through demonstration that includes some audience participation and/or performance (for example, demonstrating knot tying, basic tennis shots, a dance step, crewel, basic golf, reading aloud, working a calculator, working a slide rule, timing an engine, sketching a landscape, a card trick, shooting dice, solving a puzzle, tying a bow tie, folding a flag, walking like a model). Offer a careful demonstration for your listeners to follow. Help them personally with any difficulties they may be having. Be specific about the items or steps of the process you want them to remember the most.
4.   Prepare an informative talk on your favorite hobby. Use visual aids and/or demonstration.

5. Analyze speech manuscripts or editorials and find, if possible, one example of each of the following types of support: illustration, analogy, statistics, and testimony.

6. Analyze speech manuscripts or editorials and find, if possible, one example of each of the following ways of increasing interest: specificity, conflict, novelty, curiosity, immediacy, humor, vital concerns, figures of speech (pp. 252–53).

7. Prepare an informative or instructional four- to six-minute speech in which you attempt to generate audience participation. Use overhead, direct, and redirect questions. Make sure you cover your material and stay within the minimum and maximum time limits.

8. Assume you have just spoken to your classmates on a topic that is currently in the news. Now prepare for a two- to three-minute open forum. Anticipate the key questions, and give some thought to answers. Remember to follow the five basic rules for answering questions.

12

The psychology of persuasion

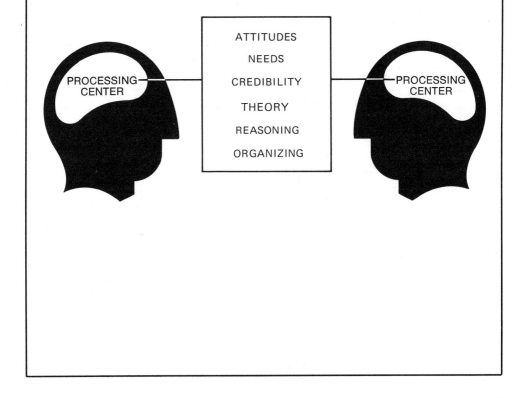

PROCESSING CENTER

ATTITUDES

NEEDS

CREDIBILITY

THEORY

REASONING

ORGANIZING

PROCESSING CENTER

General learning outcomes

- We should learn about human attitudes.
- We should learn about human needs and how they relate to persuasion.
- We should learn about credibility.
- We should learn how to apply theory to persuasive messages.
- We should learn the importance of evidence, proof, and reasoning.
- We should learn to detect strategies, theories, and fallacies being directed at us.

DEFINITIONS

Since ancient times, we have tried to find simple explanations of what motivates people to do what they do. To find out Aristotle suggested that, "the proper study of man is man himself." The assumption is that all humans are much alike. At the physiological level this presents few problems, for despite obvious differences in height, weight, and color, all people are quite similar. We could hardly have a science of medicine were this not true. On the other hand, Plato argued that to study man one must study the world around him; for Plato, man was a reflection of his society.

Today, we say that one must understand both humans and their environment in order to understand human motivations.

The Social Imperatives

To live in a democracy we must understand how people are persuaded. Persuasion is the major means of settling problems, selling ideas and products, and changing people's attitudes. Persuasion is the heart of advertising and political campaigns. Persuasion is central to leadership and interpersonal relations; it is the substitution for force.

CAMPAIGNS. As receivers, we hear and see endless appeals on radio and television and in print. Rarely are these "one-time" persuasion efforts. Although they could stand alone, they are almost always part of larger campaigns of persuasion.

One division of a major automobile maker spends over $95 million a year on advertising. You had better believe there is a master plan or campaign. This plan schedules and coordinates all of the commercials, the car shows, the news releases—even "punt, pass, and kick" contests—for best effect. Persuasion *is* the business of advertising and marketing. It is clearly also in the consumer's best interests to understand the techniques of persuasion.

In a democracy, hard-fought persuasive political campaigns replace revolution and force as instruments of change. Political campaigns sell candidates, programs, and promises. Candidates' speeches are carefully prepared to meet the main issues at the right time. Even timing the announcement of a candidacy is part of the campaign strategy. We can become better citizens by understanding these techniques.

SOCIAL COMPLIANCE. When political issues get very heated, we are tempted to put persuasion aside in favor of more direct action. Even a democracy needs a means to ensure that persuasion, not force, is used. The means of achieving compliance usually comes in the form of *laws*. We avoid violence or unfair action, in part, to escape legal punishment. *Social pressure* also persuades us to comply even with programs that are unpopular—for example, a dress code in school or a large social program like busing. That social pressure all too often may cause us to break the law is also painfully clear. The offer of *rewards* also persuades us to restrain ourselves to do things we might not otherwise do. Employers reward with promotions, teachers with grades, parents with allowances.

LEADERSHIP. Leaders of organizations, private and public, have great need of persuasion talents. The modern leader has little harsh clout left. To fire a person a week for no reason other than to keep everybody honest is really a practice of the past. Unions, labor laws, social pressure, and government programs motivate leaders to use persuasion. A reckless loss-of-job threat loses much of its sting in the face of supplementary unemployment programs and welfare programs. Employee benefits, training, affirmative action, communication programs, working conditions, grievance procedures—these are the tools of the modern persuasive leader. It's the *threat* of the strike rather than the strike itself that usually causes changes in behavior, if not attitude. Most union-management problems are successfully resolved through negotiations and persuasion. We hear and read about the minority that are not.

INTERPERSONAL RELATIONS. How we treat others near us is a large part of how we influence them. Interpersonal persuasion is an important part of campaigns, social compliance efforts, and leadership. How we perceive others—and they us—affects our personal persuasion. For all the efforts of the mass media, we still spend most of our communication time talking and listening to others. Improving your interpersonal sending and receiving is strong reason for studying persuasion.

Attitudes

Persuasion is an attempt to change or maintain the *attitudes* of others. These attempts to change attitudes are usually directed at some related behavior: obtaining a vote, selling a product, achieving compliances.

An attitude is a tendency to respond in a given way. It may express itself in the way one *thinks* (cognitive aspect), the way one *feels* (affective aspect), or the way one *behaves* (behavioral aspect).

Opinions are essentially the same as attitudes; for some an opinion connotes a more superficial or less enduring form of attitude. The concept of attitude also encompasses *beliefs* and *values*. Our beliefs are what we think. We think (or believe) a thing to be true or false. Pigs are dirty. Cats are sneaky. Attitudes, on the other hand, are more concerned with favorable-unfavorable dispositions. I don't like pigs. I love cats. We develop our attitudes, in part, on what we believe.

Value is a broad concept, usually made up of many beliefs and attitudes. Values are not always logical, but they affect how we think, feel, and behave. They build from experience, the environment, perhaps even frustration. Money has become a controlling value for many. For others civil liberties are important values. Values are *systems* that hold attitudes together. Knowing a person's value system often enables us to predict attitudes on smaller issues. Knowing a person holds a strong, positive value about women's liberation might allow us to predict that person's attitude about the Equal Rights Amendment.

Attitudes are thought to serve different functions. As receivers we can see how our attitudes function to decode persuasion. As senders our success may depend on how accurately we assess why an audience holds a specific attitude.

Some attitude purposes are quite *practical*. We form favorable attitudes toward persons who make us feel good about ourselves. We usually form favorable attitudes toward things that reward us: high grades, money, special privileges. The practical function also surfaces in unfavorable attitudes. We usually form very practical attitudes against punishment or low grades.

Many of our attitudes *express our values*. Their function is to maintain and promote our value systems and our self-concepts. If we strongly value clean air, we would have unfavorable attitudes toward smoking and fluorocarbons. We feel more consistent, more comfortable, that way.

Some attitudes serve to *defend our egos*. All of us are somewhat directed by our own self-interests. Egoism is thought by some to be a major motivator of all human conduct. We defend our own welfares and advancements above all else. Take care of number one! The function of this attitude has been called *ego defensive*. It is most often difficult to change and frequently destructive. Attitudes serve various functions. Among them are practical ones, value-expressive ones, and ego-defensive ones.[1]

A single attitude is seldom simple and seldom unrelated to other attitudes. Larger attitudes may be thought of as a cluster of related notions, some more important than others. Some attitudes involve more notions than others. For example, consider an attitude about marijuana. It's like a leaf or daisy with plus and minus petals (notions) sized according to importance.

[1]Daniel Katz, "The Functional Approach to the Study of Attitudes," *Public Opinion Quarterly*, 24 (1960), 163–204. (Katz also considers knowledge to be a function of attitude).

Figure 12.1
An attitude about marijuana

In Figure 12.1 the prevailing attitude is negative (-22, $+15$) and gives a measure of strength. We say more about how we resolve these uncomfortable differences in positive and negative feelings later. For now it helps us see the complex nature of attitudes.

Measuring attitudes is difficult because we can't see them. We infer attitudes from what people do or what they tell us. Consider the statement of attitude in Figure 12.2.

The attitude our plant cluster (Figure 12.1) illustrates would appear to fall in number 3 on the graph in Figure 12.2. However, we're not really sure. Although marijuana's illegality greatly affected (-9) this person's attitude toward *use*, he or she might lean toward legalization. Suppose a person, Daisy, did check number 3 in Figure 12.3. If that were really the only position she cared about, she might be difficult to persuade. But suppose a range of positions matched her attitude. Perhaps she could also live with 2 and 4. We could label these acceptable positions.

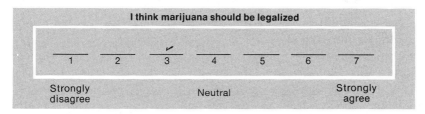

Figure 12.2

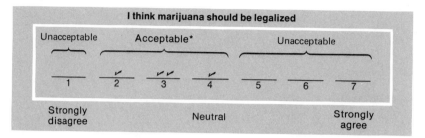

Figure 12.3

Perhaps she found positions 5, 6, 7, and 1 unacceptable. Now we have more attitude information.

Although position 3 is *most* acceptable, Daisy's range includes the neutral position. Persuasion looks more promising.

Next, suppose Daisy had a large range or latitude of *noncommitment* on the following scale:

I think natural gas prices should be deregulated

Unacceptable	Noncommitment	Unacceptable

| 1 | 2 | 3 | 4 | 5 | 6 | 7 |

Strongly disagree   Neutral   Strongly agree

Figure 12.4

Assuming she is interested or involved enough to listen, we could infer that Daisy would be easy to persuade (either way). However, if her range was very narrow and her most acceptable position was still 4, she might be very difficult to persuade. She has rejected all the other positions! See Figure 12.5.

In general, the wider the range of *rejection* (unacceptable positions), the more ego defensive Daisy becomes and the more difficult to persuade. The wider range of *acceptance* or the range of *noncommitment*, the less Daisy's ego is involved and the easier it is for her to change her attitude.

I think natural gas prices should be deregulated

Unacceptable	Noncommitment	Unacceptable

| 1 | 2 | 3 | 4 | 5 | 6 | 7 |

Strongly disagree   Neutral   Strongly agree

Figure 12.5

These three positions have been called *latitudes* of acceptance, rejection, and noncommitment.[2] They have also been referred to as ego-involvement theory.

When inferring attitudes about others we should remember to discount seemingly obvious causes if other plausible causes are also present.[3] Our impressions of others and our attitude attributions to them can often be more accurate by simply *taking another look*. Try to observe the people or person in different contexts. Determine also if people are under special external pressure. Is there free choice or does the job or situation dictate all or part of the behavior? Another, often overlooked, way of gathering more information before attributing attitudes is to ask the opinions of other respected observers.

The Concept of Multimotivation

Seldom are we persuaded by one thing alone. Success and satisfaction foster motivation. So do failure and dissatisfaction. We are motivated by *need* and by *plenty*. We learned earlier that we are persuaded through social compliance and laws. We have, then, avoidance needs as well as growth needs.

Our human motives have been defined by Krech and Crutchfield as *survival, security, satisfaction,* and *stimulation*.[4] These are grouped into *deficiency* motives (survival and security) and *abundancy* motives (satisfaction and stimulation). Deficiency motivation is characterized by needs to avoid danger, threat, disruption, discomfort . . . Abundancy motivation is characterized by desires to grow, discover, create, enjoy, achieve . . .

While we are being motivated in this manner, we are also being persuaded by appeals both to our *logic* and our *emotions*. When we are persuaded to buy a product, take a position, or join a cause, how much of our behavior is based on reasoned discourse? How much on appeals to our emotions? More evidence that humankind is multimotivated!

Sometimes the sender doesn't influence us as much as the *people* between the sender and us. On hearing a political candidate take a stand on a hot issue, we might suspend judgment until we check with others. Friends, family, and people we respect are often *intermediary* persuaders. Opinion leaders are intermediaries who screen and shape the attitudes of all of us. Between us and a persuasion source may be several *significant others*. In complex campaigns and in shaping attitudes on social issues persuasion is probably a multistep process rather than a two-step flow.

The various motivations just discussed are in part *verbal*, in part *nonverbal*. Some experts think the nonverbal has more impact than the verbal. That our non-

[2]From assimilation-contrast theory. See Muzafer Sherif and Carl Hovland, *Social Judgment* (New Haven: Yale University Press, 1961).

[3]Harold H. Kelley, "The Processes of Causal Attribution," *American Psychologist*, 28, no. 2 (1973), 108.

[4]David Krech and Richard S. Crutchfield, *Elements of Psychology* (New York: Alfred A. Knopf, 1958), p. 279.

verbals may unintentionally contradict our verbals should intrigue would-be persuaders. Our nonverbal codes, except in isolation, are interpreted quite accurately, particularly in expressing emotions such as love and leadership.

In sum, all of us are multimotivated. While one particular appeal may be the big one that triggers a change, other factors come into play in the total persuasive effect.

Persuasion, Influence, and Motivation

In simple terms *persuasion is a means of influencing others.* It involves *attitudes.* Attitudes are a tendency to respond in a given way. People respond in terms of how they *think, feel,* or *behave.* Attitudes express our beliefs and values. They also reflect and defend our egos. Larger attitudes are clusters of related notions. Attitudes usually fall within a range of latitude. This range, if known, is extremely useful to the persuader. To restate, *persuasion is a means of influencing others' thinking, feeling, and/or behavior.*

In this definition *persuasive influence* must protect a receiver's right to *choice.* "Your money or your life" may involve influence or motivation, but it does not afford viable choice. If the receiver is to be given choice, *persuasive* influence must exclude physical violence. We can now add the words *through nonviolent techniques* to our definition. However, social pressure and compliance efforts are usually acceptable means for social persuasion.

Much motivation, violent or otherwise, comes from the social and physical environment all around us. One must reckon with it. However, this chapter concentrates on *rhetorical messages intended to persuade* others through finding common cause with them.

Persuasion is rarely a one-time or one-shot effort. Almost always each message is part of a larger plan or campaign. Senders and receivers must consider this fact while encoding or decoding a specific appeal.

Senders must analyze and predict audiences to be effective persuaders. If a receiver understands who the sender is trying to persuade, he or she can gain insight into the sender's strategy. If choice really is operating, then most persuasion is self-persuasion. Receivers persuade themselves. If we do persuade ourselves, we have still more reason to learn why we do the things we do. Every good *sender* starts with knowing audience attitudes. Every good *receiver* should start with knowing him or herself and recognizing the techniques of persuasion.

Our simple definition of persuasion spoke of *a means of influencing others.* We extended *others* to include their attitudes. This led us to define persuasion as *a means of influencing the thinking, feeling, and behavior of others.* Our discussion of choice led us to add the words *through nonviolent techniques.* The word influence was taken to mean through *intended rhetorical messages.* However, there are other forms of influence.

In sum, *persuasion is a nonviolent rhetorical means of ethically influencing the thinking, feeling, and/or behavior of others.* There is no lasting persuasion without honesty, freedom from violence, receiver choice, tolerance for strategy, fair hearing, and a willingness to comply with persuasion from legitimate authority. In a democracy, ethical persuasion should be the major means of social influence.

HUMAN NEEDS

All people are thought to have the following kinds of needs: physiological, safety, belonging, esteem, and self-actualization.[5]

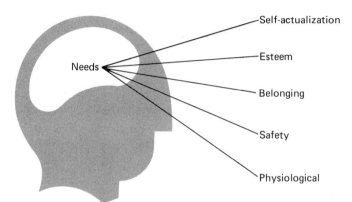

Figure 12.6

Physiological Needs

Biologically we are all strikingly similar. Doctors use the same anatomy chart for each of us. They search for the heart in the same place in each of us. The human body operates according to a master plan that governs survival. The body is composed of 21 trillion cells, which are organized into body systems, tissues, and bones. The human body is a tough, adaptable, survival-oriented organism—but one with limitations. It can't survive without oxygen for longer than ten minutes; it can tolerate no more than ten degrees change in body temperature; it must have food, water, rest, and even love. These needs are essential to self-preservation. When the biological needs are not being met, important social needs will be ignored.

The primary physiological needs are: (1) oxygen; (2) food; (3) water; (4) rest; (5) exercise; (6) avoidance of bodily damage; and (7) excretion. Although these needs start within the body, they must be met from outside the body. Even at the basic level of food and water, we can choose how we will meet our needs. But whether we choose water, milk, or beer, we must satisfy our basic need for fluids.

[5]Abraham H. Maslow, "A Theory of Human Motivation," *Psychological Review,* 50 (1943), 370–96.

Safety Needs

We are concerned here primarily with psychological safety. We desire security, we avoid personal violence, harm, or disease. Most often, we prefer a safe, predictable environment to one plagued by unknown events. This protective desire may prompt us to be concerned with insurance and with jobs that offer security first and high wages second.

Like physiological needs, our needs for psychological safety do not dominate our lives except in times of emergency or danger. Many people see change as a threat to their security. A change in a work routine, even when carefully explained, often causes visible anxiety. The change in environment experienced by first-year college students is often an extreme threat to their safety needs. As a consequence they may be quite open to persuasion that promises more security in terms of campus organizations, housing, trips home, and friends. The first year of military service is similarly threatening. All of us have a strong desire for psychological safety.

Belonging Needs

Some use the term *love* for this group of needs. People must be loved and in turn must express their love. Sharing our lives with others is important to us and we often react quickly if we think that this need will be denied. We find satisfaction for belonging needs most often through our families and close friends. But beyond this we desire the approval and acceptance of our classmates, our fellow workers, and the many groups of people with whom we identify ourselves. We alter our behavior and perhaps even our standards in order to be accepted, to belong, to be loved by our chosen friends and groups. We must give as well as receive love to be well adjusted. Our lonely-hearts clubs offer evidence of this powerful need to give and share love. All too often dishonest persuaders have taken advantage of this need by only pretending to care for suffering people.

Esteem Needs

Once our physiological, safety, and belonging needs have been satisfied, our esteem needs come to the fore. We have a more active desire for recognition and respect, as well as a need to evaluate ourselves and achieve self-respect.

In our culture esteem needs are very important. Americans are often accused of being self-centered. Threats to our ego or self-esteem, whether real or not, often prompt swift reactions. Our radio and television commercials appeal to our esteem needs by emphasizing the prestige attached to certain expensive cars or by suggesting that our status in a group is threatened if we don't buy particular products.

The satisfaction of esteem needs leads to self-confidence and a feeling of personal worth. Attempting to meet esteem needs often leads to frustrations and personal conflicts. People want not only the recognition of their chosen groups but also the self-respect and status for which their moral and social standards call. When the price of acceptance is behavior that conflicts with one's standards, heroic choices are called for in order to remain well adjusted. People play many roles to satisfy some of the different groups to which they belong.

Some poorly adjusted individuals have esteem needs so great that they will seek achievement (or what they consider achievement) at the price of their own self-respect and morals. The so-called achievement motive is normal, although it can be carried to extremes.

Self-Actualization Needs

This might be called *self-fulfillment* or *self-realization*—the desire to reach the height of our personal abilities and talents. "What a person *can* be, he or she *must* be." This need becomes more important as the previous four needs are satisfied. In our culture it is very important. The large number of people of all ages who take courses in art, writing, or drama to satisfy creative urges is one response to self-actualization needs.

Picture this system of needs as steps. The higher needs become important only as the lower ones are largely satisfied (see Figure 12.7).

How satisfied is the average person? It's hard to say. Maslow suggests that the average person achieves the degrees of satisfaction shown in parentheses in

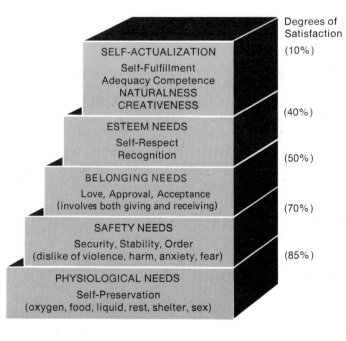

Degrees of Satisfaction

Figure 12.7
Steps to satisfying human needs

SELF-ACTUALIZATION
Self-Fulfillment
Adequacy Competence
NATURALNESS
CREATIVENESS
(10%)

ESTEEM NEEDS
Self-Respect
Recognition
(40%)

BELONGING NEEDS
Love, Approval, Acceptance
(involves both giving and receiving)
(50%)

SAFETY NEEDS
Security, Stability, Order
(dislike of violence, harm, anxiety, fear)
(70%)

PHYSIOLOGICAL NEEDS
Self-Preservation
(oxygen, food, liquid, rest, shelter, sex)
(85%)

Figure 12.7. Since a satisfied need is not a strong motivator, the smaller figures should indicate the areas in which we are most open to persuasion.

Appeals that a persuader might use can be roughly sorted as follows:

MOTIVE TERMS AND THE BASIC NEEDS

Physiological Needs	*Safety Needs*	*Belonging Needs*
1. Bodily comfort	1. Fear	1. Loyalty
2. Sex attraction	2. Conformity	2. Family affection
3. Physical enjoyment	3. Companionship	3. Sympathy
4. Hunger	4. Saving	4. Mothering
5. Activity	5. Conflict	5. Respect for Deity
6. Rest and sleep	6. Cleanliness	6. Sentiments

Self-Esteem Needs	*Self-Actualization Needs*
1. Pride	1. Creativeness
2. Reputation	2. Curiosity
3. Power	3. Constructiveness
4. Achievement	4. Ambition
5. Social distinction	5. Independence
6. Appearance	6. Freedom from restraint

CREDIBILITY

Credibility refers to the receiver's attitude toward the source. Aristotle used the term *ethos* to say the same thing. He set forth the general rule that "there is no proof so effective as that of the character." It may be more fact than fiction that "What you are speaks so loudly I can't hear what you're saying."

Source credibility is related to Aristotle's notions of *good will, good character,* and *good sense.* In modern times, source credibility has been discussed in terms of *good intentions, trustworthiness,* and *competence* or *expertness.* Source credibility involves trust and confidence based on the intent, position, knowledge,

Figure 12.8   The closed mind and source credibility   © 1961 United Feature Syndicate, Inc.

and sincerity of the speaker. Those with high source credibility generally produce greater attitude change. Both reason and research tell us that an untrustworthy speaker, regardless of his or her other qualities, will be less persuasive. Of course, an expert car thief would have a credibility born of his or her *competence* should he or she elect to explain his or her trade.

In its 1908 catalog, Sears Roebuck used the credibility of its bankers to persuade the customers that it was a respectable and responsible company (Figure 12.9).

Pragmatic ethical proof is credibility that is established during the sending of the message. It refers to the audience's impressions of the honesty, character, wisdom, and good will of the speaker.

Ethical proof is established or maintained when:

1. Others perceive us as having attitudes similar to theirs;
2. We use humor effectively;
3. We use evidence in our messages;
4. We deliver the message well.

We can destroy credibility if (1) we're perceived as faking our attitudes; (2) our humor is inappropriate; (3) our evidence is unfair; and (4) our voice and language are unsuitable for the occasion.

Figure 12.9 From Joseph J. Schroeder, Jr., ed., *1908 Sears, Roebuck Catalogue* No. 117 (Northfield, Ill.: DBI Books), p. 18.

ERNEST A. HAMILL, PRESIDENT
CHARLES L. HUTCHINSON, VICE PRESIDENT
CHAUNCEY J. BLAIR, VICE PRESIDENT
D. A. MOULTON, VICE PRESIDENT

JOHN C. NEELY, SECRETARY
FRANK W. SMITH, CASHIER
B. G. SAMMONS, ASS'T CASHIER
J. EDWARD MAASS, ASS'T CASHIER

No. 5106

THE CORN EXCHANGE NATIONAL BANK
OF CHICAGO
CAPITAL $3,000,000
SURPLUS $3,000,000

CHICAGO, October 22, 1907.

TO WHOM IT MAY CONCERN:
    We are pleased to testify to the responsibility of Sears, Roebuck & Company. The company enjoys the highest credit with their Chicago banks, of which this bank is one.
    We believe anyone who has dealings with this company will be treated in the fairest manner possible. We confidently assure anyone who is thinking of placing an order with them, that, in our judgment, there is absolutely no risk in sending the money with the order.
    Yours very truly,

Frank W. Smith

Cashier.

In writing to the above bank as to our reliability, be sure to enclose a 2-cent stamp for reply.

PERSUASION THEORIES

Persuasion theories assume that when new information is inconsistent with a person's notions and attitudes, it will lead to some confusion and tension. This tension may motivate people to adjust their attitudes or behavior. All of us seek an agreeable, balanced, *consistent* set of relationships between our notions of the world and our latest perceptions of it. *Consistency* refers to a kind of mental agreement between a person's notions about some object or event and some new information about it. It also involves the attitudes and images a person holds of the world. Inconsistency causes the tension that causes the motivation that may cause a change in attitude or behavior. Consistency theories provide us with many practical principles of persuasion.[6]

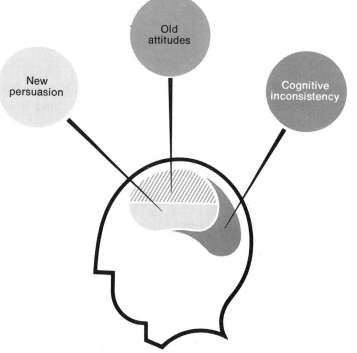

Figure 12.10.

[6]See Charles E. Osgood and Percy H. Tannenbaum, "The Principle of Congruity in the Prediction of Attitude Change," *Psychological Review*, 62, no. 1 (1955), 43; F. Heider, *Psychology of Interpersonal Relations* (New York: John Wiley, 1958), p. 190; T. M. Newcomb, "An Approach to the Study of Communication Arts," *Psychological Review*, 60 (1953), 393–404. See also T. M. Newcomb, "Individual Systems of Orientation," in *Psychology: A Study of a Science*, ed. S. Koch (New York: McGraw-Hill, 1959), volume 3, pp. 384–422; M. Rosenberg and R. Abelson, "An Analysis of Cognitive Balancing," in *Attitude Organization and Change*, ed. C. Hovland and M. Rosenberg (New Haven: Yale University Press, 1960), pp. 112–63; M. Rosenberg, "An Analysis of Affective-Cognitive Consistency," in *Attitude Organization and Change*, pp. 15–64; Leon Festinger, *A Theory of Cognitive Dissonance* (Stanford, Calif.: Stanford University Press, 1957), p. 3.

We seek to somehow keep our attitudes in harmony or consistent with the world around us. When faced with differing attitudes we tend to average them out according to their strength or power. Persuasion is then the result of this pressure. However, when inconsistency is so great as to be unbelievable, it backfires. During World War II, our shipbuilding production rate was so high that American propagandists reduced the actual figures for fear the enemy would not believe them and therefore be less likely to surrender.

These theories also suggest that we will avoid situations and messages that make us feel uncomfortable. We tend to communicate in such a way as to help us reduce this tension or strain. Attitudes consist of two elements: feelings and beliefs. We like to keep what we feel about an issue or person in balance with what we *believe*. When we are out of balance we must change either our feelings or our beliefs. The persuader who causes us to feel imbalanced or inconsistent has a good chance of changing our attitudes, if we don't simply reject his or her data.

Social judgment refers to our perception of how close a sender's attitude on an issue is to our own. If you see another's attitude as falling within your range of acceptance (as discussed previously), then, according to persuasion theory, you will judge it to be even closer to your central attitude than it really is. You *assimilate* the difference. Your attitude moves closer to that of the sender. If you see the sender's position as falling within your range of rejection, then you judge it to be even further from your central attitude than it is. You *contrast* your attitude with that of the sender, and you see it as more different than it actually is.[7] The theory also suggests that if you really have your ego involved in an issue, you'll have a much larger latitude of rejection. If you're firmly against abortion, for example, you will reject a wide range of proabortion appeals. Little ego involvement suggests a narrower range of rejection and a greater openness to persuasion. Persuading a person with a heavy ego involvement, on the other hand, is likely to be very difficult.

Both-Sides Persuasion

When your audience is "against" your message, is it more persuasive to use only those arguments "for" your side? Or, is it better to include those against? Research clearly shows that "presenting the arguments on both sides of the issue is more effective."[8] At least the opposition knows you have considered its side.

[7]See C. W. Sherif, M. Sherif, and R. E. Nebergall, *Attitude and Attitude Change: The Social Judgment-Involvement Approach* (Philadelphia: W. B. Saunders, 1965).

[8]Information and Education Division, U.S. War Department, "The Effects of Presenting 'One Side' Versus 'Both Sides' in Changing Opinions on a Controversial Subject," in T. M. Newcomb et al., *Readings in Social Psychology* (New York: Holt, Rinehart & Winston, 1947), pp. 566–77; see also C. I. Hovland, A. A. Lumsdaine, and F. D. Sheffield, *Experiments on Mass Communication* (Princeton, N.J.: Princeton University Press, 1949), pp. 201–27; Ralph L. Rosnow, "One-Sided versus Two-Sided Communication under Indirect Awareness of Persuasive Intent," *Public Opinion Quarterly*, 32 (Spring 1968), 95–101; and Glen Hass and Darwyn Linder, "Counterargument Availability and the Effects of Message Structure on Persuasion," *Journal of Personality and Social Psychology*, 23 (August 1972), 219–33.

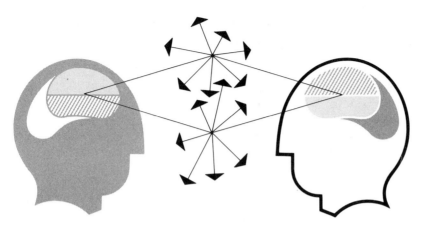

Figure 12.11

If the audience is already sold on your message, should you still give both sides? Obviously it is not as necessary. If you knew that the audience would later be exposed to counterpropaganda, what would you do?

Research has found that the groups persuaded with both sides of an issue were more resistant to counterpropaganda than those persuaded with one side. Only 2 percent of the group hearing one side maintained the desired attitudes when exposed to counterpropaganda. Sixty-one percent of those hearing both sides maintained the desired opinions. The researchers concluded that "a two-sided presentation is more effective in the long run than a one-sided one (a) when, regardless of initial opinion, the audience is exposed to subsequent counterpropaganda or (b) when, regardless of subsequent exposure to counterpropaganda, the audience initially disagrees with the commentator's position.[9]

Both-sides persuasion has appeal. It is an honest call for fair play. Opposing arguments are not omitted and, therefore, those who disagree are not as upset. The audience is more inclined to listen. Both-sides persuasion helps insulate audiences against counterarguments. However, speakers must be sensitive to the audience and aware of its attitudes, arguments, and issues. One speaker, after thoroughly researching both sides of his subject, reported that he became convinced of the "other" side. Both-sides persuasion is, then, (1) a most effective form of motivation and (2) a most logical form of preparation. It's a little like inoculating your receivers against the opposing arguments.[10]

[9]Arthur A. Lumsdaine and Irving L. Janis, "Resistance to Counter-Propaganda Produced by a One-Sided Versus a Two-Sided Propaganda Presentation," *Public Opinion Quarterly*, 17 (1953), 311–18.

[10]For a discussion of inoculation theory, see W. McGuire, "The Effectiveness of Supportive and Refutational Defenses in Immunizing and Restoring Beliefs against Persuasion," *Sociometry* 24 (1961), 184–97.

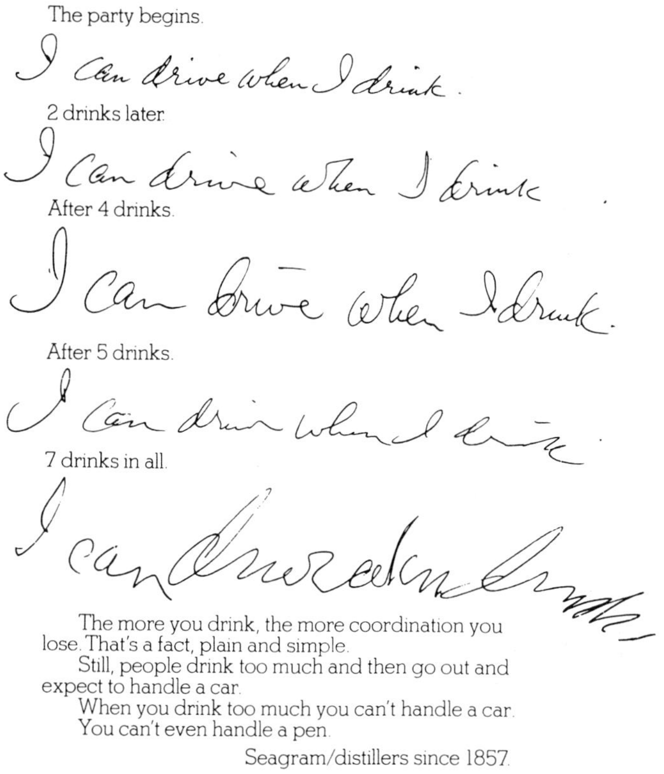

The party begins.

I can drive when I drink.

2 drinks later.

I can drive when I drink   .

After 4 drinks.

I can drive when I drunk.

After 5 drinks.

I can drin when I drin.

7 drinks in all.

I can drurealen ln

The more you drink, the more coordination you lose. That's a fact, plain and simple.
Still, people drink too much and then go out and expect to handle a car.
When you drink too much you can't handle a car.
You can't even handle a pen.

Seagram/distillers since 1857.

Figure 12.12   ''Moderation Messages''   (New York: Seagram Distillers Co., 1975.)

Both-sides persuasion almost always involves some concession. The advertisement in Figure 12.12 is a good example. Seagram concedes the bad effects of too much alcohol. The handwriting in the Seagram ad is also a clear and interesting use of the logical supports of persuasion.

Following are characteristics of good both-sides persuasion:

1. *Objectivity*: fair, honest, bases bias on evidence.
2. *Suspended judgment*: avoids positive statements, creates honest doubt.
3. *Nonspecific opponents*: does not identify audience as the opposition, suggests audience is undecided, creates a common ground.
4. *Critical willingness*: motivates audience to reconsider the "other" side.
5. *Qualified language*: does not overstate the position and the evidence, is careful of generalization.

6. *Audience-sensitive:* adapts to feedback signs, considers alternative actions before making the speech.

7. *Ethical:* above all, honest; presents opposing arguments in an objective manner.

He who knows only his side of the story doesn't know that . . . .

J. S. Mill

LOGICAL SUPPORTS OF PERSUASION

Forms of Support

EVIDENCE.   "Evidence consists of source materials external to the advocate or audience which may be used to lend support or proof to a conclusion."[11] The sources of evidence are observable objects or things.

If you were to go to Baldwin School, for example, and count 525 students, that number would be a fact that you had observed. It would still be a fact if a document written by the principal said there were 525 students in Baldwin School.

The most useful sources of evidence are: (1) authority; (2) examples; and (3) statistics.

Figure 12.13

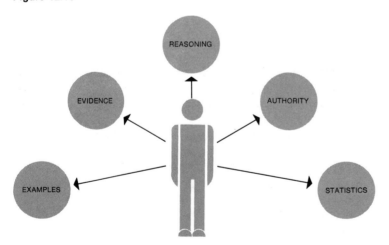

[11]George W. Ziegelmueller and Charles A. Dause, *Argumentation: Inquiry and Advocacy* (Englewood Cliffs, N.J.: Prentice-Hall, 1975), p. 49.

AUTHORITY

This evidence is usually in the form of quoted testimony from a person better qualified than the speaker. The value of an authority really depends on how expert the person is. Authority was discussed earlier under credibility, which is made up of the intent, trustworthiness, and competence of the source.

The idea being supported determines in part who the experts are. If you are trying to prove that the driver who crashed into your car ran a red light, the expert is the lone person who was standing on the corner and saw the whole thing. With this kind of testimony you often need more than one witness. If you are to prove you have seen a bird considered extinct, such as the passenger pigeon, you will need the testimony of a qualified ornithologist. In this case this expert will insist on firsthand observation of the actual bird.

Authorities are qualified to give expert testimony because of their first-hand observations or because of their special training in observing. The authority should be an expert *on the topic under discussion.* You would not ask a doctor of medicine to diagnose a problem in an airplane engine.

Other problems of authority involve what your audience knows and thinks of the person quoted. The bias the audience assigns your expert may be very troublesome. When the audience does not know who your chosen authority is, then you must explain why his or her testimony is authoritative (for example, "John Doe is Professor of Economics at Cornell University and a member of the U.S. Tax Commission").

EXAMPLES

An example is a specific illustration that supports a point you are trying to make. A hypothetical example may be a real aid to clearness and is often persuasive, but it is *not* proof. For evidence you must present real, factual examples.

To prove that a person can operate normally in a state of weightlessness, for instance, you could cite one example of an astronaut who has done so. However, a single factual example, though proving its own case, may be so exceptional that it does not truly support a generalization. Suppose you were arguing that all models of a particular type of car were poorly and carelessly assembled and you supported this statement with only *one* example of a car that was indeed assembled poorly. Your proof becomes suspect.

STATISTICS

A joker once said, "First come lies, then big lies, then statistics." (Or was it, "Figures don't lie, but liars figure!"?) Despite the jokes, we live by statistics. We accept data on births, deaths, and accidents as facts. However, statistics as a method bewilders many people. You do not have to be a statistician to realize that a *mean* (an average) is not always the best measure. Let's take an example of eleven educators and their yearly incomes:

Table 12.1

	SALARY		SALARY
Educator A (Administrator)	$29,000	Educator G	$15,000
Educator B (Administrator)	28,500	Educator H	13,950
Educator C	20,500	Educator I	13,600
Educator D	18,250	Educator J	13,300
Educator E	17,200	Educator K	13,000
Educator F	15,500		

The mean income of these eleven educators is $17,982. But the problem with this number is obvious: The two administrators make the figure unrepresentative, particularly if one is concerned with "teachers'" salaries. The middle figure in the salary list is $15,500. This is the *median*—in this case a more meaningful figure. If we take away the salary of the two administrators, the average income of the teachers is $15,589 and the median is $15,000. You could then figure the amount each income differs from the average. The average of these differences is the *average deviation*.

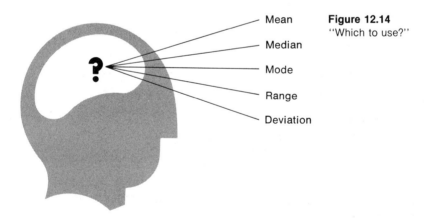

Mean
Median
Mode
Range
Deviation

Figure 12.14
"Which to use?"

Statistics can very quickly become complicated and (if you are not careful) meaningless. The lessons are: (1) to select the right kind of statistics for your point; (2) to know how and when they were collected; and (3) to know the credibility of the source. As a receiver, remember that figures (statistics) don't lie, but liars *do* have the opportunity to figure.

Reasoning and Proof

INDUCTIVE AND DEDUCTIVE PROOF.   The reasoning by which we arrive at a conclusion or generalization through observing specific cases is called *induction*. If you were to observe 500,000 spiders and if each had eight legs, you could reasonably conclude that spiders have eight legs. The induction is perfect for the 500,000 cases. There were no exceptions. But to be very scientific, this induction is merely a prediction (although a highly probable one) when applied to all the spiders in the world.

Here are some requirements for safe inductive reasoning:

1.   Is the example a fair one?
2.   Are there a number of examples?
3.   Do the examples cover a period of time?
4.   Are exceptions explainable?

Deductive reasoning may be defined as "... the analytic process used in moving from generalities to structurally certain conclusions."[12]

Assuming we are happy with the generalization, "All spiders have eight legs," we can then conclude *deductively* that this particular eight-legged thing in our garden is a spider. Inductive proof starts with particular cases and proceeds to a generalization. Deductive proof starts with a generally accepted law or principle and applies it to a particular case.

CAUSE AND EFFECT.   Suppose we see a person accidentally shoot another person and see the victim fall dead with a bullet in the heart. We could say the *effect* was death and the *cause* was the bullet or the person with the gun. Even this simple observation is full of problems. If the shooting were deliberate, would it in any way change things? Or suppose you found a dead person (the effect of something) with a bullet in the heart. Can you conclude absolutely that the bullet is the cause? This is reasoning from effect to cause. The bullet is certainly a possible cause, but as any Magnum P.I. fan knows, the victim might have been killed by arsenic poisoning, then shot to hide the real cause!

One more example: Suppose a person dashes into your classroom, shoots a gun at your professor, and dashes out; your professor falls to the floor and everyone runs out screaming. You observed the cause and concluded that the effect was murder or attempted murder. (A role play?)

Now suppose your car battery is weak, you observe it's 10° below zero, and you conclude that your car isn't going to start. This is before-the-fact reasoning. The conclusion is based upon circumstances you observed before the disputed fact. You are reasoning from *cause to effect*.

[12]Ibid., p. 90

If, when you get up tomorrow morning, you say "It's 10° below zero; my car won't start; I'll be late for school," you are reasoning from *effect to effect*. Both your faltering battery and your tardiness (and the thermometer reading) are the effects of a common cause: low temperature. In arguing from effect to effect, you must first sort out the effect-to-cause and cause-to-effect elements and then apply the general requirements for arguments based on causal relations. These are good questions:

1. Is the cause able to generate the effect?
2. Is the cause the only possible cause?
3. Has coincidence been mistaken for cause?
4. Was the cause operating freely?

Fallacies

A fallacy is an idea or opinion founded on mistaken logic or perception.

OVERGENERALIZATION.   This is a common fallacy. Snap judgments based on too little evidence or experience belong in this category. We are not talking about language and the dangers of the word *all*, but rather the concept of *allness*

"Still cheating?"

Figure 12.15

"They're all dumb."

"What discrimination?"

"The dance caused the rain."

itself. This fallacy results in going from the general case to a specific case, or vice versa. It is similar to the problems of induction and deduction.

It is in the exceptions to rules that overgeneralization causes the most trouble. We would all agree that is wrong to kill a person. However, a specific case of killing in self-defense is for most of us an exception to this rule. To take another example, there could be several exceptions to the rule, "Alcohol is harmful."

Two special kinds of overgeneralization are *sampling* and *thin entering wedge*. An example of sampling would be: A group of star high-school football players were being shown a certain campus when they observed a dozen unusually attractive women. To a man, the generalization was "Wow! What coeds this place has!" The coach recruiting them did not bother to tell them that the women were all fashion models who had just come from a faculty program. A rash of teenage delinquencies may cause some to conclude that all teenagers are juvenile delinquents. This would be an unfair generalization.

The worst part of a sampling fallacy is that it does start with facts. There *were* twelve stylish females on a given campus; teenage delinquency *has been* recorded. The kind of overgeneralization known as *thin entering wedge* proceeds from limited data to probability predictions. Weather forecasters are stuck with this problem. So, to some extent, are economists and political pollsters.

FALSE CAUSE.   This fallacy, also known as *non sequitur*, is the fallacy of assigning a wrong or false cause to a certain happening or effect. It also involves refutation with irrelevant arguments. Superstitions belong in this category. If you blow on the dice and win, was it the blowing that brought you luck? We still sell rabbits' feet, and most hotels have no floor labeled *thirteen*. There are four special kinds of false cause:

AFTER THIS, THEREFORE BECAUSE OF THIS

This fallacy is also known as *post hoc, ergo propter hoc*. It is the fallacy of thinking that an event that happens after another must be its result. If a new city government comes into power after a rough winter and the roads are badly damaged, it may indeed be easy to hold the new government responsible as you survey one ruined $50 tire: "We didn't have roads like this until after their election." After this, therefore because of this! The great Roman Empire fell after the introduction of Christianity—care to try that one? Superstitions also fit in this category.

THOU ALSO, ALSO KNOWN AS TU QUOQUE

This fallacy consists of accusing one's attacker of a similar, but irrelevant charge. A discussion between a Brazilian student and several Americans about Communist infiltration in Latin America became quite heated. Suddenly, the Brazilian said, "Communists? How about segregation in your country?" The retort was equally unrelated: "How about Nazis in Argentina?" In an army mess line a steward put a perfectly good salad right in the middle of a soldier's mashed potatoes. When told what an ignoramus he was, the steward retorted in a most effective (if illogical) way, "Yeah, what about those poor guys in Vietnam?" Or, how about "Tell it to the Marines!"

EITHER-OR

Certainly, some things in this world are either one way or another. You are either living or dead; the lake is frozen or it is not; there is no such thing as being partially pregnant. However, when a statement or problem with more than two possible solutions is put in an either-or context, we have a fallacy. "The fight is either Jan's or Jim's fault." It may be neither's fault, or it may be the fault of both. There are shades of gray in most things. All too often, either-or arguments only slow real solutions: science versus religion, capitalism versus socialism, suburban versus city living, and so forth.

LOADED QUESTION

This trick usually involves asking two questions as if they were one. You're in trouble no matter how you answer. In a speech it may take the form of a great many questions, the combination of answers leading to fallacious reasoning. The answers sought are *yes* or *no*. "Have you stopped cheating? *Yes* or *no?*" If you answer *no*, you are an admitted cheater. If you answer *yes*, you are an admitted former cheater. Either way, the loaded question stacks the deck against you.

BEGGING THE QUESTION.   This fallacy assumes the truth or falsity of a statement without proof. There are special kinds: *arguing in a circle* and *direct assumption*. The fallacy of *arguing in a circle* uses two or more unproved propositions to prove one another. Professional boxing should be outlawed for it is inhumane; we know it is inhumane because it is a practice that should be outlawed. Take the course "Speech and Communication Theory" at Northwestern University because it is the best in the country. Why is it the best in the country? Because it is taught at Northwestern University.

In the fallacy of *direct assumption* language is carefully selected to help conceal bald assumptions. Many statements may be used or just a word or two may be inserted. In a discussion of big-time college football, an opposition speaker started with the words, "It is my purpose to show that buying professional players is not in the best interest of college football." This statement begged the whole proposition by assuming that colleges buy professional players. Unless the statement is proved, it remains only an assertion.

IGNORING OR DUCKING THE ISSUE.   This fallacy can be tricky and vicious. It almost always involves using irrelevant arguments to cloud or duck the real issue. This fallacy has several types. Each is worthy of a word of warning:

AD HOMINEM

When a speaker makes a personal attack rather than arguing the issue, that is an *ad hominem* argument. *Ad hominem* changes the issue from an argument on the proposition to one of personalities. "Anyone with your short hair and rotten sense of humor has got to be a Republican!" is a good example of *ad hominem*.

FALSE APPEAL TO AUTHORITY

When the authority is legitimately connected to the subject, as Aristotle is to logic, we have no problem. However, if in our reverence of Aristotle we use him to oppose modern probability theory, we are guilty of false appeal. Roger Staubaugh and Johnny Bench are well-paid experts in their special fields. They are not authorities on laser theory or even shoes, shaving cream, or cars. If you are impressed because Dr. Whosis says that alcohol causes cancer, find out if Whosis is a medical doctor or an English professor!

APPEALS TO IGNORANCE

An appeal to ignorance is a mean trick in which one covers up arguments by overwhelming an audience with impressive materials that they know little about. A twelve-cylinder vocabulary can screen many a feeble argument. An improper use of statistics (or even a proper one) for people ignorant of the theory or the numbers involved is a good example of *appeals to ignorance*. This is not to say that vocabulary or statistics is the problem. The problem is the intent with which the speaker adapts them to the audience.

MESSAGE ORGANIZATION

The logical dimensions of message organization are served by asking yourself the debater's *stock issue* questions:

1. Have I shown a real *need* for a change?
2. Will my *solution* meet that need?
3. Does my solution involve any unmanageable disadvantages?

If better schools (need) demand higher taxes (solution), but the higher taxes drive you out of the community, you may have a solution with unmanageable disadvantages.

There is a normal thinking pattern thought to exist in all of us. It suggests a logical arrangement for persuasive messages. All such arrangements start with attempts to get attention.

The famous psychologist William James once said, "What holds attention determines action. . . . The impelling idea is simply the one which possesses the attention. . . ."

Attention may be thought of as a readiness to respond. To think of attention alone as controlling behavior is a little frightening and, of course, goes beyond James' meaning. It does, however, show the importance of attention. If one thinks of hypnosis as a state involving complete, undivided attention,[13] it does appear that "that which holds attention determines action."

Our attention, like all perception, is selective. Because of this, the persuasive speaker must concentrate on keeping the audience involved in the subject. Other things compete for the listeners' attention: sounds, sights, people, ideas, and so on.

Arrange your persuasive message so that your audience will receive it in a natural thinking order. Hollingworth suggests a sequence of: (1) attention; (2) interest; (3) impression; (4) conviction; and (5) direction.[14] Monroe's system, which he called the *motivated sequence*,[15] suggests key steps in this natural order: (1) attention; (2) need; (3) satisfaction; (4) visualization; and (5) action. First, our attention must be caught. Second, we must be made to feel a definite need. Third, we must be shown a way to satisfy this need. Fourth, we must be made to see how the proposal applies to us personally. Finally, a definite suggestion must be made as to how we should act.

Whichever system of message organization you decide upon, the following psychological order is involved:

1. Creation of attention and need.
2. Relating of the need to the specific audience.
3. Explanation of the solution in terms of the need.
4. Consideration of all important objections and counterarguments.
5. Reinforcement of your message through verbal reminders, summaries, and visualizations.

A list of some of the systems, arranged in terms of introduction, body, and conclusion, includes:

	Hollingworth	*Monroe*	*Ross*
INTRODUCTION	Attention	Attention	Attention
BODY	Interest	Need	Need
	Impression	Satisfaction	Plan
	Conviction	Visualization	Reinforcement
CONCLUSION	Direction	Action	Direction

[13]Hypnosis is probably allied more closely to normal sleep.

[14]H. L. Hollingworth, *The Psychology of the Audience* (New York: American Book Company, 1935), pp. 19–32.

[15]Alan H. Monroe, *Principles and Types of Speech* (Chicago: Scott, Foresman, 1949), pp. 308–9; see also Alan H. Monroe, Douglas Ehninger, and Bruce Gronbeck, *Principles and Types of Speech Communication* (Glenview, Ill: Scott, Foresman, 1978), p. 143.

A WAR ON WORDS*

General End: To persuade.

Specific Purpose: To persuade the audience to reject the terms "man," "woman," "masculinity," "femininity," "husband," "wife," "father," "mother," etc. in their traditional form; and to effect a change in the usage and accepted meaning of such terms.

Introduction (Attention)	I What if this week Dr. Ross asked us to define who we are, or what our roles are? In doing so I wonder how many of us would use such terms as "man," "woman," "female," "male," "husband," "wife," "mother," "father," "masculine," "feminine"? And if so, I wonder how many of us would be stereotyping ourselves?
(Psychological Needs)	II For far too long cliches—such as: "Little boys are made of snakes and snails and puppy dog's tails; and little girls are made of sugar and spice and everything nice"—have represented the image of the male and female in society. Traditionally, males have been depicted as heroic, active, and aggressive, while females pale in the shadow of masculinity.
Body (Overview of Problem)	I The problem with such stereotypes is that they pervade our culture, and threaten our psychological stability.
(Achievement, Competence, Esteem, Self-Actualization Needs) (Safety Needs)	A From textbooks to television stereotypic definitions of these terms have been—and too often still are—reinforced.
	1 Male and female stereotypes in student textbooks emphasize the boys as "doers" and the girls as observers.[1]
	2 Females are depicted as "sub-mankind" in basal readers.[2]
	3 In television advertising, females are primarily associated with personal hygiene products, while men are associated with cars, trucks, gas, oil, etc.[3]
	B The acceptance and use of such terms threatens our psychological stability by placing unreasonable pressure on us to conform to such tags.
	1 Men must be "big," "gruff," and "aggressive."
	a Some men physically "fail" to measure up to the "big" description.
	b Some men psychologically aren't—and don't want to be—"gruff" and "aggressive."
	2 Women must be "petite," "sweet," and "meek."
	a Again, some women physiologically are not "petite."
	b Not all women are—or wish to be—psychologically "sweet," and "meek."

* From a student speech by Marcy L. Krugel, Wayne State University.

[1] David Sadker, Myra Sadker, and Sidney Simon, "Clarifying Sexist Values," *Social Education,* 37 (December 1973), 759.

[2] Sadker, Sadker, and Simon relate the following negative dialogue that appeared in a basal reader: "We are willing to share our great thoughts with mankind. However, you happen to be a girl." *Venture, Book 4* (Glenview, Ill.: Scott Foresman & Company, 1965); Sadker, Sadker, Simon, "Sexist Values," 757.

[3] Joseph R. Domineck and Gail E. Rauch, "The Image of Women in Network TV Commercials," *Journal of Broadcasting,* 16 (Summer 1972), 259–65.

Figure 12.16 A model outline   Adapted from a speech by Marcy L. Krugel, a student at Wayne State University.

Figure 12.16 *(cont.)*

(Objection)   C But, some would argue—and have argued—What's in a word?
                        1 S. I. Hayakawa asserts that "words influence and to an enormous extent control future events."
                        2 Benjamin Lee Worf concludes that language shapes perception.
                        3 Barbara Herrnstein Smith pinpoints the specific semantic problem.

(Both-sides   a The original adjectives are "handy" and "informative"; not "vicious" at all.
Persuasion)   b But these adjectives acquire a sexual impact.
                            (1) Women are expected to be passive, so passiveness becomes a feminine trait; thus, an aggressive woman is masculine.
                            (2) Men are expected to be aggressive, so aggressiveness becomes a masculine trait; thus, a passive man is feminine.[4]

(Solution)   II In order to solve these problems, a change in the usage and accepted meaning of these words must be initiated.
                        A We must sweep these stereotypic definitions from our culture.
                        1 Textbooks must stop codifying roles in relation to gender.
                        2 Basal readers must concentrate on equality.
                        3 Television must depict men and women in diverse areas and aspects of life.
                        B Further, society must objectively redefine its terms so that they no longer pose as prescriptive formulas of behavior.

(Visualization)   1 The terms "husband" and "wife" should merely denote a legal relationship.
                        2 The terms "father" and "mother" should denote a legal status.

Conclusion   I So, what is a "man"? What is a "woman"? They are both human beings
(Reinforcement)   who should be free of the sex-typed labels of "masculinity" and "femininity."

(Action Step)   II Consequently, we must reject the traditional meaning of these terms: to
(Self-actual-   liberate us *all* from a sex-typed fate; to allow our own very individual
ization)   "me's" to be.

[4] Barbara Herrnstein Smith, "Women Artists: Some Muted Notes," *Journal of Communication,*
24 (Spring 1974), 146–47.

SUMMARY

Persuasion is an important study of human motives. It is the major means of settling problems, selling ideas and products, and changing people's attitudes. If we are to live in a democracy, we must understand how people are influenced.

Attitudes refer to the thinking, feeling, and behavioral intentions that govern our predispositions toward people, situations, and things. An attitude may also be defined as a readiness to respond. The dimensions of attitude have been described as cognitive, affective, and behavioral.

Persuasion is the ability to (1) assess the causes of motivation in human affairs and (2) assess the available means of influencing attitudes and behavior. It is a rhetorical means of ethically influencing others' thinking, feeling, and/or behavior.

A persuader has a moral responsibility for the strategies employed. Strategy *is not* unethical unless it is dishonest, unfair to the facts, or so subtle that it gives no clue to the receiver. Receivers must be afforded some choice.

Motivation refers to specific deficiency and abundancy needs in the human experience. We are motivated by both need and by plenty: survival and security but also satisfaction and stimulation. We desire consistency in our attitudes and our behavior, in what we feel and in what we think.

Maslow provided us with a useful classification of human dynamic needs. In the order of their importance, these needs are: physiological, safety, belonging, esteem, and self-actualization. A satisfied need is no longer a motivator, according to this theory. Motive appeals are useful triggers of human needs.

Credibility, or *ethos,* refers to the receiver's or audience's acceptance of or disposition toward the source. It is related to Aristotle's notions of good will, good moral character, and good sense. In modern times, source credibility is discussed in terms of good intentions, trustworthiness, and competence or expertness. High source credibility generally produces more attitude change in the receiver. Ethical proof includes practical factors like attitude similarity, language, humor, voice, and evidence.

Theories of consistency offer many practical principles of persuasion. They refer to a mental agreement between a person's idea of some object or event and some new information about that same object or event. Persuasive communications tend to be effective when they reduce inconsistency or dissonance and to be ineffective when they increase dissonance.

In social-judgment or involvement theory, the audience's initial attitude serves as an anchor for making judgments. If a message does not fall too far outside its range of acceptance, it it likely to be assimilated. If it falls well beyond the range of acceptance, it will be judged more discrepant than it actually is (a contrast effect).

Both-sides persuasion has been shown to be superior to one-sided persuasion when the audience is initially opposed to the point of view being presented or when, regardless of initial attitude, the audience is exposed to counterargument. A rational form of persuasion, the both-sides approach is characterized by objectivity, suspended judgment, nonspecific opponents, critical willingness, qualified language, audience sensitivity, and ethical conduct.

Logic dimensions of persuasion include: evidence, reasoning and proof, and fallacies. The most useful sources of evidence are authorities, examples, and statistics. Induction is that process by which we arrive at a conclusion or generalization through observing specific cases or instances. Deduction starts with a generally accepted law or principle and applies it to a particular case. Causal reasoning may proceed from cause to effect, effect to cause, or effect to effect.

Finally, there are four major types of fallacies: (1) overgeneralization; (2) false cause; (3) begging the question; and (4) ignoring or ducking the issue.

A natural thinking order suggests the following procedure for organizing persuasive messages:

1. Creation of attention and location or establishment of need.
2. Arousal of interest and problem awareness by relating the need to the specific audience.
3. Explanation of the solution in terms of the problem, need, previous experience, knowledge, and personality of the audience.
4. Evaluation, when necessary, of all important objections, counterarguments, or alternative solutions.
5. Reinforcement of the message throughout the speech, particularly toward the end, through verbal reminders, reviews, summaries, and visualizations.

There are many plans similar to this one. Hollingworth suggests that the fundamental tasks of a speaker are attention, interest, impression, conviction, and direction. Alan H. Monroe calls his system the motivated sequence. The key steps are (1) attention; (2) need; (3) satisfaction; (4) visualization; and (5) action.

STUDY PROJECTS

1. Prepare a three- to five-minute talk in which you attempt to persuade the audience to belief or action. Use the primary needs and motive appeals discussed. This is an exercise and you need not have a detailed outline. Indicate the theories and appeals you are using. (See Appendix C.)
2. Prepare a detailed outline for a four- to six-minute persuasive speech. In the margins of your outline state those needs, theories, or appeals that you are using (safety, belonging, esteem, self-actualization, dissonance, and so forth). (See Appendix C.)
3. Prepare a detailed outline for a five- to seven-minute persuasive speech that is based on a motivated sequence.

I. Attention		I. Attention
II. Need		II. Need
III. Satisfaction	or	III. Plan
IV. Visualization		IV. Reinforcement
V. Action		V. Action

   Indicate the primary motives, appeals, and other devices (safety, esteem, self-preservation, and so on).
4. Clip three newspaper or magazine advertisements and evaluate them in terms of the sequence in project 3.

5. Report on a radio or television commercial that made use of both-sides persuasion.

6. Prepare an eight- to ten-minute persuasive speech, taking the side to which your class audience is mostly hostile (for example, pick the more unpopular side of a social issue). Meet the "other side" arguments first and give in where you must before turning to your side.

7. Prepare a detailed outline for a two- to three-minute persuasive one-point speech using the logical supports of persuasion (authority, examples, statistics, and so forth).

8. Evaluate the logic of your classmates' speeches. Watch for fallacies. Be prepared to cross-examine the speakers.

9. Search the daily print media and locate two fallacies; define and explain them.

10. Prepare a four- to five-minute persuasive speech that will be followed by a three- to four-minute open forum. Remember to stay in control by following the principles, rules, and suggestions in Chapter 11.

Appendix A

Communication models

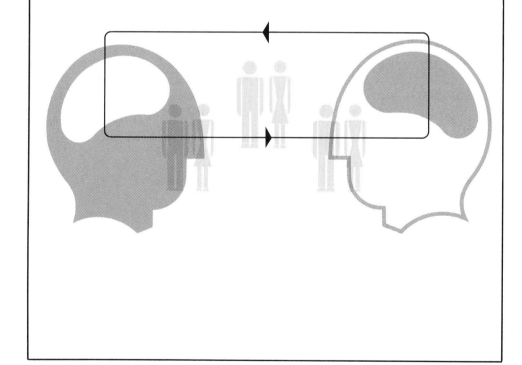

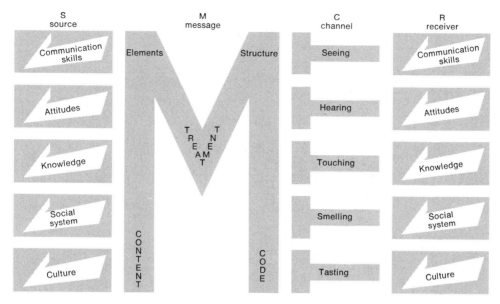

Figure A.1 Berlo model   From *The Process of Communication*, p. 72, by David K. Berlo, Copyright © 1960 by Holt, Rinehart & Winston. Reprinted by permission of Holt, Rinehart & Winston, CBS College Publishing.

Becker suggests a cube of information with layers and slices producing minicubes or cells. The receiver is figuratively strained through a changing framework of layers of information. Dark cells suggest that some pieces of information are not available for use.

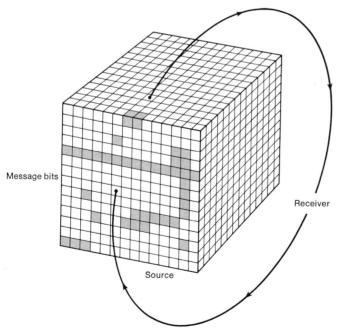

Figure A.2 Becker model   Presented by Samuel L. Becker at the Wayne State University special graduate seminar, "Potpourri '70: Communication Relations," July 20, 1970.

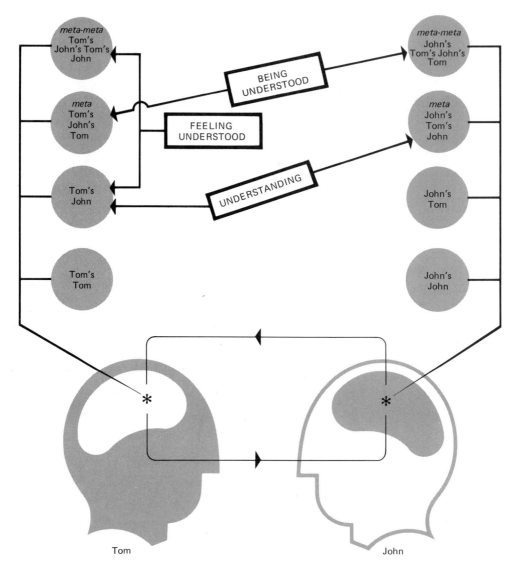

Figure A.3 Perceptions of understanding model   For explanation, see Raymond S. Ross and Mark G. Ross, *Relating and Interacting: An Introduction to Interpersonal Communication* (Englewood Cliffs, N.J.: Prentice-Hall, 1982), Chapter 1.

Appendix B

The employment interview

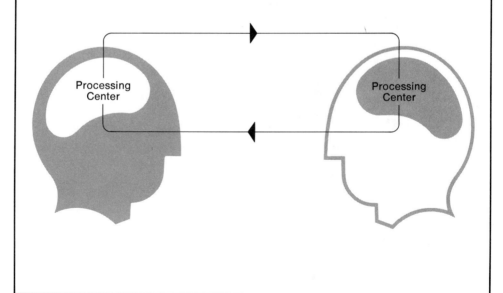

WHAT THE EMPLOYER WANTS TO KNOW

"What do you hope to achieve on a job like this?" This question, or one like it, is a typical opener. The interviewer is probably looking at your application or a resume of your experience and training. The substance of your answer may not be as important as the maturity with which you answer. In the most general sense, the interviewer wants to know more about your *motivation,* your *maturity,* and the *kind of person* you are. When answering such general questions, you should keep the following concepts in mind:

Do You Fit The Job?

In a specific sense, the employer wants to know if you "fit" the job. You have probably already met some of the requirements in your application and/or resume, or you wouldn't have been invited to the interview. You should be prepared to expand upon your work experience and your education and training. These matters are critical to an employer, but so are your oral explanation and expansion. The Dunhill Personnel System's advertisement illustrates the importance attached to motivation, maturity, and character (Figure B.1).

Figure B.1
By permission of Dunhill Personnel System

We could have told you he wasn't right for the job.

He shows up at your door ready to conquer the world, full of unbridled enthusiasm with an itch for excitement.

Do you hire him? Not if you've tried Dunhill Personnel first.

Our consultants are the best trained, most highly skilled in the personnel industry. They are specialists at understanding your business, ascertaining your needs and carefully screening for particular qualifications.

It's easy to overlook hidden flaws when confronting charisma. The Dunhill Personnel System is designed to see beyond the obvious to the essence of each candidate.

Those who are presented for your final decision are the finest — supremely qualified, but not over-qualified.

If you had asked Dunhill Personnel to screen for that aggressive super-talent, we would have found that the above candidate, though highly qualified, tends to bite off more than he can chew...and wouldn't be satisfied for long with just one company.

Find us in the telephone directory and find the right person for the job.

Dunhill Personnel System
The right people for the job.

Do You Fit The Organization?

Your work experience and training can help answer the question "Do you fit the job?" Both personal data and your communication behavior enable the interviewer to determine how well you fit the organization, or how well the organization fits you. You may not want to work in an ultraconservative or perhaps ultraliberal organization. (Of course, a lot may depend on your alternatives!)

The personal data on your application or resume may help answer this question, but your commentary is very important. What to emphasize or omit about yourself is often not only a difficult, but a critical decision. Give this considerable thought. See how your priorities, value system, and general outlook match those of the organization.

How you present yourself verbally and nonverbally is also part of the assessment. All the communication behaviors discussed in this text come into play. Your use of voice, language, gesture, organization of answers or statements, dress code, listening ability, emotional control, and responsiveness are all part of how you are judged in terms of motivation, desire to work, maturity, and general character or personality.[1]

Figure B.2 "I think I have your man. Heavy marketing background, right salary bracket, and your corporate philosophy seems compatible with his value system." Reprinted by permission of Donald Trawin and *Fortune Magazine.* Copyright Time, Inc., 1981.

[1]For more on the employment interview, especially from the employer's viewpoint, see L. J. Einhorn, Patricia Hayes Bradley, and John E. Baird, Jr., *Effective Employment Interviewing* (Glenview, Ill.: Scott, Foresman, 1982); see also Charles J. Stewart and William B. Cash, Jr., *Interviewing: Principles and Practices,* 3rd ed. (Dubuque, Iowa: Wm. C. Brown, 1982), especially Chapters 7 and 8. See also Donna Bogar Goodall and H. Lloyd Goodall, Jr., "The Employment Interview: A Selective Review of the Literature with Implications for Communication Research," *Communication Quarterly,* 30, no. 2 (Spring 1982), 116–23.

WHAT YOU SHOULD KNOW

The Character of the Organization

Our discussions in this text of specific purpose and audience analysis pertain here. An interviewer is usually impressed if you know something about the organization and its current successes and problems. According to Professor Richard Hatch, you should know the following things when you walk through the door:

The exact name of the company or organization
What that organization does, in as much detail as you can possibly find out
At least two or three recent developments in that organization
The exact nature of the job you're going to talk about
The duties of the job
The qualifications the job requires
How much pay the organization is willing to offer
The name of the interviewer and how to pronounce it
The position of the interviewer with the organization
The kind of work you really want to do
The major qualifications you have in relation to that job
The weaknesses you have in relation to that job—and how you'll deal with them
How much money you think you should be paid
The geographical location where you want to live
Other things you want from a job
Several intelligent questions you can ask about the job[2]

The Legal Constraints on the Interviewer

If you are not asked the following questions, it doesn't mean that the interviewer isn't interested in you. It is because these questions are illegal.

How old are you?
When were you born?
Do you plan to start a family soon?
Are you married?
To what clubs or organizations do you belong?
What does your husband (wife) do?
What was your maiden name?
How long do you plan to work?

[2]Richard Hatch, *Communicating in Business* (Chicago: Science Research Associates, 1977), p. 235.

What is your race?
What is your religion?
Have you ever been arrested?[3]

According to the Equal Employment Opportunity Commission (EEOC), Title VII (Affirmative Action) regulations, and recent court decisions, these questions and others like them are legal grounds for discrimination suits. When these questions are not job related, they can lead to discrimination on the basis of sex, race, color, national origin, age, or religion. The laws are meant to protect you, and you should know when you are being treated illegally.

When these questions are job related, it is a different matter. Although it is generally illegal for an employment interviewer to ask if you can speak a foreign language because it may reveal your national origin, it would be an appropriate question if the job called for you to teach English to a class of Chicano students.

The influence of these legal constraints on interpersonal communication is considerable, especially if you, the interviewee, are not aware of them. The interviewer may appear disinterested, cold, or even hostile. For example, a friendly interviewer of the same ethnic group as you may not legally ask if you are native born. He or she can ask if you are a United States citizen. However, if you say that you are not, he may not ask the country of citizenship. It is even unlawful to ask you about the identification of a nearest relative (even for emergency purposes). He or she can ask for the name of a person to contact in case of emergency. Perhaps you are proud of your military experience. The interviewer can ask if you are a veteran, but cannot ask about your discharge. The interviewer can ask about experience, career goals, prior employers, previous jobs, education, references—in short, those things that are clearly job related.

To further complicate matters, while it is illegal for the interviewer to ask some questions, it is not illegal for you to volunteer such information. You may feel that certain information would make you a more attractive candidate or overcome a hidden objection. For example, a woman applicant, realizing that a job calls for travel, may offer the information that even though she has two children, it is not a problem since she is divorced and her children are living with their father. The interviewer may appreciate the applicant's information but is in a legal bind regarding his or her reaction. One expert recommends the following cold but legally safe response to such situations:

Thank you for volunteering that information. However, since our organization is an equal opportunity employer and we are interested only in job-related factors, what you have told me will have no bearing on whether or not you are recommended for the position, except for the fact that you are free to meet the job requirements for travel.[4]

[3]Thomas L. Moffatt, *Selection Interviewing for Managers* (New York: Harper & Row, 1979), p. 137.
[4]Ibid., p. 142.

The reason for this cold doubletalk is that trained interviewers become nervous when they hear illegal information (from their perspective) being volunteered. At worst, an interviewer may be concerned about being set up for a discrimination suit. Knowledge of these legal constraints will not only protect you against discrimination, but will also help you understand the behavior of the interviewer.

WHAT YOU SHOULD DO

Prepare a Resume

If you have filled out an application, then you already have some idea of what the organization is looking for. However, the same legal constraints that apply to the interview also apply to application forms, and they may therefore appear brief or restrictive. Some that have not been revised recently may even include illegal questions.

You can anticipate that an employment interviewer will want to see a one- or two-page resume. What you volunteer in a resume is your business. The legal constraints do not pertain, but what you volunteer about age, sex, marital status, national origin may modify the persuasiveness of the resume and perhaps affect what is discussed in an interview.[5]

Some typical kinds of information found in short resumes may help you organize your own information. Most employers expect but may not legally demand a resume to include:

A   Personal data
    Name
    Age
    Citizenship
    Marital status
B   Education
    Schooling, majors, minors
    Training
C   Extracurricular activities
D   Awards and honors
E   Work experience
F   References (two or three)

When you mail out a resume, you should write a short covering letter that indicates your special interests.

[5]Thomas R. Tortoriello, Stephen J. Blatt, and Sue DeWine, *Communication in the Organization* (New York: McGraw-Hill, 1978), pp. 160–66.

Follow Communication Guidelines

1. DO AN AUDIENCE ANALYSIS   Learn something specific about the organization, its leaders, and, if possible, the interviewer. Consider the interview as a special communication context with legal constraints on some topics.

2. BE SCRUPULOUSLY HONEST   Any hint of lying or gross exaggeration is enough to put you out of contention. You need not answer illegal questions, but be frank and honest about why you will not do so.

3. REMEMBER THE NONVERBALS   Be prompt. Whatever the reason, being late is read as a clear expression of disinterest. Be dressed appropriately. Our audience-analysis guidelines should help here.

4. THINK BEFORE YOU TALK   Organize your thoughts and language. Speak clearly and sincerely. Look at the interviewer. Ask questions if the interviewer has confused you.

5. MIND YOUR LANGUAGE   Job counselors' polls show that rejections are frequently based on candidates' poor command of language. "An interviewer won't say, 'I didn't hire you because you talked funny.' He'd get sued. But the fact is, the way you speak makes all the difference."[6]

6. LEAVE DISCUSSION OF SALARY AND BENEFITS TO THE LAST   Let the interviewer bring these up, but ask the salary range or typical rate if he or she doesn't. Detailed benefit questions are often better left until after an offer has been made.

      Some employment interviews are held during lunch. Abné Eisenberg suggests some dos and don'ts. Here are a dozen of each culled from his recommendations:

DON'T

Be late.
Rush.
Talk with your mouth full.
Talk too loud.
Ask the other person a question when his/her mouth is full.
Order a heavy meal if the other person is eating a light one.
Let the food appear to be more important than the other person.
Smoke without asking the other person if it is all right (especially a cigar).
Drink over your limit.
Complain about the food or choice of restaurant.
Use profanity.
Overeat.

---

[6]Phyllis Martin, *Word Watcher's Handbook* (New York: St. Martin's Press, 1982), p. 3.

DO

Call if you are going to be late.

Dress appropriately.

Let what your host orders be your guide as to what you should order.

If you arrive first, tell the head waiter or hostess that you are expecting to meet someone.

Be an attentive listener.

Stand up when your prospective employer approaches the table if you are already seated.

Show signs of your willingness to learn.

Speak clearly and distinctly.

Display a special interest in your employer's company or firm.

Illustrate your ability to communicate effectively.

When it is time to leave, don't linger. Leave promptly.

Graciously thank your host for the luncheon.[7]

---

[7]Abné M. Eisenberg, *Understanding Communication in Business and the Professions* (New York: Macmillan, 1978), pp. 164–65.

Appendix C

Outlines

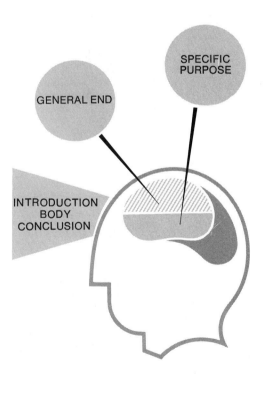

The Role of the Manager

General End: To inform.
Specific Purpose: To explain five basic functions of managing.

Introduction

I. In a well-run organization, confusion exists 25 percent of the time.
   A. Visual aid with data and another with list of functions.
   B. Studies show that communication breakdowns occur.
II. Management is getting work done through others.
   A. That makes communication the heart of all management functions.
   B. That takes a knowledge of the other basic functions.
      1. Planning.
      2. Organizing.
      3. Directing.
      4. Coordinating. } Human relations and communication area
      5. Controlling.

Body

I. The planning function.
   A. Determine objective.
   B. Consider tools available.
      1. Time.
      2. Space.
      3. Personnel.
      4. Material available.
   C. Consider possible lines of action.
   D. Select the best line of action.
   E. Determine the actual process.
      1. Who?
      2. When?
      3. What?
      4. Where?
      5. How?
II. The organizing function.
   A. Line of authority.
   B. Span of control.
      1. Number of personnel.
         a. Nature of job.
         b. Ratios (1:20, 3:7)
      2. Distance.
      3. Time.
   C. Homogeneous assignment.
      1. Like functions grouped together.
      2. Avoid several unrelated responsibilities.
   D. Delegation of authority.
      1. Cannot delegate responsibility.
      2. Clearly define limits of delegated authority.
III. The directing function.
   A. Communication.
   B. Understanding people.

Note: Outlines show various outline forms.

IV. The coordinating function.
   A. Relating to lateral organizations.
   B. Relating to the parent organization.
V. The controlling function.
   A. Reporting.
   B. Inspecting and evaluating.

Conclusion
   I. I have tried to make clear the five basic management functions.
      A. Planning.
      B. Organizing.
      C. Directing.
      D. Coordinating.
      E. Controlling.
   II. Communication is the heart of all management functions! It has to be: Management is getting work done through people—and that takes communication.

The Dietary Laws of the Jewish People

General End: To inform.
Specific Purpose: To inform the class about the ancient Jewish dietary laws that are practiced even to this day.

Introduction
   I. Jewish culture is interesting to study not only because of its religious aspect but also because the laws promulgated by Moses in ancient times are still practiced by observing Jews.
   II. The dietary laws I will discuss are the following:
      A. Consumption of meat.
      B. Consumption of fish.
      C. Consumption of dairy foods.
      D. Consumption of a living animal.
      E. Consumption of blood.
      F. Ritualistic slaughter.

Body
   I. The Bible prohibits the consumption of meat that comes from animals that do not possess cloven (split) hoofs and that do not chew their cud.
      A. Animals that belong to categories that possess both characteristics are permissible as food.
         1. Cows.
         2. Goats.
         3. Lambs.
      B. Animals that chew their cud but do not have cloven hoofs are prohibited as food.
         1. Rabbits.
         2. Camels.
      C. Animals with cloven hoofs that do not chew their cud, especially hogs, are prohibited as food.

        D. Animals that possess neither characteristic are prohibited as food.
           1. Dogs.
           2. Cats.
           3. Horses.

II. The Jewish people are prohibited from consuming fish that do not have both scales and fins.
    A. Those with both characteristics are permitted.
        1. Pike.
        2. Bass.
        3. Carp.
    B. Those with only one characteristic are prohibited.
        1. Catfish.
        2. Bullheads.
    C. Those with neither characteristic are prohibited.
        1. Crabs.
        2. Lobsters.
        3. Clams.

III. Another law prohibits the cooking or eating of meats and dairy foods together.
    A. This law based on Exodus 23:19: "Thou shalt not seethe a kid in the milk of its mother."
    B. Rabbinic legislation provided that two separate sets of dishes be maintained.

IV. The Bible prohibits the eating of any part of a living animal.
    A. This is one of the seven laws of Noah derived by the Talmud from scriptural references.
    B. This prohibition precludes cruelty to animals.

V. The Bible prohibits the eating of blood.
    A. The biblical reason given for this law is that because blood is the symbol of life it must be respected.
    B. From this law stems the practice of koshering meats.
        1. The rabbis prescribed that before the meat could be cooked it had to be soaked in water for one-half hour.
        2. After the meat is soaked, it must be heavily salted in coarse salt for one hour and rinsed with water.
        3. Meat that is broiled need not be salted.
        4. These practices all draw off the blood.

VI. Only meat from an animal that has been ritually slaughtered may be consumed.
    A. Ritual slaughter is the severing of the jugular vein in one stroke.
    B. The animal is killed instantly and painlessly and the blood removed.

Conclusion

I. There were probably also pragmatic reasons for the laws.
    A. Preserving foods was difficult for the nomadic Jews.
    B. Fish without both fins and scales are typically inedible.
    C. Many of the rules prevented cruelty to animals.
    D. These laws helped prevent disease.

II. In review, I have discussed the dietary laws of the Jewish people. An observing Jew may *not*:
    A. Consume meat that comes from animals that do not possess cloven hoofs and that do not chew their cud.

B. Consume fish that do not have both scales and fins.
C. Consume or cook meat and dairy foods together.
D. Eat any part of a living animal.
E. Consume blood (hence, koshering).
F. Consume meat from an animal that has not been ritually slaughtered.
III. These laws are not merely obsolete observances, but have real meaning to observing Jews to this day.
   A. The dietary laws in the total system of commandments represent submission to a divine discipline.
   B. The acceptance of this discipline has served as a significant instrument of group survival for the Jewish people.

A Rampant Killer

General End: To persuade.
Specific Purpose: To persuade the audience that they should have their chests X-rayed.

Attention

(Possible Procedures)
Startling Statement
Illustration
Rhetorical Question
Reference to the
Subject

I. There is a subtle killer loose in the room.
   A. It killed 40,000 people last year.
   B. It likes young people.
II. No one is immune to tuberculosis.
   A. You may be infected now!
   B. How long has it been since you had a chest X-ray?

Need

(Development)
Statement
Illustration
Statistics
Evidence
Self-Preservation

I. Despite wonder drugs, TB is our number six killer disease in America.
   A. Last year 40,000 Americans died from it.
   B. Nearly 2000 died in Michigan alone.
II. No one is immune to TB.
   A. You can get it by contagion.
   B. The most susceptible ages are from fifteen to thirty-five.
III. It maims and handicaps as well as kills.
   A. Many of those who recover cannot lead normal lives.
      1. They cannot travel in warm, damp climates.
      2. They cannot exert themselves.
         a. Cannot run to class.
         b. Cannot dance.
         c. Cannot play athletic games.
   B. TB may spread to other parts of the body.
      1. One may lose a limb.
      2. It often attacks the spine.
      3. One can lose a vital organ such as an eye or a kidney.

Plan

(Development)
Statement
Explanation
Demonstration
Illustration
Objections

 I. A yearly X-ray checkup is the surest way to avoid a serious case of TB.
  A. It can be stopped most effectively if caught in time.
   1. For the most part it is a slow-developing disease.
   2. Its growth depends on the resistance of the victim.
   3. Even if detected in its early stages, a cure would take at least six months.
  B. An X-ray checkup is the most positive means for detecting the disease.
   1. A patch test merely indicates the presence of TB germs, but the disease may not actually be present.
   2. A lesion is the positive sign when it shows on the X-ray.

 II. We can benefit from an X-ray easily and quickly.
  A. It is free.
   1. The money from the sale of Christmas Seals pays for the X-rays and other tests you get.
   2. The state is particularly interested in preserving the health of its young, college-age people.
  B. It is convenient to get.
   1. The mobile unit comes to the campus during the first week of the semester.
    a. It is open weekdays from 8 A.M. to 4 P.M.
    b. It parks near the Health Center.
   2. There is also a permanent clinic in town.
    a. It is open five days a week for adults from 8:30 A.M. to 4:30 P.M.
    b. A special appointment may be arranged after 4:30 P.M.
    c. It is located on the corner of Cass Street and Putnam Avenue.
    d. The phone number there is 831–0100.

(Meeting
 Objections)

  C. It is painless and quick.
   1. If you've ever had an X-ray, you know it doesn't hurt.
   2. You need only remove your outer garments, such as coats and jackets.
   3. You can be in and out in five minutes.
  D. The results are mailed to you.

Reinforcement

(Project the
Future)
(Methods)
Summary
Challenge
Inducement
Specificity

 I. A few minutes now can beat this killer.
  A. Avoid pain and suffering.
  B. Avoid years in a tuberculosis sanitarium.
  C. Avoid physical handicaps.
 II. Enjoy a normal life physically and psychologically.

Action

 I. Get a chest X-ray this week.
 II. It is simple and convenient.
  A. The mobile unit is on campus at the library.
  B. It will take just five minutes of your time.
  C. It is absolutely free.
 III. The X-ray examination program is an effective way to fight this disease.

Name index

Subject index